The

Mysterious Death

of

Pope John Paul I

SIMON AND SCHUSTER
New York   London   Toronto
Sydney   Tokyo

A Thief in the Night

John Cornwell

Simon and Schuster
Simon & Schuster Building
Rockefeller Center
1230 Avenue of the Americas
New York, New York 10020

1 3 5 7 9 10 8 6 4 2

Library of Congress Cataloging in Publication Data

Cornwell, John, date.
A thief in the night : the mysterious death of Pope John I / John
Cornwell.
p.   cm.
"Originally published in Great Britain by the Penguin Group"
1. John Paul I, Pope, 1912–1978—Death and burial.   2. Cornwell,
John, date.   I. Title.
BX 1378.4.C67   1989
282′.092—dc20
[B]   89–36326
                              CIP

ISBN 0-671-68394-2

*For the rector, staff and students of the Venerabile
Collegio Inglese with gratitude*

ACKNOWLEDGMENTS

My debt to the many informants who made this book possible will be apparent throughout the text.

I owe special thanks to Father Andrew Summersgill, Father Philip Caraman, Dr. Nicholas Gold, Jill Lush, Derek Wilson, John Heilpern, Tobias Wolff, Robert Lescher, John Wilkins and Jonathan Cornwell. I also owe a special debt of gratitude, as ever, to John Guest and to Peter Carson.

THE VATICAN CITY

1 Vatican Pharmacy
2 Vatican Health Service
3 Post Office
4 Porta Sant'Anna
5 IOR—The Vatican Bank (ground floor)
6 Cortile di Sisto Quinto
7 Papal Apartments
  (two top floors
  surrounding Cortile
  di San Quinto)
8 Cortile di San Damaso
9 Sistine Chapel
10 St. Peter's
11 Bronze door
12 Piazza San Pietro
13 Arco delle Campane
14 Audience Hall of Paul VI
15 Commission for Social
   Communications
16 Station
17 Governor's Palace

. . . the day of the Lord will come—like a thief in the night . . .

—*1 Thessalonians 5:2*

CONTENTS

PROLOGUE

> . . . someone carelessly had lied; that some-
> one carelessly had blundered; and that all
> concerned were determined not to own them-
> selves or anyone else . . . to be in the wrong.
> A mistake had been made; and, by quibbles,
> by evasions, by threats, by every hole-and-
> corner means conceivable, the mistake was
> going to be perpetuated.
>
> —FREDERICK ROLFE, *Hadrian VII*

This is the story of an investigation into the circumstances of the sudden death of Pope John Paul I, the "smiling Pope," on September 28, 1978, and of the allegations that he was murdered by senior prelates of the Roman Catholic Church. My inquiries were encouraged by the Vatican in the hope that I would publish conclusive proof of the falsity of a series of conspiracy theories that had been a matter of dismay to the Church for more than a decade.

John Paul I's unexpected death, after reigning as Pontiff for thirty-three days, might have been accepted as an act of the Holy Spirit, or as a simple misfortune, were it not for circumstances that raised questions about the truthfulness of officials in the papal household and the Secretariat of State.

During the two weeks following the Pope's death, Vatican spokesmen, members of his household and important official and unofficial witnesses contradicted each other. They disagreed about:

1. Who found the body.
2. When the body was found.
3. The official cause of death.
4. The estimated time of death.
5. The timing and legality of the embalmment.
6. What the Pope had in his hands at the moment of death.
7. The true state of his health in the months leading up to his death.
8. The whereabouts of personal belongings from the papal bedroom.
9. Whether or not the Curia had ordered and performed a secret autopsy.
10. Whether or not the morticians were summoned before the body was officially found.

What lay behind these points of dispute? Was there something to hide? Had the Pope been assassinated and was there a cover-up at the very heart of the Roman Catholic Church?

Who *was* John Paul I? And why should anybody have wanted to remove him after only thirty-three days?

After one day's voting, on August 26, 1978, the conclave of cardinals elected Albino Luciani on the fourth ballot. It was the shortest conclave of the century and almost the shortest in history. The British Cardinal Basil Hume declared him "God's candidate," adding, "Once it had happened, it seemed totally and entirely right. The feeling that he was just what we wanted was so general. . . . We felt as if our hands were being guided as we wrote his name on the paper!" But there were misgivings even in those first few days of rejoicing. London's influential Catholic periodical *The Tablet* editorialized:

> We are still left with the mystery of how a vastly expanded Electoral College, more international than ever before, greatly preoccupied with problems such as those of the Third World and greatly influenced by Vatican II, could so rapidly agree

about the suitability of a man to deal with all of this, a man, moreover, of whom they had scarcely heard. Either this was a spectacular intervention of the Holy Spirit or the result of a long and carefully prepared campaign. . . .

There was another theory going the rounds. Luciani had been chosen to block the powerful candidatures of such capable and experienced Italian cardinals as Giovanni Benelli, Giuseppe Siri and Sergio Pignedoli.

First, who was Albino Luciani? He was born in Forno di Canale in the diocese of Belluno, in northeast Italy, on October 17, 1912. His father was an outspoken Socialist, a migrant worker who spent long periods in Switzerland. The son attended local seminaries and was ordained on July 7, 1935. He went then to the Jesuit Gregorian University in Rome and wrote his doctoral thesis on Antonio Rosmini-Serbati, a nineteenth-century Italian priest-philosopher who was suspected for a time of heresy. Luciani worked for a while in his home parish and taught for ten years at the seminary in Belluno. In 1948 he was made acting vicar general of his diocese, in charge of catechetics, and in 1958 he was appointed bishop of Vittorio Veneto. His ministry was grass roots and pastoral. Luciani had little interest in administration, finance or politics. In 1969 he was made patriarch of Venice.

He moved perceptibly to the right, announcing during the Italian election of 1975 that Christianity was incompatible with Communism. This may account for his "traditionalist" reputation.

He published a series of whimsical letters to fictional and historical characters, including Pinocchio, Walter Scott and Figaro, and remarked that, "If I hadn't been a bishop I would have wanted to be a journalist."

In the late sixties, Luciani became interested in birth-control problems, interviewing doctors and theologians to form his own opinion, but he fell into line and defended Paul VI's encyclical, *Humanae Vitae*, which condemned birth control. He was the first member of the Italian hierarchy to speak out against test-tube babies.

. . .

In his first press conference as Pope John Paul I, Luciani enthralled
the world with his simplicity and humor. Watching a video recording
of his first homily, I was struck by his intensity. He clasped his
hands together at his breast, and seemed to plead with his audience
in a supplicating, quavering voice. He spoke slowly, huskily and
with impassioned emphasis. His voice seemed to break with emotion
at the end of his sentences. There was something childlike and
ingenuous about his demeanor. He had a habit of holding his head
to one side, of leaning forward with hunched shoulders. And there
was that ready smile, eyes wrinkled with delight. The new Pope
announced that he would dispense with the traditional pomp of the
papal coronation and the gestatorial chair. He said he wished to be
known as "Pastor" of the Church, rather than "Pontiff." He was
dubbed the "smiling Pope." Rarely had a Papacy begun with such
popular appeal.

Thirty-three days later, during the night of September 28–29,
1978, Papa Luciani, as the Italians called him, died unexpectedly
in his private apartments. The cause of death, according to the
Vatican's announcement, was myocardial infarction, a heart attack.
The Pope was not quite sixty-six. He had no history of heart disease.
He had died sitting up in bed, reading, wearing his glasses.

Rumors that Luciani had been assassinated began to circulate
on the very day he died. Newspapers in Italy, and bishops as far
away as South America, wondered aloud why there was no autopsy
in view of the suddenness of his death. The Pope, his doctor claimed,
had been in excellent health.

Civiltà Cristiana, the Rome-based organization that represents
the traditionalist cause of Archbishop Marcel Lefebvre, conjectured
that the Pope had been murdered by "liberals" in the Vatican
because he planned to renounce reforms promulgated by the Second
Vatican Council of the mid-sixties. Lefebvre had founded a break-
away seminary eight years earlier in Switzerland where he was
training priests who refused to recognize the decrees of the council,
notably the abolition of the old Latin Mass and liturgy.

The traditionalists believed that Vatican Freemasons lay behind
the assassination. Their reading of recent Church history was that
young Freemasons had been recruited and planted as moles in
Roman Catholic seminaries during the forties and fifties. By the

sixties, many of these moles had become leading theologians and had been chosen as *periti,* or expert advisers, during Vatican II. It was due to their efforts that leading cardinals and bishops had been suborned, and many great Roman Catholic traditions—from the Latin Mass to the order of exorcist—had been abandoned.

Lists had been published in right-wing magazines citing Masonic code names of Roman Catholic prelates, including Archbishop Paul Casimir Marcinkus, head of the Vatican Bank; Cardinal Jean Villot, secretary of state; and Cardinal Sebastiano Baggio, the head of the Congregation of Bishops, who had brought sanctions against Lefebvre in 1976.

The Masonic master plan, according to these extremists, was to let Satan loose in the heart of the Church.

The fifteen-year reign of John Paul I's predecessor, Paul VI (1963–78), had indeed seen a widening gulf between the forces of reaction and reform. The Church seemed to tear itself apart over issues such as birth control, clerical celibacy, liturgical reform, the status of Marxism within Catholic thinking, questions of conscience and authority, and even the primacy of the Papacy. Paul dithered in the divide, seemingly unable to make up his mind whether he wished to preside over a major devolution of papal power and a fragmentation of the Church, or return to an absolute autocracy of earlier popes. The controversies that swirled about him would have daunted the most resolute of Pontiffs, much less the indecisive Montini. Even the popular John XXIII, his predecessor, had described Montini as "a little like Hamlet."

Paul VI's tendency was to set opposing forces in motion. His appointment of the French Cardinal Jean Villot as secretary of state, it was thought, gave French liberalism a strong voice on major issues. Villot, it was said, had urged the Pope to excommunicate Lefebvre. At the same time Paul appointed the conservative Cardinal Giovanni Benelli as substitute secretary of state, where he pushed a tough, centrist policy. Benelli funneled all major and minor decisions of the expanded commissions and congregations across his own desk for the Pope's approval.

In a class and faction of his own was Chicago-born Archbishop Marcinkus, the powerful head of the Vatican Bank, who had managed to outflank Benelli and establish a direct reporting line to Paul

VI. Marcinkus was a crucial figure in Paul's Papacy because of the huge increase in new commissions and congregations following Vatican II. The new emphasis was on consultation, research, "talk shops," not only in Rome but all over the world. Where was the money to come from to pay for it? And the Vatican's three thousand employees were clamoring for new pay deals and pensions. Marcinkus's job was to bring American know-how to Vatican finance, and he did so with great energy and a spirit of independence. One year into his presidency of the bank, he was allegedly embroiled in a billion-dollar counterfeit bond fraud. There were rumors of further scandals.

Contemplating all the conflicts and all the "scandals," surveying the threatened fragmentation of the Church, the traditionalists believed that their Masonic conspiracy fitted the facts. Was it not evident that there were men within the Vatican intent on destroying the Church? Would they stop at anything to foil attempts to expose them? Was not John Paul I the sort of Pope who might do so?

The case for assassination depends heavily on the ten discrepancies listed above. Some of these points of dispute had been generated by semiofficial agencies such as Vatican Radio. In a broadcast at 2:30 P.M. on September 29, 1978, Vatican Radio announced that the Pope had been reading the *Imitation of Christ,* a popular Catholic work of devotion, at the moment of his death. This was corrected on October 2. But some Vatican observers were equally skeptical about the new version which said the Pope had been reading sermons and discourses when he died. Still other sources claimed that he was reading an address he was to make to the Jesuits.

There were other discrepancies according to ANSA, the Italian news agency, which had excellent sources inside the Vatican and no obvious ax to grind. On October 5, ANSA reported that it was not the papal secretary, Father John Magee, who had found the body, but a certain Sister Vincenza, a nun in the Pope's household. ANSA said the body was found not at 5:30 A.M., as the official bulletin had it, but at 4:30 A.M. What had officials been up to in the papal apartments during that critical extra hour? ANSA's report stated that the Pope was holding a list of removals and new appointments to the Curia when he succumbed.

The oddest dispatch, also published by ANSA, had been over-
looked in the excitement immediately following the Pope's death.
At 7:43 P.M. on September 29, ANSA put out a story concerning
the morticians who had treated the Pope's body. The Signoracci
brothers had embalmed several previous popes and some leading
Italian victims of violence, such as Aldo Moro, the distinguished
Italian politician, kidnapped and murdered in May of 1978. Two
of the brothers, ANSA noted, Ernesto and Renato (the other two
are Cesare and Arnaldo), were awakened at dawn and picked up
from their homes by a Vatican car at 5:00 A.M. This dispatch would
have had the brothers called out before the Pope's body had been
officially discovered. The Vatican did not repudiate nor did it explain the report.

In the aftermath there were many conspiracy theories. In 1983,
Jean-Jacques Thierry's *La Vraie Mort de Jean Paul Ier* depicted
Cardinal Villot, the secretary of state, as substituting a double for
Paul VI and planning the Pope's murder when he discovered the
nest of Freemasons in the Vatican.

Also in 1983, Max Morgan-Witts and Gordon Thomas published
Pontiff. They suggested that the assassination hypothesis was a
rumor put about by the KGB to discredit the Vatican. This theory
fit with the assassination attempt on John Paul II in Saint Peter's
Square on May 13, 1981, by Mehmet Ali Agča.

Also in 1983, a thinly disguised roman à clef, *Soutane Rouge*,
by Roger Peyrefitte, combined a KGB plot with a conspiracy involving the Mafia, the Freemasons and the Vatican Bank. His plot
depicted prelates within the Church involved with crooked financiers
and members of a pseudo-Masonic Italian lodge, P2.

Peyrefitte's pope was not a reactionary murdered by liberals in
league with Masons, but a liberal reformer bent on destroying cor-
ruption. The background to Peyrefitte's intrigue had a basis in well-
known fact. The Vatican Bank had forged strong links with Roberto
Calvi—or "Salvi," as Peyrefitte calls him—the power-hungry head
of the Banco Ambrosiano in Milan. Calvi in turn was linked with
Michele Sindona—or "Bidona"—a Machiavellian Sicilian lawyer
and financier who had been jailed in the United States and Italy
for fraud. Both these men were friends of the president of the Vatican

Bank, Archbishop Paul Marcinkus—"Larvenkus"—and both were also closely associated with Liceo Gelli—"Mellifluo"—an Italian financier who controlled the unofficial Masonic P2 lodge (Q3 in *Soutane*). On June 17, 1982, following the collapse of the Banco Ambrosiano, Calvi was found hanging under Blackfriars Bridge in London, murdered or a suicide.

Peyrefitte has "Larvenkus," together with the secretary of state, Cardinal "Hulot" (Cardinal Villot), murdering the Pope with a poisoned syringe. The deed is done in association with Salvi, Bidona and Mellifluo. The immediate motive of both prelates was to avoid their imminent dismissals. Larvenkus's dismissal would have exposed the wider involvement of the Vatican Bank in Mafia and Masonic dealings.

In 1984, the P2/crooked-financier/Mafia conspiracy resurfaced in a nonfiction investigation, *In God's Name*, by David Yallop. Here again were Sindona, Calvi and Liceo Gelli, and the familiar clerical suspects—Cardinal Villot and Archbishop Paul Marcinkus, now joined by Cardinal John Cody, archbishop of Chicago. These three, Yallop contended, acting alone or with other suspects, may have plotted or connived to murder John Paul I with digitalis. Yallop's original contribution consisted not so much in the story line or in new evidence (most of the circumstantial evidence had been in the public domain since 1978) as in his preoccupation with motive. Yallop's portrait of John Paul I, like Peyrefitte's, is one of a liberal reformer, but he casts him also as a saintly and courageous firebrand. The heroic stature of the Pope, which dominates Yallop's plot, casts a dark shadow across the evil clerical tormentors and suspected assassins.

Thierry and Peyrefitte had flown their kites without even pretending to produce any new evidence; thus the Vatican could ignore their insolence, following the old Scholastic maxim: "Quod gratis asseritur, gratis negatur"—"What is asserted without proof can be denied without proof." But Yallop put the conspiracy thesis on a new footing. The melodrama of his allegations lay not only in the heinous crime of murdering a pope, but in the spectacle of bishops capable of murder on one day celebrating Mass on the next. This was an implication that was not lost on the Catholic faithful who read the book in very large numbers in America and Europe.

And what motives could the conspiracy theorists ascribe to these men? In the case of Marcinkus they had not far to seek. The golf-playing prelate from Al Capone's backyard, Cicero, near Chicago, was up to his neck, they sought to demonstrate, in malfeasance. His name had been linked with financial scandals as far back as 1972, the year in which he was investigated by the FBI in connection with a billion-dollar counterfeit bond fraud. His friendship with Sindona and Calvi was well established, and they in turn were allegedly linked with Gelli and P2. Morgan-Witts and Thomas assert that John Paul I had Marcinkus under strict review. Peyrefitte and Yallop claim that John Paul was about to fire him. All four authors claim that the new Pope was about to expose Marcinkus's and his associates' involvement in massive fraud and dangerous political chicanery. The repercussions in the financial world, and the implications for Vatican finance, would have been incalculable. What would Marcinkus not have done to avert such a disaster?

Peyrefitte suggests that Villot, "Hulot," was fearful of dismissal. Yallop goes further: Villot's motive, he asserts with scant evidence, was the fear that John Paul was going to throw out the Church's teaching on birth control. The implication is that Villot was so deeply concerned for the integrity of the Church's moral teaching that he was capable of destroying the very source of its doctrinal authority. However flimsy the evidence for these alleged motives, Villot was essential to all the conspiracy theories, for he was the camerlengo—the prelate who directed Luciani's obsequies, and who was associated with most of the contradictions that remained unanswered and unresolved.

Yallop went a step beyond Peyrefitte, adding a third clerical suspect, Cardinal John Cody, the controversial archbishop of Chicago. Yallop's attempt to create a motive for Cody makes colorful reading, but he fails to produce a shred of even circumstantial evidence. Cody's appearance among the conspirators remains a red herring. Cody died in 1983.

By the time Thierry, Peyrefitte, Morgan-Witts, Thomas and Yallop hit the bookstores, Villot was dead, Calvi murdered or a suicide, Sindona in prison and Gelli languishing in South American exile. One man, however, was both alive and more or less in charge of his destiny. Archbishop Marcinkus, temporarily embarrassed at being a prisoner in the Vatican as a result of a warrant issued for his arrest in Italy on fraud charges, was still president of the Vatican Bank.

In the case of Marcinkus, Yallop had produced a single dramatic allegation. The sergeant of the Swiss Guard, Hans Roggen, had apparently declared in an interview that at 6:45 on the morning of the Pope's death, he had seen Marcinkus lurking in the Vatican precincts. It was an unprecedentedly early hour, Yallop claimed, for the late-rising banker. Marcinkus did not in those days live at the Vatican, but twenty minutes' drive away at the American clergy house, Villa Stritch, named after another cardinal-archbishop of Chicago. When Roggen informed the archbishop of the Pope's death, according to this interview, Marcinkus simply stared, uttering not a word.

Quite apart from this dramatic item, Marcinkus had become the central figure in the catastrophic collapse of the Banco Ambrosiano in 1982, with losses of $1.3 billion. The leading debtors associated with the debacle, or so it seemed, were ten shadowy companies apparently controlled by the Vatican and by Marcinkus personally. Documentary evidence of the Vatican's link with those companies existed in the form of letters of patronage, or "comfort," issued by the Vatican in the months preceding the collapse. In any conspiracy theory involving the Vatican, Marcinkus would be a suspect by the mere fact of guilt by association.

The time was also ripe to take account of that extraordinary ANSA dispatch about the Signoracci brothers being swept off to the Vatican by an official car at 5:00 on the morning of the Pope's death. Both *Pontiff* and *In God's Name* include the early arrival at the Vatican by the morticians, supporting a theory of a Mafia-style "cleanup" before the death was officially announced.

The Signoraccis had made a further dramatic disclosure in 1983. According to Yallop, they declared that the Pope died not at 11:00 P.M. on September 28, but closer to 4:00 A.M. on the twenty-ninth. Associated with this disturbing charge were other strange rumors, all emanating from inside the Vatican: that John Paul I's personal items—his will, his slippers and his spectacles—had mysteriously disappeared; that the body was prematurely embalmed without any of the blood or internal organs being removed; that Villot had masterminded a cleanup operation in the Pope's bedroom in the early hours of September 29, including the seizure of whatever it was that John Paul was reading. John Paul I's death certificate, against all precedent, remained unpublished.

In the face of such evidence and rumors, the Vatican had very little to say, apart from a blustering press release. Why had Marcinkus not defended himself against these scurrilous allegations? Why had he not brought a legal action, as he did in the case of a novel, *In the Name of the Father,* published in 1987, that depicted him as ordering the murder of Yuri Andropov, the Soviet general secretary?

The strange circumstances of John Paul's death remained unresolved. The published theories had not solved the mystery but simply drawn attention to it. The circumstances of the death, the rumors, innuendos and allegations, suggested a cover-up, but of what? And if the Vatican had been guilty of a major act of public deceit, could this be dismissed as the aberration of individuals? Or was it indicative of the moral health of the institution?

Such is the traditional secrecy and the lack of accountability of the Vatican that the circumstances of John Paul's death might well have remained forever in the realms of enigma and half-truth had it not been for a single Vatican prelate. An American archbishop, John Foley, the former editor of a Catholic diocesan newspaper in Pennsylvania and a comparative "new boy" in the Vatican bureaucracy, invited me to investigate the Pope's death and the aftermath. The manner in which I was chosen for the task was, I am convinced, a matter of pure chance. I was by any yardstick an unpromising choice for championing the cause of the Vatican.

I had been a lapsed Catholic for more than twenty years. My departure from the faith had been no long slide down a slope of indifference; I had spent seven years studying for the priesthood in seminaries in England. I left the Church as a result of a conscientious decision to reject both vocation and belief in God. The departure was difficult: there were painful memories of an intellectually narrow and overdisciplined youth, but there were happy memories, too, of companionship in community and fleeting periods of spiritual contentment. The legacy faded in time; I had no great ax to grind, and I did not look back. In my subsequent career as a journalist I was rarely involved with religious topics.

In 1987, however, I was working on a project that took me abroad
to study contemporary claims of "supernatural" phenomena. I investigated the story of Padre Pio, the Stigmatic; the latest scientific
evidence on the Holy Shroud of Turin; the Marian apparitions to
the children of Medjugorje in Yugoslavia. I was examining the
phenomena from the standpoint of science as well as faith, and I
was intrigued by both the religious and psychological overtones.
There was no question of partisanship.

The investigation brought me to Rome in October 1987 in pursuit
of official ecclesiastical answers to the controversy over the Medjugorje apparitions. I was suddenly and surprisingly encouraged by
Archbishop Foley to consider a quite different project: the true story
of the death of John Paul I.

I was aware of the rumors that had persisted since 1978 and I
had an open mind on the question. There had, after all, been a
near miss with John Paul II. I was not inclined to believe easily
that senior prelates in the Church had conspired, or even acquiesced, in a plot to kill John Paul I. But I had not the slightest
doubt that were I to discover a shred of evidence indicating that
conclusion, I would pursue it relentlessly and publish my findings.

I have no brief for the Roman Catholic Church, for the Vatican
nor for individuals within these institutions. I had walked into the
Vatican off the street and found myself in the right place at the
right time.

For an ex-Catholic former seminarian, the writing of this book
has been something of a sentimental journey, an unusual opportunity
to review my attitude toward the practices and beliefs of Catholicism
and the conduct of the Roman Catholic clergy at the very center of
the Church. Here and there my personal feelings and reflections
on these themes have unavoidably crept into the narrative.

No conditions were imposed on my research, nor on my conclusions. My interviews with official representatives and principal witnesses were taped and attributable. There were obstacles and
obstructiveness, but these arose because of individual reluctance
rather than official policy; there are people within the Vatican with
minds and wills of their own.

Early on I realized that the process of my investigation would be
as important as my findings; that I had been granted a privileged

look into the workings, the personalities and the behavior of priests and prelates in one of the most secretive institutions in the world. My story inevitably embraces the tensions that exist between a high spiritual calling and the demands of bureaucracy, worldly ambition, politics and mammon at the administrative heart of the Roman Catholic Church.

The Vatican expected me to prove that John Paul I had not been poisoned by one of their own. As I attempted to arrive at the truth through a series of intriguing and often baffling encounters, both inside and outside the Vatican, the evidence led to a conclusion that seems to me more shameful even, and more tragic, than any of the conspiracy theories.

PART
I

Full in the panting heart of Rome
Beneath the Apostles' crowning dome
From pilgrim lips that kiss the ground
Breathes in all hearts one only sound:
—God Bless Our Pope!

—POPULAR CATHOLIC HYMN

1

On a morning late in October 1987 I set out for the Vatican from a hotel on the Via Vitelleschi close to the Castel Sant' Angelo. It was warm for the time of year and I felt exhilarated as I turned from a side street to view the grandeur of Saint Peter's Basilica in misty sunlight from the Via della Conciliazione, the ceremonial route that sweeps grandly from the Tiber River to Saint Peter's square. The tourists had mostly departed and the pavements were empty except for those familiar figures of Catholic officialdom, the Roman clergy. Square-shaped, wearing black cassocks and raincoats, thick-soled shoes, black berets, bespectacled, they moved impassively, separately, yet all at the same dogged pace toward their destination, the Vatican City. To the children of Rome they are known as *bagarozzi*—black beetles.

I began to walk in the same direction as the priests, toward the smallest state in the world, and perhaps the most secretive.

My appointment was with Archbishop John Foley, president of the Commission for Social Communications, an official Vatican media and public-relations office. I had been instructed by his secretary to report at the gate known as the Arco delle Campane, on the left of Saint Peter's Basilica. One of the two Swiss Guards beneath the arch stood with halberd presented as the other approached me, his gingery hair shorn to the skull, wide in his bulky cloak. He saluted and waited for me to speak as he barred my way. When I told him the nature of my errand, he shouted gutturally, "Permissions Office!" and waved me through the gate and to the left of the archway.

There was a marble-floored room with a long table and chairs, and a counter where two men sat in front of ancient telephones. A huddle of people stood before them waving bits of paper; others sat at the table filling out forms.

The Vatican's security arrangements involve stating the person and department one wishes to visit within the city-state. One of the factotums behind the counter telephones through to the visitor's destination to confirm the appointment.

The pass, when I twice succeeded in pushing my way through, was a pink piece of paper headed: "Stato della citta del Vaticano— Governatorato." It noted the time of arrival, the date and was signed by the official, or *addetto*, behind the counter. I was now free to enter the city.

Directed by Vatican carabinieri from their weather shelters, I walked on past the east end of Saint Peter's. There was a cluster of gloomy baroque buildings to my left, where a stone plaque bore the inscription: MAGNIFICENTIA OPUS EJUS—Magnificent Are His Works. I emerged into a square with a central garden of evergreen shrubs surrounding a fountain; there were tall office buildings on two sides. In the distance ahead of me I could see on a bluff the entrance to the Vatican's railway station with its grand stone entrance halls, a stranded monument to the Fascist era, a ceremonial gateway to nowhere.

There was an impression of neatness and unusual cleanliness. After the noisy streets of Rome it was as quiet as Zurich on a Sunday afternoon. I went to the first of the two buildings. Under an archway was the door of the Commission for Social Communications.

I was shown into a parlor by a black-suited valet and was left to consider the furnishings. A modern painting of Trafalgar Square. Some armchairs. A low coffee table covered with copies of the Vatican Radio magazine. The door remained half open and I saw the passing figure of a cleric, who paused momentarily and peeped in at me: it was a *bargarozzo*, and he seemed to inhabit an office in a warren down the corridor. I waved cheerfully, and he vanished.

A large bald man entered. He was dressed in a black three-piece suit with a heavy-looking gold cross at his breast. His face was as round as a bun and innocent; I guessed him to be in his early fifties. His eyes were cobalt blue, wide open and unblinking, as if he were permanently startled; one of his eyes had a slight cast. This was Archbishop John Foley.

He told me that he came from Philadelphia, where he had been editor of the diocesan newspaper until being transferred to Rome in 1984 to bring some New World know-how to the Vatican's media policies.

We launched into a discussion of modern supernatural phenomena and he told me that he had just come back from Syracuse in Sicily, where he had visited the shrine of the Madonna of the Tears.

He said, a sense of wonder in his voice, "Scientific experts have done tests on the liquid collected from the plaque of the Virgin down there and the liquid has been found to be real, human tears."

He had an even mode of delivery, separating each word and eliminating elisions and contractions. It was a voice for the pulpit, a melodic, clerical diapason. He occasionally made graceful gestures with his hands, frequently bringing them together in an attitude of prayer, flashing his chunky gold bishop's ring.

He gave me some contact names in the Congregation for the Doctrine of the Faith, the department run by the Church's guardian of orthodoxy, Cardinal Joseph Ratzinger, and as we were about to end the interview, he chatted on for a while. We found ourselves discussing the death of John Paul I.

"There are those who claim that Pope John Paul I was poisoned by us here in the Vatican. Archbishop Marcinkus is singled out as a prime suspect. It is a pity," he went on to say, "that somebody like you doesn't write the truth of what really did happen on the night of Pope John Paul's death. I am sure it would be more interesting than all that sensationalist fiction.

"I am sure," he said, "that if a bona fide journalist attempted to write the truth of that night . . . I could open up the Vatican."

I liked the Americanism, but it seemed an optimistic assertion even to an innocent in Vatican matters. I had to remind myself that I was talking to the Pope's public-relations chief.

"Would Archbishop Marcinkus allow himself to be interviewed?" I asked.

He stared hard, as if focusing on an object slightly above my head. "Oh, I'm sure I could deliver Archbishop Marcinkus. And you'd need to talk to John Magee, the bishop of Cloyne, who was the Pope's secretary. You see, we were less than frank about the circumstances at the time. There are some of us who feel that the whole truth should come out—better late than never. That should be the role of the Commission for Social Communications. There should be more honesty, more readiness to admit our mistakes and failings."

After staring back at him a few moments, I said, "I would be interested in such a project. But what would *you* hope to achieve?"

"To end all this scandal. These rumors have done a great deal of damage to the faith of millions of Catholics all over the world. They come to their parish priests and say, 'Father, is it true the Pope was murdered in the Vatican?' And we have nothing to recommend as an antidote. You even find priests who believe the allegations. . . ."

He rose from his chair. "If you are interested in pursuing the project, why don't you call me? In any case, why not go down to the tomb of the popes and consult the man yourself? Say a little prayer to Papa Luciani by his tomb."

I liked the unworldliness of this head of "Social Communications," even before he gave me a parting gift that revealed him as perhaps the most extraordinary PR man on the face of the earth. I was about to go out of the door of the parlor when he said, "Let me give you my blessing." As I stood on one leg, not knowing whether to kneel or not, he pulled himself up to his full height and said a formal and quite lengthy prayer over me, ending with a sign of the cross—deep and wide. He looked pleased with himself as he showed me to the door.

Outside the Arco delle Campane I decided to take the archbishop at his word, at least as far as visiting John Paul's tomb. I ascended the steps of Saint Peter's on the left-hand side of the basilica, and walked the length of the nave to the great baldacchino. The descent into the area of the tombs of the popes is just beyond the high altar. A twisting staircase takes pilgrims down into a recently renovated catacomb, past the casket containing the bones of Saint Peter and into a series of subterranean corridors reminiscent of the London underground. In shrines and chapels were situated the tombs of the more recent popes, including Pius XII, John XXIII and Paul VI. In a grotto I found the slab of gray marble inscribed: JOANNES PAULUS PP I. There were angels with arms crossed on their chests on each corner of the sarcophagus. There was a single dead rose on the top.

As I stood contemplating the tomb of the "smiling Pope," pilgrims came and stood for a few moments; many of them put a hand on the marble and then crossed themselves. Those that came in pairs or groups would make brief whispered comments: "Papa Luciani . . ." "assassinated . . ." "disgraceful. . . ." I heard a teenage English girl say to her companion: "Was this the one that was done in?" They moved on, giggling softly in the gloom.

Ten years after his death, John Paul I's tomb was still attracting more interest than the memorials of all the other popes put together. Ten years after his death, the Roman Catholic Church was still smarting at the "murder"-conspiracy rumor. And the fact that this powerful institution should be irritated by the allegation to the extent of considering a surrender of its customary secrecy was in itself both impressive and deeply curious.

That afternoon, in connection with my researches into supernatural phenomena, I had been invited to lunch at the English College, the Venerabile Collegio Inglese, the theological seminary in Rome under the direct patronage of the Pope for English candidates for the priesthood. I was hoping for permission to use the college library. I set out with trepidation, for this was my first visit to a seminary since my departure from the Church at the age of twenty-four. I found the college off a narrow lane called Via di Monserrato near the Piazza Farnese in the old city.

There was a man sitting in a porter's lodge wearing a thick white sweater. He looked up from his puzzle magazine and opened the door electronically from behind a barred window.

I entered a high-ceilinged corridor with marble plaques and a papal coat of arms featuring the triple tiara—symbolizing sway over heaven, earth and hell. There was a long sweep of polished black-and-red tiles leading to a high, frosted romanesque window. I caught a whiff of incense and institutional beeswax polish which brought back a flood of memories. In my own day as a seminarian, one might have seen cassocked students walking purposefully in silence along such a corridor; now a young man, dressed in gray pants and bomber-jacket, came down the wide marble staircase to my right, nonchalantly smoking a cigarette. He went out into a garden at the far end of the corridor.

Eventually I heard a sound of humming on the staircase and in time the college rector, Monsignor Jack Kennedy, appeared—bluff and balding, hand in pocket, clothes casual. Twenty years ago he would have been buttoned and trussed in a black cassock with purple piping and a high, glossy dog-collar propping up his chin. This jovial rector of the eighties looked as if he had just come off a golf course. "Call me Jack!" he said, with a firm handshake and a Lancashire accent.

He took me straight into the college chapel, where he genuflected before the Blessed Sacrament tabernacle. I hung back, but he beckoned me to the high altar. He wanted to show me a painting that hung at the east end of the church. It depicted the Trinity, with God the Father holding the body of the dead Christ, which was spilling blood on a map of England; Saint Thomas of Canterbury and Saint Edmund knelt, gazing upward. On a scroll at the bottom of the picture was the quotation: "Veni mittere ignem in terram"—"I have come to spread fire upon the earth."

"It's by Durante Alberti and it's four hundred years old," said the monsignor. "During the days of the persecution of Catholics in England, the students would come and sing a Te Deum before this picture every time news arrived of the death of another martyr who had been a member of the college."

He took me upstairs and showed me the library, one whole section of which housed a unique collection of works dealing with penal history in England during the Reformation. Coming back down the staircase I noticed a portrait of Pope John XXIII and a bust of John Paul II. There was a framed list of students who had died, most of them by hanging and disembowelment, for the Roman Catholic faith in England. Queen Elizabeth and her government officers would have called them spies and traitors; here they were venerated as glorious martyrs. An atmosphere of militant sixteenth-century popery seemed very much alive and on the offensive within the walls of this thoroughly English institution in the heart of Rome, with its direct links with the Pope and the Vatican. "The college," said the rector, "is truly pontifical. I can only be sacked by the Pope himself. He's the boss here."

At lunch in the oak-paneled refectory, I sat with the college staff at a center table beneath a vaulted ceiling depicting the patron saint of England, Saint George slaying the dragon. About eighty students were seated at long tables ranged along the sides of the refectory. A reading pulpit high against the wall stood empty. There was a roar of voices. The students were dressed in casual clothes, but I thought I recognized in them a similarity with the seminarians of my youth: a hint of primness, a faint air of fastidiousness in their table manners. Many of them were bespectacled, their hair cut short, and they favored somber colors and clerical grays. I had a vague sense of being an intruder.

Over tagliatelle and a glass of white wine, I told the rector of my conversation with Archbishop Foley and his remarks about the papal poison plot. He inclined an ear intently. Then he said, with some vehemence, "That *would* be an important project. If you want to write the truth about Pope John Paul I's death and put a stop to that murder-theory nonsense, we'll give you all the help you'll need."

As the conversation around the table proceeded, I had an intimation of the sort of pressure that I might endure were I to accept the project. I quailed at the thought of being regarded the "Vatican's man," a writer "roped in" to provide a "riposte." I sensed a ghostly, combative, anti-Protestant enthusiasm pervading the atmosphere of the old English College, where the enemy lines were clearly drawn and the staff and students still thought of England as "the mission." It reminded me of a hymn we used to sing—"Faith of Our Fathers"—which had the refrain: "We *will* be true to thee till *death!*"

And yet, as I looked about me at the eager clerical faces, I realized that I had distanced myself irretrievably from such a milieu. I felt no sense of antipathy, but never again would I even pretend to the frame of mind of a militant, apologist Catholic.

I was an interloper, and it was an interloper's sense of curiosity about the post–Vatican Council Church, and the center of its power, that was intriguing me deeply, tempting me to plunge into the "murder" project. Despite all the years I had spent as a cleric, I had no idea what the Vatican was *really* like. I felt that my journalistic curiosity was my best protection against blandishments from any quarter.

The rector was saying, "If you decided to take on that book about the murder of the Pope you could come and stay here and live in the college for as long as it takes. We'll give you all the help you need."

I had already decided to tackle the story of John Paul I's death. I knew that it was unlikely to be the kind of book the Vatican expected of me.

2

J decided to return to Rome in the hope of setting up a meeting with Archbishop Marcinkus in early December. Two weeks in advance of this planned trip I had called Archbishop Foley's office from London hoping that he would now agree to make good his promise to "deliver" the Vatican. His secretary, Sister Pia, had answered. No, the archbishop, whom she called "the president," could not come to the phone; it would be best if I wrote. I explained that the post being what it was between Britain and Italy there would not be enough time to correspond before my arrival. I reflected wryly on the "president's" role as head of Vatican communications. At last we agreed that I should make an appointment to call the archbishop at a specific time on the next day.

For seven days running I called. On each occasion I got through at the appointed time only to be told that "the president has a visitor," "the president is on another line," "the president is out in the corridor."

At last, I told Sister Pia, "I have an idea. Why doesn't the president call me?"

There was a shocked silence. Then she said, "I'm not sure that would be feasible. The president doesn't normally do that."

"Perhaps I could conduct a conversation with him via telex or fax?" I asked. "Do you have such things in the Communications Commission?"

The patient sister failed to react to my sarcastic tone. She said, "Oh, yes, certainly!" She gave me the numbers.

On the Monday, a week before my planned trip to Rome, I composed the following message to Archbishop Foley:

"My publisher supports the project concerning Pope John Paul I . . . but I need your assurance that I can have access to significant figures. Regards, John Cornwell."

All day long I failed to make contact by telefax. All six of the numbers given were permanently engaged or out of order. Late that afternoon I sent the message by telex and it went straight through.

The next morning I received a telephone call from the Vatican.

"Hi there! I'm Marjorie Weeke. We received your telex. We've got a bit of a problem on this project of yours." The voice was deep and hurried. I had heard the accent in New York City: a sort of side-of-the-mouth utterance of self-mocking desperation.

I said, "Are you a nun?"

"For God's sakes! I'm a kind of executive here, supposedly. . . . Anyway, the president has asked me to sort this out."

"The president promised that he would try to get me an interview with Archbishop Marcinkus."

"Yeah. Well, we need a whole lot more accreditation. We'd need a letter endorsed by all the bishops of England and Wales and the cardinal-archbishop that you're an okay guy. Look, it's not me— it's the Vatican."

"But I don't know these bishops and cardinals . . . who wants that kind of endorsement anyway?"

"Look, I'm trying to help you here. You've got to understand how this place works."

"Perhaps the best thing would be for me to forget the whole project."

"Let me give you some advice. You know George Leonard. He's a monsignor over at the Catholic Media Office there in London.

He's a fixer. Give him a call and give him something to fix; you know George, he'll enjoy that."

"But I don't know George Leonard. It's not going to work."

"George Leonard. Best of luck!" And she put the phone down.

One of my few contacts with Roman Catholic institutions was the London weekly, *The Tablet*, for which I'd written occasional reviews and articles. Its editor, John Wilkins, had once worked as a producer for the BBC. He listened sympathetically. "They might be getting cold feet. You've got to understand how their minds work. The Vatican has its own strange way of doing things. They're incredibly secretive. But I don't think all is lost. I think you should keep them to their word. I'll talk to the cardinal."

"But, John, I'm not going to do a whitewash job for the Catholic Church."

"That's all right, there's no question of that."

I felt grateful for Wilkins's offer, but I doubted that he could get a letter out of Cardinal Hume that would make both me and the Vatican happy.

Before resigning myself to writing off the project, I thought I would try one more contact. That afternoon I rang the English College in Rome to talk with Monsignor Kennedy.

He was jaunty and welcoming. "When are you coming, I've got a room for you."

"I feel reluctant to come out unless I have an undertaking that Marcinkus will talk to me. Now they're asking for a letter of accreditation from the English hierarchy. I can't get that. I'm not sure I want it."

"Who asked for that?" he said.

"Archbishop Foley."

"Don't worry about it, you come out and we'll try to fix up everything from here; but you know what the Vatican is, a decent letter would come in useful."

"If I could just get to Marcinkus."

"I occasionally play a round of golf with him. I'll see what I can do from my end. Once you're here it will all be easier."

Later that afternoon I had a phone call from John Wilkins.

"Relax," he said, "everything's been fixed. A letter went out to Rome via telex from Cardinal Hume this morning. It's a superb letter and he points out that you should be allowed total freedom as an independent investigator."

"How did you manage it?"

"George Leonard," he replied. "George Leonard fixed everything."

3

In Via di Monserrato the great doors of the English College were shut against me and I stood in the deserted lane ringing the bell. Eventually a priest turned up from an afternoon walk to take me and my bags through a side door to the quadrangle and into the long corridor where I had been greeted by the rector several weeks earlier. He explained that Rome was on holiday for the Feast of the Immaculate Conception.

He had a wide, ruddy Irish face with gray watery eyes behind ecclesiastical steel-rimmed spectacles. His graying hair stood out like a halo. He carried my bags up the staircase and into a corridor on the first floor. A line of portraits of English cardinals adorned the walls—Wiseman, Manning, Newman, Hinsley, Godfrey, Heenan. He told me a joke about the English College in Rome—there were three conditions for being made a Catholic bishop in England: you must be male, you must be a baptized Catholic and you must have been a student of the English College. "The first two conditions could be dispensed with," he said, "but never the third." He had a quiet, gentle voice and a self-deprecating way of lowering his eyes when he smiled.

We passed through a long, elegantly furnished room with sofas and occasional tables and more portraits of ecclesiastics. The priest called this the *salone*. He carried the bags to my room and before leaving drew my attention to the college timetable on the back of the door: visitors were invited to follow the same schedule of the day as the staff and the students, starting at 7:15 with morning prayers. The priest knew the purpose of my visit. He said playfully, "If you're going to cross-examine Marcinkus, you'd better try to understand how his mind works. Find out what his golf game is like."

My room was, like much of the college, a mixture of faded grandeur and monastic austerity. It was lofty, with orange, silver and gold sunflowers depicted on the wood-paneled ceiling; there was a narrow bed, a desk and chair, a wardrobe and chest of drawers, simple and institutional. A crucifix hung on the wall, a picture of an angel was on the chest of drawers. On the desk was a telephone and a copy of an immensely fat red book called the *Annuario Pontificio: Città del Vaticano*. A high window looked down into the quiet courtyard and there was a view of a Renaissance clock tower above the college roofs.

I picked up the *Annuario*. It had cloth covers and a red silk marker, with the gold coat of arms of the Pope stamped on the front. This curious manual, of more than two thousand pages, was almost as wide as it was high, and packed with information about the establishment of the Roman Catholic Church in its links with the Papacy. Here were all the offices, commissions, councils, tribunals, departments, congregations, foundations and academic institutions, with historical notes; there were names, telephone numbers, ranks and career details of all relevant officials so that, no doubt, those in the know could tell who was in, who was out, who wasn't on the way up. At a glance I could see the layers of bureaucratic prece- dence, rife, I imagined, with potential for self-comparison and ca- suistic intrigue: how, for example, did a *minutante* of the second class in the first grade of minor officials in the Secretariat of State compare with a *scrittore* of the first class in the *"addetti" tecnici* section of the minor officials of the second grade of the same sec- retariat? It was the ultimate ecclesiastical handbook, an anatomy of the Vatican and an invaluable introduction to my work at hand.

I found, for example, that this seminary in which I was now about

4

J was woken by bells. It was now dark and I groped for the bedside lamp to find that it was seven o'clock in the evening.

I wandered back down through the corridors and found the house empty and in semidarkness. I could hear singing from the church and I walked slowly to the doors and opened them gingerly.

The church was ablaze with candles, filled with flowers. The priests and students were vested in white, standing in a semicircle around the central altar. It was the Mass of the Feast of the Immaculate Conception. The organ was in full flood and columns of incense rose to the rafters.

The celebrant was a small man with a furious white beard and the rounded glowing face of an old cherub. As I took my seat behind a pillar, he began a resounding homily on the Virgin Mary. Looking about the church at the faces of the young seminarians from England, the spectacle of them gathered together on my first evening in the college seemed to temper my creeping cynicism about the world in which I was about to be embroiled.

After Mass we went into the refectory for a buffet supper.

I found a free place at the table where the college staff collected. On my right was the Mass celebrant with the beard. He introduced himself as Monsignor Jim and told me that he was eighty-four and the former rector of the English seminary in Lisbon. "I'm used to bossing people about," he said gruffly.

Monsignor Kennedy, sitting opposite, was chatting affably to another visitor, a quiet little clergyman, the only man dressed in clerical black and Roman collar. He was introduced to me as a visiting bishop from England. There were two younger priests, tall, bespectacled and serious, tutors in philosophy and theology; a silver-haired canon with cinematic good looks, known to everyone as Harry; then there were two Vatican monsignori, resident in the college, svelte and prosperous-looking, with flashing spectacles and knowing chatter.

A brief conversation started up among the clergy about John Paul I. Some snatches of it were memorable:

"He was a simple man from the Veneto . . . Coming to Rome was a complete trauma. It was like coming to Africa . . ."

"He wasn't up to it . . . He took one look at his in-tray and flipped . . ."

Monsignor Jim, having got his bearings on the purpose of my visit, was a formidable talker. Amid an impressive monologue on the obsequies of dead popes, he told me something of great interest. "They said, you know, that John Paul I didn't have an autopsy because they never perform them on popes. That's not true. Clement XIV had one—he was the chap who suppressed the Jesuits in the eighteenth century. He was terrified of being poisoned and there was a story about a crucifix that he was worried about; he stopped kissing the feet of the Christ because he thought the Jesuits would put poison on them. When he died his body decomposed so rapidly that the Vatican thought that the Jesuits had succeeded. They put a mask over the face of the corpse because it looked so dreadful."

Monsignor Jim's conversation gave me an idea. How many popes in history, after all, had died of poisoning? After supper he led me to the library and helped me to get my bearings. I took an armful of books to a carrel in the deserted reading room; they included Pastor's *History of the Popes*, the *Catholic Encyclopedia*, Gualino's *Storia Medica dei Romani Pontifici*. From the ninth century onward, I discovered, poisoning had been a fairly common occurrence among the popes, although it was more often a case of rumor than proven fact.

John VIII, the first pope to be assassinated, was poisoned in 882 by members of his entourage; the potion took so long to work that he was clubbed to death. Ten years or so later the body of Pope Formosus, poisoned by a dissident faction in his court, was exhumed by his successor Stephen VI, solemnly excommunicated, mutilated, then dragged through the streets of Rome and thrown into the Tiber.

In the tenth century John X was poisoned in jail by the mad and tyrannical Marozia, his mistress's daughter and the mother of John XI; Benedict VI was poisoned, as was John XIV. In the eleventh century it was the turn of Sylvester II, known as "the Magician" for his alleged dealings with the devil, and then Clement II, and his successor Damasus II (although there is evidence that he might well have died of malaria).

As the generations rolled by, more information was forthcoming on methods and motives. Celestine V may have been poisoned by his successor Boniface VIII, who had thrown him into a dungeon after engineering his abdication; Benedict XI was said to have died of powdered glass in his figs; Paul II passed away after eating "two big melons," poison again suspected. Then in 1503 Alexander VI, the notorious Borgia Pope, probably died of poison intended for another. The manner of his death convinced his household that it was white arsenic in the wine: his flesh turned black, froth formed around a monstrously distended tongue, gas hissed and exploded from every orifice. His body was so swollen after death that the undertakers had to jump on his stomach to enable them to close the coffin lid.

Not all plots succeeded. A decade after Alexander VI's death, Leo X was elected, a man so avid for money that he auctioned cardinals' hats. A Florentine surgeon was hired by five cardinals to murder him by introducing poison into his anal passage while pretending to treat His Holiness's piles. The conspiracy was discovered and the ringleader, Cardinal Alfonso Petrucci, was strangled with a rope of crimson silk.

But had papal assassination ceased with more enlightened modern times? According to a scurrilous little book entitled *The Vatican Papers* by one Nino Lo Bello, such a murder had occurred as recently as 1939. In early February of that year Pius XI, aged eighty-two, had been planning a special address against Fascism and anti-Semitism in a denunciation of the concordat with Mussolini. Il Duce thus had a powerful motive to do away with the aging Pope. The story goes that just twenty-four hours before Pius was due to read his discourse to a special audience of bishops, he was given an injection by one Dr. Francesco Petacci. As well as having medical duties inside the Vatican, Petacci was the father of Mussolini's mistress, the starlet Clara Petacci (later to be hanged alongside the dictator). Conspiracy theorists believe that Petacci injected the Pope with poison, for he died the next morning before he could make the speech, the text of which was never found. The source of all this, according to Lo Bello, was the private diary of the powerful French cardinal of that period, Eugène Tisserant.

Against this background the case of Pope John Paul I had a distinctly familiar ring. Turning to the new *Oxford Dictionary of Popes*, by J. N. D. Kelly, I read the entry for John Paul I:

> . . . about 11 p.m. on Thursday 28 Sept., he died of a heart attack while lying in bed reading some papers containing personal notes. His light was still on when he was found dead about 5:30 a.m. next day. Rumours of foul play, fanned by the lack of an autopsy, were later (1984) blown up into the claim that he was poisoned because he planned to clean up the Vatican Bank, demote important curial figures, and revise *Humanae Vitae* . . .

Kelly's account goes on to comment that evidence in the conspiracy theory "was a tissue of improbabilities," and yet I noted that the only substantial biographical references cited were Peter Hebblethwaite and David Yallop. Even a cursory glance through the history of the popes convinced me that insalubrious rumors have a way of sticking down the centuries.

As for short reigns, I could find only five popes in the entire history of the Papacy who had lasted for fewer than thirty-three days: Urban VII (September 15–27, 1590)—thirteen days; Celestine IV (October 25 to November 10, 1241)—seventeen days; Sylvester III, antipope (January 20 to February 10, 1045)—twenty-two days; Marcellus II (April 9 to May 1, 1555)—twenty-three days; Damasus II (July 17 to August 9, 1048)—twenty-four days. Only one of these popes—Damasus II—was suspected of having been murdered. And of these short reigns, perhaps that of Marcellus II seemed closest in atmosphere to that of John Paul I. According to Kelly:

> Few elections have aroused such eager hopes as Marcellus's . . . he seemed the chief pastor for whom the crisis-ridden Church was crying out . . . He cut the expense of his coronation to a minimum, reduced the size and cost of his court . . . Then, after reigning twenty-four days, worn out by restless activity and the burden of responsibilities, his frail constitution gave in and he died of a stroke.

He was five days short of his fifty-fourth birthday.

The bells in the college clock tower were striking eleven when I went down the "cardinals' corridor" toward my room. Standing in the shadows by the staff kitchen off the *salone* was the visiting bishop, whom I had seen at supper. Although it was still remarkably warm for the time of year, he was screwing the top into a hot-water bottle with a knitted woolen covering in preparation for bed. His face was sallow and thin, and his head lolled a little to one side. He gave me a wry, self-conscious smile.

"Hallo," he said. "I'm very interested in what you are doing. When somebody told me that the Pope had died, I said that of course he was dead—meaning Paul VI. It was all so sudden, and so soon, you see. And yet it shouldn't have surprised me, because he was a sick man. I remember the day Cardinal Hume rang me to say we had a new pope. He was here in Rome, of course, and I was in England. He was absolutely thrilled with Luciani. But I said to him, 'Has he provided you with a clean bill of health?' One had heard that he'd been continually in and out of sanitoria. This came as a surprise to the cardinal. Then there was all that typically Roman rumormongering about the death not being natural; the whole place was rife with it."

The bishop clutched the woolly bottle close to his chest. "He was a strange little fellow," he went on, smiling to himself, "always bringing children up to talk with him at the audiences, and all that stuff about Pinocchio. Whenever I saw him on television I used to say to myself, 'My God! That's Peter Sellers! They've made Peter Sellers a pope!' "

With this he began to wander away from me, saying in a fading voice, "I'd better go to bed or I'll say something indiscreet."

After he had gone I sat a while in the *salone*. I was wondering if my sense of humor was at fault. The bishop's comments about John Paul had been passing jests, perhaps not worth a second thought. It would surely be unfair to put too much significance on a weary prelate's remarks as he made his way to bed. And yet the comment had struck me very forcibly: "strange little fellow . . . all that stuff about Pinocchio . . . Peter Sellers!"

How much was that view shared among other high officials in the Church? It occurred to me that I had never heard of any pope in living memory being referred to by the Catholic clergy in such a slighting way. It was quite unlike the catalogs of criticism leveled at other popes in our era: Pius XII for his alleged anti-Semitism, Paul VI for his indecisiveness, John Paul II for his autocratic tendencies.

The bishop's passing remarks reflected on John Paul I's sheer paltriness—"a strange little fellow. . . ."

5

The clock tower on the other side of the quad rang a complicated peal at every quarter, then there was a storm in the early hours with thunderclaps, and torrents in the guttering. I slept fitfully and woke before dawn to the sound of footsteps, the purposeful, even pace of clerics on their way to church before dawn. I had a brief, uneasy impression that I had been transported back into a familiar past; I turned over and went back to sleep.

It was already nine o'clock when the rector poked his head around the door.

"I've talked to His Excellency Paul Marcinkus. Give his secretary a call on this number." He handed me a piece of paper.

Even as the rector was retreating down the polished tiles of the corridor, I was calling the Vatican.

An Italo-American voice answered: "Secretary to Archbishop Marcinkus."

"Good morning, Sister," I said.

"I'm not a sister," said the voice, a little peeved. "We're not all nuns in this place. Now . . . I know all about this. You come to the Bronze Door tomorrow at nine-fifteen. The archbishop will see you then. The carabinieri will show you the way."

. . .

In the kitchen off the *salone* I ran into one of the sleek monsignori
I had met at supper the previous evening. He was now dressed in
casual lay clothes and standing by a boiling kettle. He introduced
himself affably. He was a square-looking man, brushed and
scrubbed and pink as from a hot bath. His eyes were extraordinarily
youthful and innocent behind gold-rimmed spectacles. He was my
first full-time Vatican bureaucrat and I engaged him in conversation
with some fascination.

"I'm having a few days off," he said. "I'm absolutely shattered.
I'm reading a life of Queen Victoria to unwind. I'm intrigued as to
how you got into this. The death of Pope Luciani needs some serious
sorting out. The morticians had to break his back you know, because
of rigor mortis. You realize that Marcinkus will need the permission
of Cardinal Agostino Casaroli, the secretary of state, before he can
be quoted. And he does nothing without the Pope giving the go-
ahead."

The monsignor chatted away with a ready smile, but occasionally
his eyes would give a sudden sidelong conspiratorial look and he
would purse his lips as he made a little foray into the confidential.

"How do you get employment in the Vatican?" I asked. "Do you
apply for an advertised post?"

"Oh no!" he said, with some vehemence. "You get asked. I was
here in this college as a student and I went back to England to join
my diocese. Then one day the bishop asked me to come back to
Rome to this job and I've been here ever since—that's almost twenty
years ago. That's a typical pattern except for the ambitious, who
hang around Rome trying to get noticed. The only trouble with being
in Rome is the Italians. I won't drive in this country. In fact, I
won't drive anywhere south of Dover. I walk to and from the Vatican
four times a day. I've worked out that I walk fifteen hundred miles
a year. It's not so bad working in the Vatican. At least it's better
paid than an ordinary parish priest back in England. But I still
don't get paid more than a sergeant in the British army. Bishops
here do even better than monsignori; they get everything free, including their food and an apartment.

"There's just one thing to be careful of here in the college. I
gather you were in the library last night. Do you know there's a

ghost in the second library? You don't see anything, you just feel cold, then you become paralyzed and have to get out. It's some ancient spirit. Did you know this building was once the site of a temple to Silvanus? Of course, the whole of Rome is a bit like that, including the Vatican—full of pagan shades and ghosts."

I observed him carefully to try and detect a hint of humor. He seemed in deadly earnest.

"Can't you exorcise the library ghost?" I asked.

"Oh no. Much too powerful; it laughs at us. Anyway, ordinary priests can't exorcise—it's very dangerous. The last time one of the students experienced the library ghost the rector came up with the spiritual director and they sprinkled some holy water about. But it didn't do any good."

As I left the kitchen I told him I was off to the Vatican.

"Are you going into Saint Peter's?" he asked.

"Possibly."

"I haven't been inside Saint Peter's for twelve years," he said with a deadpan expression. "Can't stand it. It's just a desert of stone."

Intrigued by his history, I asked the monsignor his age. He turned out to be some twenty years older than my guess.

At noon I entered the Vatican by the Arco delle Campane to meet Archbishop Foley's assistant, Marjorie Weeke. I had a shopping list of requests for Vatican assistance and I was eager to get started. She had given my name to the Vatican carabinieri and I was allowed to proceed through to the Piazza Santa Marta and the Communications Commission without going to the permissions office.

I was shown into the parlor with its incongruous picture of Trafalgar Square and within moments I heard a deep querulous voice behind me: "Hi! I'm Marjorie Weeke." I turned to find a woman dressed in a plaid skirt and white blouse; her pale, thin wrists protruded from the sleeves of a black velvet jacket. She had the large baleful eyes of a thwarted child, set in a curiously wizened, bloodless face.

She took notes as I ticked off my list of requests.

I told her that I wanted access to the papal doctor, Buzzonetti; I wanted to meet the morticians. Since Sister Vincenza was dead I needed to know the whereabouts of other nuns in the papal household. The Pope's second private secretary, John Magee, was now a bishop in Ireland—would she write to him about me and recommend an appointment? And could I have an introduction to John Paul I's Italian secretary, Don Diego Lorenzi? Was there a file containing the Pope's medical records? Where was the death certificate? And the Pope's will?

My list was connected with the straightforward circumstances of the Pope's death. If there was nothing to hide, then there could be no difficulty in swiftly reconstructing the basic facts from a few interviews and documents.

She raised her eyebrows: "I don't know about all this. I think it will make their hair stand on end. The Vatican isn't exactly full of up-front guys and they have a way of dumping things in irretrievable archives."

Our meeting was interrupted by a phone call. She stood up and said, "I've got problems at the Pope's Wednesday audience. Come over there with me and we'll talk as we go."

We walked out of the palazzo and headed across the square toward the back of a modern building shaped like an aircraft hangar. She moved slowly, as if in pain, and stopped occasionally to make a point.

What, I was intrigued to know, was an American woman doing in the Vatican?

"Oh, they've got this crazy idea that Americans invented the media, and they ought to have some of us around in their communications activities. But the problem is getting them to take any notice. This whole poison plot is a result of their usual old-fashioned way of doing things. They go on doing things as they always have. I hear you're all set up with Marcinkus. That's unheard of, you know. He never speaks to anyone.

"He's now fighting a case in New York over a book that depicts him as the murderer of Andropov. He's trying to get an injunction. The poor guy, they make him out to be such a monster. You'll see. He's no such thing. People who know him are very devoted to him. He's a kind of sportsman, really.

"The key to exploding this whole assassination theory is Papa Luciani's health. He was very sick, you know, and could have died at any time. But I can't help you directly with all those requests. You'd better see Dr. Joaquin Navarro-Valls, the director of the Press Office. That's more his department than mine. . . ."

We had now reached the Hall of the Audiences, which Marjorie entered by a system of side doors, vetted as we went by security guards.

It was a shock. One more door and we were suddenly on the stage of a vast auditorium, with dazzling arc lights and the echoing roar of thousands of pilgrims. I looked out at a sea of faces on the rising tiered terraces. Groups were singing hymns and waving banners which identified different nationalities and affiliations; some were praying in unison or calling out messages. There was a steel band playing a rousing Italian march. And just a few yards below me was the familiar figure of Pope John Paul II making his way along a line of besuited men at the very front of the audience, separated from him by a barrier. He was shaking hands, patting heads, moving inexorably along through plucking, sighing, weeping devotees. He was a man for the limelight and his glowing heroic profile projected an extraordinary charisma of confidence and good looks, a natural focus in the surrounding crowds. On the stage facing out toward the audience were some fifty men draped with sashes, and knots of tough-looking security men wearing dark glasses. I counted five TV film crews with their handheld cameras and lighting equipment, all vying for the best position.

"We've got problems with these TV men," she said. "I'll have to go and sort them out. Do you want to stay on or slip away? Get in touch after you've seen Marcinkus."

Marjorie Weeke set off in the direction of the Pope, who was now waving at a crowd that seemed barely under control. Then, to the consternation of the men in dark glasses, the stocky figure in white plunged straight into the pilgrims and started to work his way up through the auditorium, causing waves of movement. People were holding up religious objects to be blessed; some were weeping and making distraught gestures with their hands. Sections of the crowd burst into spontaneous applause, again and again. Despite the efforts of the henchmen the Pope was eventually engulfed. I was beginning to be affected by the shrill atmosphere of hysteria in the hall. I decided to leave.

Before passing through the stage door I turned and saw Marjorie Weeke trying to shepherd a crew of gesticulating Japanese film technicians. Finally she too was submerged in the crowd. The exercise of papal ministry, it seemed, required considerable stamina.

I walked back to the English College in the rain, to arrive in time for lunch.

I sat next to the priest with the halo of hair, who listened to my description of the papal audience with amusement. "I stay away. I can't stand the papal triumphalist circus," he said with some feeling. "Incidentally, I saw Marcinkus at an ordination in the North American College last year. It wasn't long after he'd become a wanted man. I got up close because I was fascinated to know what he looked like, and how he'd taken it. He looked absolutely haggard. I watched him very closely because I was wondering whether he was just a businessman or also a man of prayer. He didn't look particularly spiritual. He looked shattered."

Later, in the *salone*, which served as a staff common room, I met the second of the two monsignori who had been at supper the previous evening. He was a fast-talking, polished Vatican official in one of the many new commissions spawned by the Second Vatican Council. There was something brisk and military about the way he bustled up to offer his services, and he had the same boyish youthfulness as his colleague. Twenty years of celibate life in a college routine seemed to act as a sort of aspic.

He was a little purple around the gills, and his hair was curly and silvered. He twinkled with energy and goodwill. He said he was the friend of an acquaintance of Don Diego, the dead Pope's Italian secretary, and offered to arrange a meeting. "He's the man you want to see to get a close view of the Pope during that short Papacy. You see, there were two secretaries living in the papal apartment permanently, sharing all meals and the whole working day with the Pope. Don Diego actually came with Papa Luciani from Venice. He is rather—ingenuous is not quite the right word, but not very complex.

"I'll just tell you another little snippet which I picked up from a

very close friend of mine, who's totally reliable. A few days before
coming down to the conclave after Paul VI's death, Luciani visited
a parish priest in this friend of mine's hometown, and he had to
rest awhile because his feet were swelling up, which is a sign of
certain sorts of heart problems. That's a tiny thing, but all these
little bits could add up to something. Another thing I've heard is
that there had been problems with his health before he became a
bishop. There was a doubt. You're going to need to document that
somehow."

We sat down at the far end of the *salone* where there were
armchairs and a sofa beneath the somber gaze of clerical portraits.
"My view of the Marcinkus affair," he went on, "is that he's a
perfectly nice guy who was taken for a ride; there just weren't enough
checks and balances on the running of the bank. It has all created
a terrible milieu of damage, of scandal. Even loyal Catholics are
at a loss. They read all sorts of things about the Church and finance
in the newspapers. But there's no solid information coming out. All
we can do is hang our heads in shame. It particularly affects our
young people. They love the Church, they want to defend it, so why
not give them the facts? One simply doesn't have a defense, because
there's no information. You know, to hand over two hundred and
fifty million dollars in compensation for the Banco Ambrosiano
collapse and then say there's no moral culpability at all is difficult
to comprehend. It doesn't wash. The Vatican is running a deficit
of thirty to forty million dollars a year currently. When you're so
deeply in the red you don't give away two hundred and fifty million
dollars just as a gesture of goodwill. There was some sense of
responsibility. The whole thing isn't finished yet.

"As for the murder theory, I know what the Vatican is like, and
I know that they would have asked themselves—how can you have
a woman discovering the Pope's body at that time of the morning?
The Italians will say 'See! The Popes are always sleeping with
women.' Anyway, if it were the case that they changed the truth
for this reason, then it was a simple case of stupidity. But the
trouble is that the outside world doesn't buy that naive stupidity
story. They think we're devious and conspiratorial. Which to a
certain extent is true, but not in the normal, worldly way.

"What a place! Let me give you some advice. As you go about

your investigations you've got to learn to distinguish in what you're told between *ufficiale* and *ufficioso*. The latter doesn't mean 'officious'; it's very special to the Vatican and it means information that has special weight, or spin, and means that it's been okayed upstairs at the Secretariat of State, but they're not coming right out and stating it fully, if you see what I mean. They can always deny that they actually said it; *ufficioso* material has a special flavor of what's being thought, what's being said, even. Although they won't admit they're saying it."

He gave a nervous, rapid laugh at the absurdity of it all, although I detected a hint of regret that he should be regarded as part of it.

"Anyway," he said finally, "it will be interesting to discover what special flavor pervades Marcinkus's conversation with you when you get to see him."

6

The entrance to the Vatican Press Office is under an arched walkway at the end of the right-hand side of the Via della Conciliazione opposite Saint Peter's Square. There is a spacious marble vestibule and an auditorium for press conferences. The full-time Vatican correspondents hang out in a smoke-filled room where desks and telephones and a few typewriters are provided. I poked my head into this room late in the afternoon of that first day, after making a telephone appointment to meet the director, Dr. Navarro-Valls. There was a group of elderly-looking men talking to a rascally looking priest. The journalists ignored me; the priest looked up sharply, but I had already gone.

On the other side of the vestibule was an office where I found Sister Giovanna, a fresh-faced, gray-eyed nun who was all concern and smiling kindness. The director was expecting me and she led the way.

I entered a windowless office with a high-octane smell of antiseptic; the pervasive, razor-sharp whiff was so striking that it evoked the atmosphere of an operating theater. Behind the desk, which shone like glass, stood a man in a well-cut brown suit. His gold-rimmed spectacles gleamed and glittered, and his dark, wavy hair glistened with a rich dressing. He had a broad mouth with thick, womanish lips and a great row of strong-looking teeth. His hand felt as if it had been scrubbed in cold water and carbolic.

"So!" he said in a quiet, even voice with a Castilian inflection. "You are going to settle this question of Papa Luciani's death once and for all. Of course I will help you as much as I can. But first of all, let me tell you something that is pertinent to these matters. I must tell you, Mr. Cornwell, something that should interest you. I tell you that I am not just a—how do you say—a literary or . . . philosophical doctor. No! I am a REAL doctor."

He rolled his *r*'s grandiloquently. "You understand what I am telling you? I am an actual *medical* doctor, both in training and many years' practice."

He looked at me intently across the desk, his bloodless, spotless hands joined in the highly professional manner of a consultant. He paused as if to allow time for me to take in this information.

"There are several of us here in the Vatican," he went on, in a low conspiratorial voice, "several of us with . . . competent medical qualifications, who do not believe that Pope Luciani died of what the papal doctor has said he died of."

He looked at me intently.

I could scarcely believe my ears. I was sitting opposite the director of the Vatican Press Office, who was just by the way a doctor, and he was telling me, ten years after the event, that in his view a mistake had been made in the diagnosis of Luciani's fatal illness.

"Myocardial infarction," he went on, "was the suggested cause of death, but that does not seem to us a particularly likely diagnosis. You see, death was instantaneous and without pain. The manner of his death is not really consistent with the myocardial infarction theory."

Again, he let this sink in.

"It is very well attested that Luciani suffered an embolism in the eye in 1975. We also know that he had extremely swollen ankles. I could show you photographs of his ankles, very swollen, as he took walks in the Vatican Gardens. He had problems with his circulation, which is well known. It is more than likely that he suffered a pulmonary embolism on the night in question, and as a result death was instantaneous. The patient does not know it has happened. No pain. Bang! It can often happen in exactly the situation in which he was found. The patient lies down, puts his feet up, the clot rushes up through the body . . . and bang! All over."

He waited a little for this to take effect.

"So! You see! This explains many things. Clears up many things. This man did not have time to press the warning button by his bed. He had no warning of what was coming. It does not seem to me that he had a heart attack. I can put you in contact with a man called Professor Giovanni Rama who treated that embolism in 1975; he could give you an idea of the likelihood of this theory of mine."

"But can you get me access to Dr. Buzzonetti, the Pope's doctor? Surely he should have something to say on this matter?"

He thought for a moment and shook his head. "This I am not certain of. I can only do my best." He extended his hands in a gesture of helplessness.

"Can I see his medical records?"

He shrugged, and again the extended hands. "This may be secret. This is a question of his estate. I do not know."

"Can I see the death certificate?"

"I don't know."

"And the morticians, the gentlemen who say they were brought to the Vatican before the body was found. I *must* see them."

"That would be up to Dr. Buzzonetti, I should think."

"I can't conduct this inquiry unless I see Buzzonetti and the Signoraccis."

He shrugged and smiled. The meeting was over and he rose to show me to the door.

"Any way we can help you . . ."

"Signoraccis and Buzzonetti," I said.

He was shaking his head and smiling.

Out in the Via della Conciliazione I was struck by the enormity of what Navarro-Valls had told me. If the cause of death had indeed been an embolism, and if there had been a clear history of this complaint, why had the Pope's doctors missed it? Were they not aware of his medical history a month into his Papacy? Had the Pope been properly looked after?

And now there was this bizarre attempt to set the record straight ten years after the event, without the benefit of collaboration with the original doctors or a postmortem. As I took a seat in the bar next to the Holy Spirit Bank, I reflected that I had little faith in Navarro's intention to deliver the papal doctor, or the morticians, or any of the documentation. I felt baffled and angry.

7

In preparation for my meeting with Marcinkus I had put some
notes together on the facts of his life. Paul Casimir Marcinkus
was born in 1922 in Cicero, Illinois, of Lithuanian immigrant
parents. His father was an orphan who had traveled to the United
States in 1914, settling first in Pittsburgh and finally in Chicago,
where he met a girl he had known in Lithuania in his childhood.
Paul Casimir was the last of four brothers; there was also a younger
sister. His father made a living by cleaning office windows.

Marcinkus expressed an early interest in a priestly vocation. Aged
thirteen he was enrolled in the Chicago diocesan day seminary where
he received a classical education. He excelled at team games, ball
games, he was a champion swimmer. At eighteen he moved on to
the Saint Mary of the Lake senior seminary at Mundelein, Illinois,
where he studied philosophy for three years, and theology for four.

He was ordained in 1947, aged twenty-five, and posted to the
southwest side of Chicago where he spent a year in a parish working
mostly among young families: as he once commented, ". . . there
were very few funerals, very few weddings, but an awful lot of
baptisms." It was to be the only year of his life spent exclusively
in pastoral work. In the seminary he had shown an aptitude for

canon law, the internal legal system of the Roman Catholic Church;
he was taken out of his first parish to work at the diocesan tribunal
for marriage cases, dealing mainly with separations and annulments;
meanwhile he continued to help out in a city parish where the
congregation was ninety percent black.

A year later he was sent to Rome to study for a doctorate in canon
law. A Roman postgraduate education might be a path to higher
office, perhaps a bishopric, but Marcinkus claims that he had no
ambition beyond returning to the Chicago marriage tribunal. "I
reckoned that if I could only be a little sharper, a little quicker,
know a little more, maybe I could be more help to people with
marriage difficulties," he once said.

In 1952 he was in London doing research at the British Museum
when he received a letter from the Vatican inviting him to spend
two months working in the English Section of the Secretariat of
State. His name had been forwarded by professors at the Gregorian
University to Secretary of State Giovanni Battista Montini (later Paul
VI) as a promising administrator; this was his probation. He passed
muster and was sent to the Pontifical Academy for Ecclesiastics
and Noblemen, where for several months he studied diplomacy and
relations between church and state. Meanwhile he continued his
research, working often until two in the morning.

His first posting as a diplomat was in 1955, working with the
papal nuncio for Bolivia. Here he is credited with having started a
"lend-lease" program for clergy, bringing diocesan priests from the
United States, Britain and Ireland to work in the rapidly expanding
cities of La Paz, Cochabamba and Santa Cruz. His aim was to
increase the reputation of the clergy in Latin America by recruiting
"Nordic" priests, as he termed them, rather than priests from the
Mediterranean countries—"We had enough of them already in
South America," he was known to say. After two years he was
transferred to Ottawa, where he involved himself with immigration
and education problems while enjoying parish work during long
vacations in the Fitzroy Harbour resort area.

By 1959 he was back in the English Section of the Secretariat
of State where he remained, working on translations and the Pope's
English correspondence until the election of Paul VI. During these
years he was not unnoticed. He made a name for himself as a fixer,

particularly among clerical and lay visitors from his diocese. He was a byword for ceaseless energy, rising at six to say Mass. He was seen all over Rome driving a borrowed Chevrolet of immense size—ferrying tourists to the catacombs and visiting bishops to the golf course, or collecting his team of teenage Italian baseball players.

Marcinkus's opportunity to rise rapidly within the Vatican came with Pope Paul VI's decision to travel the world. Marcinkus had got to know the new Pope by teaching him English; the Pontiff asked him to help organize the Eucharistic Congress in India in 1964. Marcinkus's organizational skills proved so impressive that he masterminded nine subsequent visits, including New York, Fatima, Chile, Turkey, Switzerland, the Philippines and Uganda. He was now acting as interpreter for the more important meetings between the Pope and world leaders. He used the opportunity to improve the administration surrounding papal protocol; he apparently introduced a system for keeping minutes of the Pope's meetings, a hitherto unknown practice. He had shown an aptitude for organization, frankness, loyalty and hard work; he was known as "the Pope's man." His preoccupation with the Pope's physical safety abroad earned him the nickname "Gorilla." During the Vatican Council he was a whirlwind of activity, especially in the service of the three hundred American bishops, organizing charter flights, hotel and office accommodation and communications. In 1963 he built Villa Stritch, a million-dollar apartment complex for visiting American prelates, named after a former archbishop of Chicago; he became its first rector.

When Cardinal Alberto Di Jorio, president of the IOR, the Vatican Bank, reached the age of eighty, Paul VI decided that Marcinkus was the ideal replacement. He was moved into the bank in 1969; it was a position of enormous power and influence, outflanking the Secretariat of State and the powerful and ambitious Cardinal Giovanni Benelli. From now on Marcinkus reported directly to the Pope. He continued to organize foreign trips, which gave him an opportunity to be close to Paul VI on a daily basis, and to decide who got to see the Pope in foreign lands. In time he was to add the progovernorship of the Vatican City to his duties. Not only would he control the Pope's purse strings, he would be in charge of the personnel and the entire fabric of the Vatican City, including the buildings, furnishings, vehicles, gardens and the operation of the Vatican supermarket and pharmacy.

It was an unprecedented power base for an American inside the Vatican. It was resented, especially by the Italians, and his forthright manner did nothing to allay fears about his ruthlessness and ambition. The criticisms and allegations started early. In 1972, in the first major scandal, which came to be known as the counterfeit bonds case, he was accused of having placed many millions of dollars' worth of stolen and counterfeit securities in the Vatican vaults in a Mafia conspiracy that stretched from New York to Zurich. It was in the course of this imbroglio that Marcinkus first crossed swords with Benelli. Marcinkus was exonerated by an FBI investigation, but his bad press has continued unremittingly to this day.

The details of the various scandals touching Marcinkus—the Banco Ambrosiano collapse, the deaths of Sindona and Calvi, insalubrious assertions about the conduct of his private life—will emerge later in this narrative, but reading through scores of press clippings from all over the world it became clear that he had acquired an almost universal reputation as a worldly prelate whose career had been dogged by controversy. The consensus was ungenerous: where there's smoke there's fire. But what astonished me at this point in my research was the lack of a single friendly testimonial. Was there nobody prepared to give a character reference on behalf of the powerful archbishop? I began to ring around in search of his cronies.

I discovered that he had formed some lifelong friendships among a small group of priests during his early days as a student of canon law in Rome. The basis of their relationship was primarily, and perhaps inevitably, the golf links. The three men I managed to contact were now in their eighties, but they were sprightly and in social circulation, and still came to Rome where they would spend time with Marcinkus in the Governor's Palace. My approaches elicited the following judgments:

"The point is that most of the stories about him come from inside the Vatican. There are all sorts of creeps in there on the inside who are paid retainers to whisper unattributable dirt about their brethren to newspapers and so on. The fact is that people who could have defended him haven't lifted a finger because he's not liked. The Italians can't stand him. The only one who has supported him is this present Pope, John Paul II. The Pope accused a journalist of making a 'brutal' attack on Marcinkus. That's a savage word to use in Italian, and it shows how fiercely *he* regards the onslaught of criticism. A prominent archbishop went in to see the Pope, saying, 'We'll have to get rid of him.' And the Pope said, and I have this on impeccable authority, 'Tell me, if you were being heavily criticized and I took immediate action, would you be pleased? Until there's something definitely proved against him, he stays where he is.'

"He's *not* liked. He's better with ordinary people because he's got the common touch and he knows how to talk to them. But he's helped a lot of people in his time, especially priests and nuns with problems about buildings. He's always giving a helping hand to lame ducks. He's never done anything for himself, but he could have made a mint of money in his position.

"He's done tremendous things in the Vatican City . . . built huge underground depots and started up all sorts of schemes for young people. He's even planted some of those giant redwood trees in the Vatican Gardens—the sort they have on the West Coast that you can drive a car through. He has a genius for tidiness; he's a very good cook. When I stay with him we regularly eat in. . . . We sit by a big window playing cribbage. Then there's golf. He hits the ball a mile, but he also has the delicacy of a surgeon. He plays a straightforward game, though. He gives us all handicaps."

"He's not a pietistic type, or sanctimonious. You know what I mean? As a priest he's what you might call conservative . . . as we say in Latin, *sentire cum ecclesia*—he goes along with the thinking and dogmas of the Church. I'm impressed with the way he keeps going despite the constant negative media coverage. His golf is not as good, though. . . . Actually, I think he has a little trouble with his knee; a number of times on the drives he didn't get off the tee at all last time. But I'm sure it wasn't any of this media attention."

"Does he drink?" I asked.

"He drinks," said my informant, "but not to excess. I've never seen him under the weather, even slightly. But, of course, a man like that can consume a little more than the rest."

"How does he like to spend the evening? Does he like his food?"

"Yes, I guess so."

"So what does he do of an evening?"

"You really wanna know? He loves Westerns, cowboy videos . . . stuff like *The Plainsman*, you know, with Gary Cooper as Wild Bill Hickok, and Jean Arthur as Calamity Jane. I tried to get him on to other sorts of movies, but no, he likes that stuff."

"I knew him when he was a boy in the minor seminary. He was always very busy; he used to get a squad of kids together and go and chop trees and clear undergrowth. I don't know whether it was nervous energy, or what. He's a very sensitive man, you know. People look on him as some kind of Neanderthal or something. He's suffered a great deal, more than a lot of people I know would have done in the same circumstances. Even people who are very close to him don't realize how much he's been hurt. He's taken an awful lot.

"Why is he attacked like this? I guess it's partly because he's an American. I've noticed that he's usually attacked when there's something political going on in Italy. The enemies of the Christian Democrats try to get at them through the Vatican; they can't attack the Pope, so Marcinkus has become the patsy, because he's in the finance area and he's American.

"One of the biggest mysteries to me is why they appointed him to the job in the first place. I remember saying, 'Why appoint *him?*' There was really nothing to recommend him. The only thing I can think is that Paul VI wanted to know what was going on. But Marcinkus had no background in that field."

The responses of Marcinkus's loyal old friends had been muted, guarded. There had been no telling anecdotes, no hint of enthusiastic hero worship. The only bright note had been the comment about Westerns. The most interesting feature was the notion that he had been the victim of intrigue, although his cronies had contradicted themselves on the score of its origin. Did it derive from the Italian political scene? Or from within the Vatican itself?

But why were they so noncommittal? Putting a charitable construction on it, I wondered whether I wasn't up against the curious, understated embarrassment that, I remembered, pervades the close companionship of priests, a tendency to close ranks against lay outsiders, to abominate sentimentality and fulsome praise.

The alternative interpretation was that even his best friends found it difficult to think of nice things to say about him.

8

On a gray and freezing morning I set off down Via di Monserrato for my 9:15 appointment at the Vatican with Archbishop Marcinkus.

Saint Peter's Square had been cleared for a papal audience for members of the Italian air forces. Men in blue uniforms were spilling out of military buses; armed carabinieri were placed along the length of Bernini's Colonnade. I was obliged to quarrel briefly with one of them in order to make my way to the Bronze Door, which is the official entrance to the Apostolic Palace and my designated entrance. The young man faced me sullenly, with a machine gun slung across his midriff: his eyes were dull and obstinate, he was ill-shaven under the chin. I tried to explain that I wished to proceed to the Vatican—to no avail. I mentioned the name of Marcinkus, of Marjorie Weeke, of Archbishop Foley. *Niente!* Finally I said, *"Portone di Bronzo"*—Bronze Door—and I had found the password: *"Ah, si, certo! Avanti!"*

At the high bronze doors, weathered and battered with age, a guard in an enveloping navy-blue cloak was standing to attention, halberd presented; he was framed against the backdrop of a corridor of marble and granite that rose into the distance along the deep and shallow steps of the Scala Regia, all dimly lit by massive iron lanterns. This is the papal front door, designed to put you in your place, whoever you are! I was directed to an office on the right. I applied to a functionary for the usual pass, which I was granted after he had telephoned my name to the archbishop's secretary. A Swiss Guard at a desk outside the permissions office directed me forward up a staircase of eerie, echoing grandeur. He watched me as I went. Emerging through a glass doorway at the top I was met by yet another guard who saluted stiffly as he bore down on me to inspect my pass. I was now in a silent and spotless square described by the three sides of an immense palazzo whose balconies were protected by glass panels—the famous three-story loggias of the Apostolic Palace. In the top corner of the side to my right lived Pope John Paul II, along with the household of Polish nuns and his secretary, Father Stanislav. At each portico and doorway around the square were more Swiss Guards—scrubbed, well-shorn bully boys in Renaissance fancy dress—brimming with curiosity about everything that moved. I was directed diagonally to the right across this square, known as the Cortile di San Damaso, to an archway leading to a smaller courtyard.

As I set off I was startled by the sudden arrival of a shimmering dark-blue limousine that sped through an archway from behind me, made a loop and screeched to a halt on the cobbles before a stairway, where red carpeting had been laid right out into the square. At the same moment a sleek, well-fed prelate in cassock and long coat emerged hastily from the doorway of the palace. There was a flash of scarlet, a gleam of purple and amethyst; the Swiss Guards sprang to attention and saluted. The chauffeur ran around the car and opened the door; the prelate went straight from the red carpet into the plush interior of the limousine; the chauffeur saluted, shut the door, ran smartly to the driver's seat and sped away. The deep hush descended once more. Important matters, it was clear, were being conducted by very important people.

I now found myself in the silent precincts of the Vatican Bank. There were three cars parked outside. A brass plate on the honey-colored stone wall announced: IOR—ISTITUTO PER LE OPERE DI RELIGIONE—the Institute for Religious Works. A carabiniere sat in a glass cubicle. He asked my name and pointed me through frosted-glass revolving doors straight into the vestibule of the office of the president. There were deep-pile brown carpets, and on the walls a variety of modern religious paintings, including a Madonna and Child. Heavy tobacco scent. The vestibule was a wide corridor with doors leading off on both sides. At the far end, facing me, with her back to a high mullioned window, sat a small, neat woman at a desk. She was in early middle age, with cropped brown hair, dressed in a well-cut navy skirt, silk blouse and green cardigan. She rose to meet me. She had once, I suspected, been pretty in an elfin kind of way; her looks were still appealing, but her skin seemed pallid, as if from lack of sleep, her large, dark eyes doleful and apprehensive. This was Vittoria Marigonda—personal private secretary to Archbishop Paul Casimir Marcinkus for seventeen years, and party, I suspected, to a host of complicated and awkward secrets. Before I could greet her, I noticed a looming figure at the door to my side. A big man dressed all in black had come to scrutinize me. He was leaning easily against the doorjamb lighting a curled Petersham pipe of enormous capacity. As he sucked at the stem he gazed at me with very still, hooded eyes, a steady, bemused, cold-looking expression. His head was strangely huge, and steep at the sides—like a beehive—and he held a lighted match delicately above his pipe with massive, not too clean hands, blemished with dark warts around the thumbs.

"Hi there!" he said in a deep, grating voice. Then to his secretary: "Okay, Mavi, I'll take it."

He motioned me to enter the room—a spacious modern office divided by a gilt screen, a sort of trellis arrangement constructed of twisted metal squares: on one side was a boardroom with a coffin-shaped table and black-leather chairs, on the other his personal work and reception area with leather sofas, a low coffee table and armchairs, a grand curved desk covered with papers and an over-flowing pewter ashtray the size of a meat dish. Marcinkus walked to his desk with an easy athletic roll. He threw himself into an executive-style swivel chair.

We sat for a few moments, appraising each other. Was I sitting opposite a man, I wondered, who was guilty of the various allegations that had been circulating about him?

He had the hands and shoulders of a powerful athlete. His face was a leathery mask, the tanned and battered phizog of an outdoors man; he had a blunt nose and a firm, severe mouth. There was no attempt to return my smile of greeting: gray-green eyes gazed unblinkingly at me beneath half-closed lids, giving him a sardonic, almost drugged look. Across his wide forehead was imprinted a single deep and crooked line.

He was dressed in the full pastoral rig of a Roman Catholic priest—black suit (a hint of dandruff on the shoulders), black silk stock and deep, slightly grubby Roman collar, with no hint of archiepiscopal purple. On the wall immediately above his head hung a collage in metal of the Resurrection, with thickets of reaching hands and arms.

His physical presence unnerved me; I was used to clerical bureaucrats who by his age had got a little soft and flabby, even a trifle effeminate after a lifetime ensconced in cushioned offices and chapels. He was dressed as a priest, but physically he looked as if he had spent his working life in a breakers' yard. Never had I encountered in one person such seeming conflict (or could it be uneasy reconciliation?) between the sacred and the profane.

How should we begin? I had hoped to use this meeting as a warm-up, so that he would start to relax in my presence. But even as I framed an innocuous question in my mind, he astounded me: Archbishop Paul Casimir Marcinkus, depicted as a villain in at least three books, kicked off our conversation by launching at once into an unsolicited alibi.

"You see, John, when I lived out at Villa Stritch—that's where the American clergy have an apartment building in Rome—I always used to get in here at about seven o'clock for one simple reason: if I left it half an hour later I'd be fighting traffic. You leave it to seven-thirty, eight o'clock and you spend an hour getting in."

His voice had a deep, ragged edge to it. It was a heavy smoker's voice, with a carelessness of diction wholly discordant with the dignified confines of the Vatican sanctuary. He put down his pipe and lit a Marlboro.

"So I like to get in early, read all the papers and make an early start. Anyway, that particular morning I was in early as usual and

Sergeant Roggen of the Swiss Guard came up to me as I got out of my car and said something. I thought he said, 'Hey, I dreamed the Pope was dead.'

"I couldn't understand him. So I said, 'You shouldn't dream stuff like that.' Then he said, 'No, look, the flag is at half-mast.' Then I came on up here and I saw Magee and the doctor standing over there across the San Damaso and I waved to them and came right on in here. I guess I heard like everybody else, within a few minutes on the telephone.

"Then there's all this talk about getting rid of me . . ." To my astonishment he was moving straight from his alibi to his motive. "I was completely unaware there was any plan to replace me. Even if there had been, I wouldn't have been in any way upset. In fact, the reverse was the case. I went to see John Paul a few days before he died and he was very kind, very fatherly; he thanked me for all the work I'd been doing and said he hoped I would stay on."

His voice was grave; he spoke slowly. I felt a sense of deepening tension in the room. I attempted to interrupt with a specific question: I wanted to know whether his conversation with John Paul I had been minuted. But he plowed straight on:

"Then there was Calvi." Again he was leading the interview; now he was dealing with the billion-dollar Banco Ambrosiano collapse and his association with Roberto Calvi, the bank's president. "People say I knew Calvi. I met him two or three times. I had lunch with him once, I blessed a building of his once, but I never knew him or spent any time with him; I never visited his house or anything. I couldn't have spent more than nine hours with him in my whole life. Maximum!"

He spoke the last sentence with finality; I felt a sense of panic. He had evidently decided that he had given all the answers that could possibly be required. At this rate, I estimated, our interview would be over in a few minutes and I would be crossing the quiet square and going back down that echoing staircase no wiser than when I had come up.

I said, "Monsignor—is it all right to call you Monsignor?" (the title is an unelaborate formula, referring to the bureaucratic rather than religious status of a wide range of Vatican clerics). "All we ever read in the newspapers and various books is about you as the worldly, golf-playing prelate. I want to know a bit about you as a priest . . ."

Before the words were out of my mouth he was off again, actually answering my suggestion as if it were a question to be dealt with without delay:

"All the years I've worked here I've been doing as much pastoral work as my time would allow. I had a group of Italian kids here I was doing baseball with. I tried to do some spiritual work that way, trying to give them the idea that religion is not just something you go to church with, but a way of life. . . . Using sport, trying to give them an idea how you can live according to your principles. . . . We used to have a lot of people coming from Chicago visiting Rome and I took it over: show them the city and do things like a guide. I'd take them to the Sistine Chapel, into the gardens, have dinner with them, make them feel welcome. . . ." He paused, as if to say, "How am I doing?" His voice trailed away a little as he said in conclusion: ". . . A normal . . . priestly role. What else do you want to know?"

His intonation, accent and delivery were, like his idiom, straight off the streets of Chicago: "dinner with them" came out as "dinner wid 'em"; "context" as "karntext," and then, "I dunno," "what else do you wanna know." All his *g*'s were automatically dropped; "doin' " and "usin' " and "visitin' " and "playin'." I was intrigued at the poverty of his vocabulary, the pidgin usage—"do things like a guide." It made me wonder about the known facts of his educational background—the seven years of philosophy and theology, the doctorate in law at the Gregorian, the courses in diplomacy at the Pontifical Academy.

"Could you tell me about your early education, Monsignor?" I asked.

"I never had any trouble with my studies, but I was never really what you might call one of the shining lights, not that I couldn't have been, but I felt there was more to life than just cracking a book. Human contact was necessary. My goal was to be a parish priest—doing well there, not being involved in Vatican finance. People mention Vatican finance: I've *never* been involved in Vatican finance. . . . That's one of the conceptions people have that's false."

It was as if Kissinger had said he'd never been involved in diplomacy. The bafflement on my face must have been clearly evident.

He conceded a little: "I handle a little bit now in relation to the Governatorato, indirectly, because I have to maintain the buildings, build things, try to coordinate activities in the Vatican City State. The bank we have here is a service organization for the Church; it's involved particularly in apostolic works. Somebody asked me one time, 'Why this?' I said, 'When my workers here come to retire they expect a pension; it's no use my saying to them, "I'll pay you four hundred Hail Marys." ' Now that's been misquoted all over the place. They use that all the time, see? I'm quoted as saying, 'You can't run the Church on Hail Marys.' It would be very nice if the Church could live without depending on these things, but you build a church you have to buy bricks, have a bricklayer. . . . And if you've got people working for you, especially today, you've the obligation of pension plans and so on. I handle their money, but they handle their own finances.

"My concept has always been, and I think this is true of everybody, it's easy to say, let's just live in poverty. But there're two poverties, in a sense: there's the poverty of the spirit—complete disattachment, using money and possessions only as a means—and the other sort of poverty is to be poor with nothing. That latter is not the poverty that's preached by Christ.

"I tell my people here, my employees in the bank, 'Listen, this is no ordinary banking business we're going through. If that's your idea, you'd better be working someplace else. We're here in a kind of hidden place helping these people fulfill their mission everywhere over the world.' I say, 'If we *do* make any money on these transactions at the end of the year it should go back into the Church,' which it does. But if I run a bank in the world and it did very well, the stockholders at the end of the year would get to buy a new Cadillac."

He paused a little, to stoke up some more columns of smoke and to fiddle with the paraphernalia of his pipe. "This is my concept, and history backs me: as soon as people get too interested and too involved in money, you know, let's build a beautiful church, and all that—not NECESSARY!—then you get caught up with the material part instead of the spiritual. . . ."

Was he not protesting a trifle too much, I wondered, on the score of matter and spirit? His interest in money for its own sake? I wanted to ask him more about how the money was made, and to whom was he accountable, as a mere "service" organization, when he *lost* money.

"I couldn't care less about money in itself," he was saying.

"Who would ever question that, Monsignor?" I asked.

"I've told this to the Italians, but it's not interesting to them. Because that gives the lie to what they've been saying about me."

He rose from his chair and looked about him for a moment: "You know, I cut something out of a New York magazine, a cartoon about a man . . ." Then, at a loss as to where it might be, he sat down again. He was smiling to himself—a pained, inward smile. "I always say, you know, when you shave in the morning you've always got to recognize that face in the mirror. You can't fake that face there. You know what it is. You can fake everybody else, but you can't fake yourself. And if I become a priest for that specific goal to help my people follow the message of Christ and try to apply it in their own lives, I've got to be one of the first guys to do it, too."

He settled more deeply into his chair. He put down his pipe and lit a fresh Marlboro.

"Yes, I live a comfortable life. Maybe too comfortable, but I couldn't care less. I like to do certain things, play golf; I used to play some tennis, I need some physical exercise, chopping trees— just to get the badness out of me. But where do you chop trees around here?"

I had a momentary, sacrilegious image of Marcinkus poleaxing his way through a line of cypresses in the exquisite elegance of the Vatican Gardens. Then I thought of his crony's remark about the giant redwoods. I began to smile, but the archbishop was in earnest.

"I used to love physical work," he repeated, "because it got the badness out of me. It made me feel better. You sit behind a desk all day long, you get groggy. You see cardinals here every day take a walk for an hour in the gardens. But that's boring to me, that sort of walking. But just because I'm walking with a golf club in my hand, it's different. See? According to certain people, see?"

The archbishop was a little angry. He drew hard on his cigarette. Who were these "certain people"? I wondered. Were they within the walls of the Vatican or without?

"If I play tennis by myself, up against a wall," he went on resentfully, "nothing's wrong. But if I go out and play tennis with somebody else—'There he goes!' they say. It's different. But the people who criticize you are the ones who do it themselves."

He gazed at me for a while, a peeved smile playing about his lips.

"If I say that," he growled, "people say I'm autoincensing myself . . . to myself, see."

The incense image, it occurred to me, was very exact: he meant, of course, that act of holy incense blessing in the Catholic liturgy. It was a grotesque gibe—and peculiarly apt within this Vatican setting. His keenest critics, it was apparent, were his priestly colleagues.

"But as I say to my kids, unless I act according to what I preach it's no good. So I tell them—chew it up a little bit, digest it and live according to it. If you don't do it, I can't make you do it. . . ."

He was now delivering an impromptu homiletic aside, as if to an invisible congregation in the far corner of the room.

His habit of suddenly forgetting my presence and sermonizing his former baseball team, or his erstwhile Chicago parishioners, was intriguing. Had there been sleepless nights during the long months of his "imprisonment" in the Vatican, I wondered, when he whiled away the small hours composing some of the moral discourses he'd never managed to deliver throughout his life as a banker?

"Is it possible," I asked, "that Pope John Paul was murdered?"

He looked at me for a while, his eyes glassily amused. Then he started to chortle wheezily to himself, coughing a little at the same time: "The furthest thing from my mind . . . would be . . ." he said breathlessly, "is that *anybody* would think of getting rid of a pope." He wheezed a little more. "A lot of times I've said I'd like to strangle a guy, but that's when you've lost your patience with him or something like that, a figure of speech. . . . And yet, if you saw the Pope . . . there's a very basic thing to that Holy Father who died. Paul VI had been in the Curia for thirty-some years, he knew the

Curia inside out, went to Milan eight years, came back. He knew how the Secretariat of State ran, he knew his way around the *Annuario Pontificio*. He knew where all the offices were and stuff. But it still took him six months to get into the groove.

"This poor man, Pope John Paul I, comes out from Venice; it's a small, aging diocese, ninety thousand people in the city, old priests. Then all of a sudden he's thrown into a place and he doesn't even know where the offices *are*. He doesn't know what the secretary of state *does*."

He paused for a moment.

"They called him the '*smiling* Pope.'" He paused again. "But let me tell you something . . . that was a very *nervous* smile."

He was grinning at me crookedly. I was grinning back, but the remark had made me feel uncomfortable.

"So, he takes over," he went on. "He sits down; the secretary of state brings in to him a pile of papers, says, 'Go through these!' He doesn't even know where to start. And here's a man who didn't enjoy tremendous health to begin with. Up in Venice he would take his nice little siesta in the afternoon. If he decided he wanted to take a little walk out in the square, he'd just get up and walk out. Take a little ride in the country. . . . Then he comes in here, he's closed in, and everybody's calling him. . . . 'You've gotta get this, gotta get this. . . . What about this . . . ' And he's got to go through 'em all. So the pressure's building up, his health isn't that great. *I* can understand how something like that could happen. Divine Providence? Divine Providence . . . He served a very important role. Pope John served a role to break the pontificate of Pius XII. This John Paul I served a very important role in the Church.

"You just have to pick up the paper every day and you find young people who got a good job and they die after a while. Did somebody kill 'em? And this one, just because they didn't do an autopsy. They *never* do an autopsy."

Monsignor Jim at the English College knew better, I reflected, but I let it pass.

His shoulders began to heave, and he started a long, raking wheezy laugh: "I used to get a picture in the past, you know, a dead pope, the guy used to hit him with a silver hammer on the head to see if he was dead. . . . Well, if he *wasn't* dead, this guy made sure! He really did it! In that sense, you know, in the bad old days . . ." For a few moments the archbishop was speechless with heaving laughter, wielding an imaginary hammer in his massive right hand. "Hey there!" cried the archbishop, still laughing. "Wake up! Bang!" He brought his huge fist down with a swipe through the air.

He sighed to himself, still smiling. "But they don't do that stuff now. And I don't remember them breaking the Fisherman's ring, you know—the old seal ring the popes used to wear. All the sealing is done by the secretary of state and stuff, but the Pope doesn't wear a Fisherman's ring nowadays; that's all been stopped."

We sat smiling at each other for a few moments. The archbishop had enjoyed the hammer episode. He seemed sufficiently relaxed for me to ask a second, more personal question.

"How do you cope, Monsignor, with the idea that millions of people out there think you are a murderer?"

He immediately began to shrug, to look toward the window—its view across Bernini's Colonnade was screened by nylon curtaining. He fiddled a little with his smoking apparatus.

"Look, first of all, these guys are off their rockers!" he said slowly. "If that's an accusation people want to believe, what can I do? I have to go on living here and trying to be faithful to what I believe in. What am I supposed to do? Jump off a cliff?"

He gazed across the room bleakly, as if recollecting some deep hurt. "And yet it's remarkable; I go certain places, and I've been going to a church and I don't go in there with all my paraphernalia, I just went in there as a priest, and nobody recognized me." He seemed to go into a reverie for a few moments, as if remembering earlier, happy days, before the notoriety began.

"And then," he continued, "I go into a restaurant sometimes with friends, and people point at me and say, 'Look! That's him!' " He looked at me defiantly through a pall of smoke across the desk. "I feel like asking them, 'What do you want? My autograph?'

"The hardest thing, I have to admit . . . I've been accused of murdering a pope and then getting involved in the Ambrosiano. Both of these things are completely unfounded. If I have any inner strength, if I believe in myself, I say to myself, this might be God's way of ensuring that I get my toe in the door of paradise. If I get

my toe in, He can't slam the door. That's the price I have to pay
for my priesthood, you know. In all of our churches today you'll
have a difficult time finding a crucifix. And yet, we're supposed to
preach Christ and Christ crucified."

He was talking in a low voice, simply, with no evident note of
self-pity or false piety. I wondered if I had touched on the vulnerability remarked on by his priest friends.

"The press tends to portray you as a thug," I said. "Why do you
think they do this?"

He gave a wry smile, opened his hands. "You read these books
about me and you get the impression I was raised by Al Capone in
the streets. That's because of Cicero, see."

"So what was Cicero really like in your childhood? Was it full
of gangsters . . . whiskey stills . . . ?"

He laughed silently. "It was a suburb of Chicago, with Lithu-
anians, Poles, Irish, Czechs . . . It was a *quiet*, residential place,
and almost everybody worked for Western Electric down the street.
There was an old hotel where people *said* Al Capone had his headquarters, but I don't know whether it was true or not. His mother
lived near the church on Sixteenth Street, but as far as Al Capone's
presence was concerned, it didn't affect any of us; and anyway, his
heyday was in the twenties."

"So what was your childhood really like?"

"I couldn't have had a more normal childhood. I was always out
playing ball games with the gang around the house. We were poor.
I remember going right through a new pair of tennis shoes on the
gravel in the playground and getting it in the neck from my mother.
This was the time of the Depression. I had twenty-five cents a day
for food and travel to school, and I was always figuring out ways to
make it stretch so I could afford a ball game or take in a
movie. . . . We had fun. I remember riding on the old running
board of a car—six guys inside, six guys hanging on the outside,
driving out with them and cheering them on. . . . A perfectly *normal* childhood.

"Cicero . . . When I was stationed in Bolivia we went out to a
movie—you know, one of these places where they put up an old
curtain. In this movie the guy walks into the hotel, see, and he
puts his name in the register—Joe Baggio di Lupo, Cicero—and

the whole audience starts to go, 'da-da-da-da-da-da . . .' " The
archbishop, cigarette between his teeth, was holding an imaginary
machine gun in his hands, spraying the room with glee, breathless
with his wheezy laugh.

When he had finished, he shook his head, smiling inwardly.

"Anyway—street gangster! I was in the junior seminary from the
age of thirteen! Hard for a lot of people to imagine what that
means. . . . I was young to decide on the priesthood, but I guess
it's how some kids say they'd like to be baseball players. It was
very disciplined. Some of our guys who decided they wanted to go
out and date all the time were asked either to make up their minds,
or what. You don't play with fire if you don't wanna get burned."

"Did *you* ever date a girl?" I asked him.

"Maybe once in a while I would go out on a date, take a girl out,
or we might have the girls with the gangs around the house. I wasn't
scared stiff of them or anything. . . ."

He sat for a while, musing, looking toward the curtains.

"You planned as a boy on becoming a parish priest," I said, "but
you ended up a banker."

"I didn't plan it," he said abruptly. "I came here to Rome to
study and I got trapped up in it. I was a little unhappy I wasn't
going home to the States, but I said if my boss, the cardinal back
in Chicago, wants to loan me out to the Holy Father—it's priestly
work. It wasn't the life I'd planned for, but in all the years that I've
been in the Vatican, I've never asked for a job and I've never
refused one if they insisted."

As he spoke this last sentence his voice almost disappeared in
a deep bass whisper.

"I don't believe that I have the right to refuse. I have a right to
let my superiors know I might not be pleased or I might not be
competent to do it. As I did for this job here. I said four times,
'You must be out of your minds!' I said, 'Why don't you get somebody
else? I have no experience in banking!' And they said, 'You have
to kind of watch over things.' I said, 'I'm incompetent for that!' The
way they do things around here! They don't come and say, 'Will
you take that job?' They come and say, 'How would you look on
it . . .' and so on and so forth. *I* had no training or background in

banking. I couldn't even do any courses because I didn't have any time. People say I did a business degree, but it's not true. And actually, you see, these people don't understand. I don't do any of the transactions; I just set the policy. What I did when I came into this job, I went to New York. I went to Chase Manhattan for a day or two; I went to a place to see how stocks and stuff operated; I went to Chicago and friends introduced me to people at the Continental Bank—they gave me a kind of three-day course, taking me through everything. I spent another day at a trust business. Then I spent the whole day in a small bank seeing how the operation worked. That was it. But what kind of training do you need? From the organizational viewpoint I've always been very methodical. It may not look like it now in this office, but I am."

He looked about bleakly. There were stacks of files on the desk, an assortment of boxes and knickknacks gathering dust on a shelf behind. A fancy clock that told world time.

"I was always one for figuring out systems and numbers. Even in the seminary as a boy I had a name for it. I was thinking the other day how I devised the coat of arms for my class. My year used to call themselves the Naturals; I don't know why, but we did. I used dice as the basic part of it, and at the side three different sets of dice. Six and one is a natural in a game of dice: that meant that we used to have six years at the seminary, then they added the extra one for us, so it became six and one. Before we went into the major seminary it was five years in the junior seminary, so that's six major and five junior: that's a natural too. Then three years of philosophy and four years of theology was seven: and that was a natural. Then I said, we've got to have a motto, and I said, 'From the Natural to the Supernatural!' That's our goal. See?"

The archbishop sat back and seemed to bask in the afterglow of a happy memory.

"I like figuring out systems," he went on. "I always had organizational talents, which became somewhat obvious here when I got involved in papal trips. I'm very methodical and, you know, I've a good memory. And that's why maybe the Pope thought I'd be a good man for this job, to bring some real organization into the place. As for financial experience . . ." he gave me a wry grin.

"Well . . . let's say I counted the Sunday collection and never got it wrong!" He laughed huskily to himself. He was in a good humor, expansive. He lit up a Marlboro.

"They call you the Pope's gorilla. . . . Does that distress you?"

He drew down his mouth a little, as if to disclaim any emotional reaction.

"After one of the early trips some Italian gave me that name and it stuck. A gorilla at home in the States is like . . . a hood. But a gorilla here in Italy means a bodyguard. Naturally, I *wasn't* the Pope's bodyguard, because we always took four or five Vatican security men. But when there was a real crush around the Holy Father, maybe I became a little more . . . spontaneous, I guess, and because of my size and so forth I could clear a way for him. But my proper function was to get the whole thing set up and make sure it was carried out."

He narrowed his eyes and drew hard on his cigarette. I was looking at his massive wrists and shoulders; it was not difficult to imagine him inflicting a great deal of damage when he became "spontaneous."

"You see, when you go to these places," he continued, ". . . I hate to be critical of anybody around here, but I remember we went to the United Nations in New York and the Pope said Mass at Yankee Stadium. Some of our Vatican people were upset because the police had their backs to the Pope—which is the way *I* wanted it. They were watching the crowd, making sure nobody gets out of line. See? Some of our people thought that was disrespectful. Now when you look at a crowd you see all these machines out there—cameras of all kinds—you don't know whether there's a gun in there or not. You watch their faces, you look into their eyes and you can see immediately if some guy's off his rocker. . . ."

"Monsignor," I intervened, "maybe some people think you're a bit of a gorilla because you deal toughly with them. You don't suffer contradiction. . . ."

He shook his head vigorously.

"I'm not going to pat myself on the back, but in all honesty I don't think I tore anybody down where I became an unfair obstacle to them. Maybe that's my character, but I'm not afraid to say no. When I got this job at the bank I asked a cardinal friend of mine if he thought I could do it. He said, 'I don't know how well you'll do it, but you're the only guy I know who will say no to a cardinal.' "

He paused a moment, his jaw sticking out defiantly. "And he was the first guy I said it to," he added. "On these trips I'm sure I made an enemy or two among our own people. It's the Pope that's taking the trip, and we're there to serve *him*, not to *be* served. Arguments break out about who gets to sit closest to him. I say it should be the bishops and so on of the host country, because *we* Vatican people get to see him all the time. Why not give someone else a break! But some of these people don't like that."

"You're a real pope's man, aren't you?" I said. "You have that reputation. But were you John Paul I's man? Rumor has it around here that he didn't like you. He was going to get rid of you. There's a rumor that after your only audience with John Paul I you came back to the bank and said you wouldn't be around for much longer."

"Nah . . . I'll be blunt: that's a lot of BS. I had one audience with him for about an hour. I came down and spoke with my people here. I said to them, 'Gee, he looks tired!' I told them it was a wonderful audience, a magnificent audience, that he wanted me to stay on, he'd be calling me back. I never said anything about him pushing me out—NEVER! And later on when I read these things about him wanting me fired, I said that's the funniest way to fire a guy! He couldn't have been nicer."

"What about Cardinal Benelli? I gather you said no to *him* once or twice."

The archbishop looked at me sharply. He picked up his pipe and started to examine the bowl.

"I didn't agree with Benelli on certain things," he said slowly, "as he didn't agree with *me* on certain things. I could give you a very good instance. . . . We were in Colombia, and this was one of the first trips that he took. Everything I'd arranged had been approved in advance by him. You see, he was the *sostituto* secretary of state. I was already over there, and he arrives. He gets off the plane and he starts saying we gotta change this, change that. I said to him, 'Your Excellency, you *can't* change it! This thing is organized.' I meant that all the security arrangements, involving police and army and so forth, was fixed on every street and rooftop. Then he bawls me out: 'I didn't *know!*' So I says, 'You *signed* everything.'

So he says to me, 'Well, I didn't know about that. . . .' And I says
to him, 'Look, if you don't read it, don't sign it! See! Now, you
signed it, so it's okay, and that's the way it's going to be.' So then
he was real *furious*. We met in the car each day and he could barely
say good morning, you know, *caritas urget nos*. Benelli was a very
forceful character. You knew where you stood with him. Was he a
vindictive type of person? I don't think so. People have bandied
Benelli's name around in association with spreading this murder
theory . . . and . . . I just can't *believe* it!"

He fell silent for a while, rubbing his jaw ruminatively. At length
he said, "I come from the States. They have a different way of doing
things around here. I call a spade a spade. But over here with
Italians you have to be careful. It's kind of Oriental . . . and your
Italian will let you know in nice language that maybe he didn't
agree with you, but when you hear it, you're not too sure you
understood what he meant. So maybe there is a subterfuge."

"There was certainly subterfuge over the Vatican accounts as to
what the Pope was reading when he died," I said.

"Knowing how their minds work here, they couldn't just have the
Pope found in bed reading something light or secular; it would have
to be the Bible or the *Imitation of Christ*. But I think that's silly
myself. *I* sometimes read Westerns. I'm not always reading heavy
stuff. You like to take your mind off things."

He sat musing for a while.

"You know," he went on, "there are only three people who were
there present in the papal apartment when John Paul I died: Magee,
Lorenzi and the sister. You don't want to take too much notice of
what anybody else says."

He stopped, as if to allow me to consider this for a while. Then
he glanced at his watch. He was beginning to look restless.

"What about Cardinal Villot?" I said. "*He* was there. What sort
of man was he?"

"Villot was frightened of his own shadow. It's inconceivable that
he would have gotten involved in anything."

"Did you know him?"

"When he became secretary of state I got to know him somewhat
because he was on our board at the bank. He was a very fidgety
person; he wanted to get rid of everything right away, just to get

them off his desk. . . . Disliked travel. He was kidding me once about going home on my vacation. I said, '*I'm* not afraid to go back to my diocese.' He didn't get it at first. Then he gives a big laugh. He says, 'No, no . . . *sono qui* . . . this is my diocese. I stay here.' I've no way of judging whether he was a good priest, but from what I saw he certainly was. I'd see him out there saying his rosary all the time . . . you know. Taking a walk. You know, the only harshness I could see in Villot, if you're going to call it that, was if you didn't agree with him you could see it. But I don't think he had a harsh thought. I'll give you a good example. The secretary, John Magee, called me when Paul VI died up at Castel Gandolfo, and I was just going out for a spaghetti. I decided to go up the following morning. About six o'clock I took a ride out. And there was Cardinal Villot standing in the archway of the courtyard smoking a cigarette. He saw me . . . winked at me. But if he'd been a harsh person he would have said, 'Where are *you* going? You have no right here.' I went right up to the Pope's bedroom, I knelt down, said a few prayers by the Holy Father's bed. See? Now I know somebody else, and if *he* were there he would've stopped me."

"And who would that be?" I asked quietly.

The archbishop shook his head, stirred himself as if to go.

"You know," he said, rising out of his chair, "Villot felt the loss of Pope John Paul I as well as anybody else. He was distraught, like anybody else. There was nothing harsh about him. But at the same time Frenchmen are a bit aloof. If he came up to my apartment with a bunch of bishops, he wouldn't be as comfortable there as an American. Frenchmen have a certain amount of awareness of their position."

He walked to the door and turned, waiting for me. As I followed him he put out his huge hand. As I grasped it, he said, "By the way, I don't believe for one moment that John Paul I was going to throw away the birth-control thing. But even if he had, Villot would have been the first to go along with it, like all the French. . . ."

Out in the corridor there was a waiting monsignor, who shot straight in to see the archbishop; the door slammed behind him. I went over to Vittoria Marigonda's desk and sat down next to her. She was smoking a cigarette and looking through a file.

She looked at me appraisingly, with doleful eyes.

"When can I see him again?" I asked.

She looked doubtful. "He's a busy man. He's got a lot on. I don't know . . . Maybe we could fit it in on a Sunday."

"He works Sunday?"

"He works every day and he lives right here. He doesn't go far. I'll give you a call at the English College." She looked at me steadily again. "What exactly is it you're trying to do?"

"How do you mean?"

"He's been hurt enough already. He doesn't need any more conniving write-ups."

I wasn't sure how to answer the question.

"How long have you worked for him?" I asked.

"Seventeen years." She brightened up a little.

"And before that?"

"I worked for a securities trader."

It struck me that Vittoria Marigonda must have a fairly detailed appreciation of every move in the entire Banco Ambrosiano collapse.

"I'd be grateful for any help you can give me," I said. "I should think you know all the ins and the outs . . ."

"Well, I'll do what I can . . . I've seen it all. . . ." She was looking at me knowingly.

As I walked down the long, echoing marble staircase to the Bronze Door, it occurred to me that Vittoria Marigonda might be my best ally and a key informant in the days ahead.

9

One of my London Catholic contacts had recommended the name of a certain monsignor, a Vatican official of many years' standing, who might talk readily and indiscreetly. The monsignor told me on the phone: "I'll meet you for lunch or for dinner, and I'll talk to you so long as you don't use my name or identify my department."

We met at the Grappolo d'Oro close to the Campo dei Fiori, where I found him assiduously examining the menu. His face was puce and puffy, with a bloom of silky plumpness; his hair, cut in choir-boy style with a fussy quiff, had begun to silver. He was in clerical uniform with a snowy white-linen collar, and as he extended a milky hand there was a show of pure-white cuff with heavy gold links.

"I prefer red to white wine," he said, "but I wouldn't trust the house carafe. Perhaps the Villa Antinori. I'll have a little antipasto, then the fettuccine—which is divine here and made with doubled egg—then, perhaps, the suckling pig with some *patate arrostitite* and a little spinach."

His voice was high, nasal and monotone. He gazed at me with vacuous bright blue eyes.

"So you've seen our friend Marcinkus—'the Chink,' as we call him. Even his coat of arms has a crozier crossed with a sword! There was a row about that—it's not strictly allowed—but he's reported to have said, 'I couldn't care a damn!' There are two Milan magistrates have got some bits of paper together, probably no more than bits and scraps, but they seem prepared to put their necks on the line for what they've got. They want to put him in the dock. The Chink has nothing in the way of documentation, and I think the main question is whether he's just culpably ignorant and incompetent or merely naively so. Who knows what he might have signed inadvertently. Why don't you try to get in touch with those magistrates, or somebody who might know them?"

As he spoke he drew down his lips, showing a bottom row of small, even teeth, like a child's. He raised his eyes slightly to show the bluey whites underneath, and put two fingers to the side of his mouth, as if to indicate a confidence, although the restaurant was as yet deserted.

"The two-hundred-fifty-million-dollar payment by the Vatican Bank to the Ambrosiano creditors was to secure the new Concordat with Italy; in my view that was the price. The Chink didn't want to pay a dime. But that payment was the price of something quite different from the Banco Ambrosiano. I'd love to ask him a couple of questions myself. Why don't you ask him if he fixed the Holiday Inn property deal here in Rome? You don't know about that? It was nothing to do with the Vatican, you know. And ask him about a certain pilgrim travel business he's involved in with a friend called Stefano Falez. Ask him, in short, if he's in business, as well as being a priest and the president of the Vatican Bank.

"There are lots of people in the Vatican who would be glad to see the back of him. There was a time, in the mid-seventies, when he and Monsignor Pasquale Macchi—he was the principal private secretary to Paul VI—used to run the place. Macchi had the Pope's ear and Marcinkus had the purse strings, and nothing happened without their say so. Macchi was an operator. He was obsessed with works of art; Paul VI thought he had a 'good eye,' so he allowed him to redesign all the coats of arms and medallions—disastrously. It was Macchi who brought in Calvi.

"When they went to arrest the Chink at Villa Stritch he'd had a tip-off. He's well protected, you see. He stayed at the North American College that night and slipped into the Vatican. He lives in the Governatorato, that huge rambling palace, all by himself. Won't even have a housemaid. I went there one night to dinner with some friends. We were all togged up in our canonicals and he met us at the door, shirt open to the waist, chest all hairy. Oh my! 'Hi, you guys!' he said. Some of my confreres nearly passed out. He said, 'This place has more doors than a whorehouse.' He had a huge bearskin rug on the floor and some Italian idiot scratched his ankle on the claws."

All this was delivered in a faintly camp, mock-modest delivery, with much eye raising.

"You see how it is. The Vatican is a court, a palace of gossipy eunuchs. The whole place floats on a sea of brilliant bitchery. To get on here you need a sponsor, you have to suck up to somebody. Macchi and Marcinkus were the ultimate sponsors in the seventies. The only reason they keep Marcinkus on is that he is protecting the names of certain people. While he's in office he'll keep his mouth shut. He knows too much. Paul VI was gullible and made a lot of big mistakes: Marcinkus is still protecting him. And he's protecting this one, too. Who knows what money Wojtyla's shunted through to Solidarity and all sorts of apocalyptic Eastern schemes. Anyway, there's nowhere to send Marcinkus. Even Cody turned him down a few years back. The Pope wanted to send him to England as the pro-nuncio, but Cardinal Hume put a stop to that—'NO WAY!' "

As the antipasta arrived he appraised me a moment. Then he said, "You're going to need a sponsor if you're going to get anywhere at all with this thing. I'd stick close to Marcinkus, but be careful of the Press Office people: Navarro-Valls is Opus Dei. Somehow you need to get the ear of Casaroli, the secretary of state. The whole media side of the Vatican is rife with dissension, but it's all in order that Casaroli can divide and rule and run everything. The Secretariat of State runs the Information Office."

He ate his food fastidiously but with relish, and made frequent pauses to gesticulate with flowing fingers and easy wrists.

"Archbishop Foley's Communications Commission," he went on, "reports directly to the Information Office, and so does the Press

Office. There's a lot of overlap between those two, and they're at daggers drawn. Navarro-Valls once did a spot of bullfighting, if you please. You won't get much out of him unless it suits his purposes. Then there's *Osservatore Romano,* which is infiltrated by Azione Cattolica, and Vatican Radio is run by the Jesuits who report separately to the Information Office. Your friend Foley isn't going to get anywhere in this place—he's not smart enough and he's too nice."

I broke in to mention that he'd blessed me as I left his office in October.

"I know," ran on the monsignor. "He's ever so holy. He's out of his depth. If you're going to get to the bottom of the death of Pope Luciani, you're going to have to understand this place."

By the main course and the second bottle of Villa Antinori, my monsignor, whom I had now mentally dubbed "Monsignor Sottovoce," had relaxed into a discourse on the anthropology of Vatican officials. "You've got to understand their life-style. They start young. The Italians are worst. They come to one of the big Italian colleges in Rome, the Capranica or the Lombard, and they're already insane with ambition. Even at the 'Greg' they never consort with anyone who is not going to further their careers. They're cautious. They get into the Pontifical Accademia to study diplomacy, and they start on the ladder, attaching themselves to particular cardinals and sucking up. They have no outside interests. They go back to horrible garrets somewhere in Rome, and if they meet up in some little trattoria with their pals, their one obsession is the office: who they did down and how they triumphed in this or that petty little bureaucratic dispute. The other obsession is living quarters: they scheme and plot for years to get apartments that are a little better than the ones they've got. Then it's their furniture. It's an endless topic of conversation. The aim is to get somewhere where they can show off a little and entertain once in a while. That's what they live for. You'll see any number of these poor creatures wandering around Rome in black, looking desperate. The kids drop bags of flour and water on them from the upper stories: *'Beh! Bagarozzi!'* they yell. What a fate! And look at this city. It's awash in money and beautiful girls, not to mention beautiful young men, and glamour. It's no wonder they become twisted by the time they're forty, with all the *dolce vita* passing them by. I'd put them all out in a parish! Somewhere nasty in Turin or Milan.

"Of course, the great prize would be to become a prince of the Church. Then you get a big apartment and you can have your 'cousin' or an 'aunt' looking after you. That's a tiny minority. There are four types of Vatican officials. There are the 'flashers'; they're just for the show, the dressing up, the vanity; then there are the 'lazy blighters,' completely demoralized and doing the minimum and merely hanging on; then you have some leaders who are really good men, who are effective and good priests; finally you get leaders who have become twisted and weird with a way of life they can't cope with. The first two sorts are the devil's victory, I always say. I always think of Cardinal Newman's comment: in Rome the view is clear from the top of the hill; down below is full of malaria and swamps.

"On the pay we get it's essential to have other means. Some of us do some teaching, or even journalism, or act as consultants to governments and all sorts of dubious agencies. You get fixed up with one or two convents as a chaplain, and that way you get spoiled with nice food and wine and so forth, and a bit of money too if you're lucky. Some of them are into the tourist business, 'pilgrimages,' acting as agents and guides. Then there are the Mass stipends. You realize the faithful make little offerings for their Mass intentions, and these little sums find their way to the Eternal City to be shared around the needy clergy."

He raised his eyes, drew down his mouth and looked askance at the ceiling. "As for outside activities, the least said the better. Among the richer ones you have your golfers and tennis players and sailing fanatics—not many of those, the Italians are not into physical exercise; some of them get into the liturgy, you know, dressing up like old sanctuary queens, poncing around on the altar . . . walking processions, we call them."

In a lull before dessert, when he tried a little ricotta cheese, he asked me if I intended seeing Cardinal André Deskur. When I professed ignorance of this prelate, he said, "Ah yes, Deskur! Well, he's a key figure. He knew everything and he was in charge when Luciani died. He is John Paul II's closest confidant. He actually lives in an apartment above the Communications Commission. He was Foley's predecessor, but he got a stroke the day Wojtyla was elected. He carried on, trying to pull the strings after he was incapable of running the thing. They put in Agnellus Andrew from England, but he undermined everything Agnellus did. His loyal little workers would be running up and down the backstairs all the time, tittle-tattling, because they knew he had the ear of the Pope. Wojtyla sent for Agnellus one day. 'I know what you're going through,' he said, 'but I want you to endure it for my sake.' Agnellus used to weep with frustration; in the end he dropped dead, poor thing.

"Whatever you do, keep well clear of Cardinal Silvio Oddi. He's just given an interview to *Il Sabato* [an Italian magazine] about the murder theory. He's gone back to the original idiotic story that it was the Irish secretary, Father Magee, who found the Pope's body after everybody had agreed it was the nun, Sister Vincenza, or whatever her name was. He *says* he conducted an official investigation into the affair. Oh, he's a reactionary, unenlightened man. You see, he's in retirement now, with no proper job. What he says has no official status whatsoever, utterly *unofficioso*.

"He wrote a catechism and had it sent up, but the Pope"—the monsignor made a gesture of disdainful rejection with thumb and forefinger—"just put it to one side. He's a terrible driver, you know. I saw him stopped by the police right in front of Saint Peter's Square: he was sitting there with his hands in an attitude of prayer, you know the Italians, but they'd well and truly got him!"

The monsignor suggested a little Prosecco champagne to take with a dessert of chocolate-and-cream *torta*, "to clear the head."

"The Italians are animals. Look how they behave. It's like Toscanini—up one minute, a disaster the next! The northerners call the southerners Arabs, and the southerners call the northerners *Tedeschi*—Germans. They can't organize anything. That's the problem with this place. They hate this Polish Pope: they can't wait to be rid of him. I'll never forget the day he was elected. I was with a crowd of Italian monsignori. When his name was announced, I had the presence of mind to take a sidelong look around me to see how they'd taken it. Their faces were frozen in sheer horror—a *foreigner*! Then the old *bella figura* complex took over, and they all put on these sickly wop grins and clapped!"

As I was settling the bill "Monsignor Sottovoce" said, "The problem with Pope Luciani was that he was out of his depth. Everybody here knew it. He was about to be rumbled when the Good Lord took him away. Hopeless. I think the Holy Spirit did a good job there, relieving us before he did too much damage. They were determined to choose an Italian during that conclave, but the Holy Spirit was equally obdurate that they weren't going to have one. During his Papacy everybody in the know said he was at his wit's end. I'm telling you that on the *very* best authority. He just couldn't cope. All this stuff about him being a tough, brilliant little fellow. Sheer rubbish. I remember standing at the Angelus address that Sunday and hearing him saying in that funny piping voice, 'There's more of Mama than of Papa in Almighty God.' Very nice! But they were having kittens over at the Congregation for the Doctrine of the Faith. And as for all that twaddle he wrote in the so-called *Illustrissimi* letters! He wouldn't use the gestatorial chair, but it was a big mistake. He was ungainly. He used to waddle along, flat-footed, like a duck. And you should have seen his Italian secretary, Don Diego Lorenzi. I once watched him sitting next to the Pope at one of the audiences, fidgeting and looking around him like a little boy wanting to spend a penny. And the Pope had some kid up next to him rabbiting on about Mama and Pinocchio. I thought—THIS TEAM ISN'T GOING TO MAKE IT.

"All these allegations about Freemasonry are nonsense, stuff put out in the sixties by that rag of a magazine—*Sì sì . . . No no*. One of the chief exponents nowadays is Archbishop Emmanuel Milingo, so that shows you the authority of the source.

"It's a pity Benelli's not still alive. He could have told a tale. He was all right if you like dictators; they used to say even the toilet paper had to go back to his desk for checking. Then he went up to Florence and got all soft and pastoral." The monsignor drew back his lips with slight disdain.

"He had quite a run-in with Marcinkus—but you've got to get up early to outsmart Marcinkus.

"Incidentally, Cardinal Oddi tried to needle Marcinkus. He complained at some meeting that the security was lax down at the Sant' Anna Gate; so Marcinkus told the Swiss Guards to give Oddi the works next time he came through. . . ." The monsignor was shaking with mirth. "Poor old bugger, they had him out of the car, went through all his pockets, ransacked his briefcase. Next thing, he was screaming blue murder at the Chink. 'Just doing their job, Excellency!' Marcinkus said with a smile.

"The man who knew every move on the morning of the death was Vergilio Noè, the former master of ceremonies—the Swiss Guards call him 'Virginella,' if you please. Yes, Noè, prissy little rosebud lips . . . eyes raised to heaven: look at me! I'm so holy!

"Poor old Villot died not long after. *Very* ironic, of course. He collapsed outside the Vatican and got taken to the Gemelli. The Vatican people rushed round and snatched the body . . . I kid you *not*! They pretended the corpse was still alive, took it back to the Vatican, and said he died holily in bed! Don't for God's sake ask me why, and *don't* say I said so.

"But the funniest thing about the murder-plot idea is the notion that the Vatican could get its act sufficiently together to pull off a stunt like that. You wait till you meet Magee, the Irishman who was Luciani's second private secretary. Magee is an interesting figure. Secretary to three popes, now a bishop in Ireland. Made the southerners furious—the Pope gave him the see down in Cloyne although he's an Ulsterman. Magee—the big Irishman—has a little voice. When he went on those foreign papal trips, he was always getting lost and left behind; they had to put two men on to look after him. He was always a bumbler. He always had to have somebody to take care of him. Now how did Magee get that job as Paul VI's secretary in the first place? He was a missionary out in Nigeria with the Kiltegan Fathers, or whatever they call themselves. Cardinal Pignedoli spotted him on an African trip. You know, Pignedoli used to be at Propaganda, so he brings Magee back to Rome and when Paul VI is recruiting, Magee gets put forward. Unfortunately Pignedoli, 'the Pig,' we called him, dropped dead. Died of disappointment when he wasn't elected Pope. He'd been slimming so that he could cut a *bella figura* in a papal cassock. He overdid it, the silly old fool."

As we were leaving the restaurant "Monsignor Sottovoce" turned to me and said, "Anyway, I wouldn't take too much notice of Magee. Everything with a pinch of salt. He's a rubrician—you know what I mean? Addicted to the rubrics, the bobs and bows and genuflections. He was always good on that sort of thing. You know, on the altar there are four different sorts of bows of the head, four different bows of the body. Magee was always expert at the different bows. He always got them right. The Pole got fed up with him. Turfed him out. Made him master of ceremonies till he drove everybody mad with his sanctuary choreography. He was a strange fellow. They called him 'The Hermit of the Papal Apartment.' He never came out of there for years, and you never saw him except at the Pope's side. I wonder how he's getting on as a bishop. He's never spoken to anybody outside about the Pope's death, but I hear he'll take two hours to tell you how he fetched Luciani a cup of coffee."

We said farewell and I watched him as he walked across the Campo dei Fiori, skirting the odd rotten apple, past the noisy activity of the flower and fruit stalls which he didn't give a second glance.

As I walked back to the English College I reflected that I had forgotten just how caustic and cynical the Catholic clergy could be when relaxed and "off duty," what persistent struggles we had with sins against charity. In retrospect I associated it with the pressures of celibacy.

But more than this I dwelt on the realization that the popular image of John Paul I bore no relation to his reputation among the clergy in Rome, to whom he had been a gauche and incompetent figure of fun. The monsignor's assessment of this widespread clerical verdict seemed to me no idle item of light gossip. And then, "The Holy Spirit did a good job there!" What did this mean? Was it a joke? My sense of humor had deserted me. In the circumstances of the Pope's death, I found the remark chilling.

On a wall close to the college gate I noticed for the first time an item of graffiti daubed in red paint: CLORO AL CLERO—POISON THE CLERGY.

10

On Saturday afternoon I went to Milan to see Don Diego Lorenzi, John Paul I's Italian secretary. I took a train to avoid the wildcat strikes plaguing Rome's Fiumicino airport and checked into a hotel near Milan Central Station.

In the morning I took a taxi to the Piazza Tripoli in the western suburb of the city. As I drove through the long straight streets, which looked brutally gray and ugly that Sunday morning, I reflected on my meeting with Don Diego. He was a crucial witness, having spent two years sharing his meals and working days with John Paul in Venice before coming to Rome as the senior of the two papal secretaries. He was with the Pope until the day of his death. In the latter part of his life the dead Pope had clearly exhibited the deepest confidence in this priest; if I needed to pin my faith on any single witness it must be him.

Eventually we drew up outside the parish of San Benedetto, where Don Diego worked. A vast red-brick-and-concrete modern church was surrounded by the institutional architecture of the Piccolo Cottolengo—a home for the geriatric and the disabled run by the Sons and Daughters of Don Orione.

At the porter's lodge I found a note waiting for me: "Dear Mr.

Cornwell, I have to say 11:30 A.M. Mass. Please wait for me here. Diego Lorenzi."

I decided to go into the concrete warehouse of a church and attend the Mass. There was a packed congregation, and I edged my way to the front pews past the suburban worshipers decked out in their Sunday best until I had a good view of Don Diego sitting on an altar stool among a crew of fidgeting altar boys and altar girls. He looked absurdly young for his forty-nine years, with a short-back-and-sides haircut and horn-rimmed spectacles. *Ragazzino* (kid), they had called him in the Vatican. A pair of brown suede shoes protruded from below his Advent vestments. There was something homespun and ingenuous about his demeanor: not a hint of affectation, every inch a simple country curate.

Shortly after I settled into my seat he rose to deliver his sermon to the accompaniment of infant screams echoing to the rafters. Don Diego plowed through his homily, which was on the theme of the Virgin Mary's humility and obedience at the moment of the Annunciation. His voice was strong and insistent, with an edge of fanaticism. He did not appear to be carrying his congregation with him.

A sigh of relief went around the church like a gust of wind when some twenty minutes later he came to a conclusion and turned to resume the service of the Mass.

He eventually emerged from the church, almost at a run. He was wearing charcoal-gray trousers and a black-and-gray-patterned sweater. As he greeted me I was surprised to discern a combination of Italian and pure Liverpudlian in his accent. He took me through the ground floor of the hospital, where Christmas packages were piled up high against the walls of the corridors, and into the community refectory.

About twenty men in cassocks were sitting around a U-shaped table. There was a crèche in one corner surrounded by cases of wine and Motta cakes. Most of the community were elderly and wore their table napkins splayed out expansively across their chests, like babies' bibs. We helped ourselves to a buffet of ravioli and pieces of chicken and settled down out of earshot of the old men. Don Diego launched at once into his story:

"I speak English well because I studied in England for four years, between 1963 and 1967. Well, here I am now aged forty-nine and still a junior curate in a parish of eighteen thousand parishioners and this big geriatric home as well. But that's how it is in the Church. I was the secretary to the Pope, senior to the other one—Magee, who is now a bishop; but from the moment Papa Luciani died I became just 'the Pope's widow'—that's what they call me. I don't exist in my own right. On the day the Pope died we were kicked right out of the Vatican. I didn't even know where I was going to eat supper the night he died. Nothing! Out!

"But I came out of obscurity in the first place. I was working for my order, the Don Orione Fathers, in the Veneto area and Luciani knew of me when he became patriarch of Venice. One day he summoned me and said, 'I want you to be my secretary.' So I said, 'Well, you'll have to ask my superior.' And he said, 'I already have.'

"Then he said, 'You're going to be bored. I don't want a secretary who runs the diocese for me like Senigaglia does.' Senigaglia was the secretary I replaced. 'I want somebody who will answer the phone and the door, and type for me, and who will give alms for the poor.' You see, Senigaglia now says that he got out because he was fed up, but Luciani felt that his former secretary was a barrier between him and the diocese.

"And there was another thing. Senigaglia was in the habit of settling down each evening with the previous patriarch and discussing the state of the world and all the big issues over a bottle, late into the night. Luciani wasn't interested in big issues or in the bottle. He liked to be in bed by eight-thirty or nine o'clock. And he turned out to be quite right about the boredom. Life in Venice was very boring indeed, but it was pretty noisy there too, right there by Saint Mark's Square, with the smell of fish and chips and all that. It wasn't exactly a preparation to be a pope.

"Now, I want you to know that everything I tell you is the complete truth. I have no motive to lie, and we have never been told what to say after the Pope died. Nobody ever came to us and said, 'For God's sake, say this and don't say that!' So I've always been open about it and talked to anybody. Magee has said nothing about Papa Luciani. He has been scared, probably because his bishopric was just round the corner. When he was elected bishop he had nothing to fear for his own career. Do you get it? So now he has no problem in saying the truth, because we've never been told anything by anybody. I'm not upset about it. This is how things went."

At the end of our brief lunch Don Diego said grace and led the way out of the refectory and through a maze of bleak corridors to a cold office overlooking an empty parking lot. We sat opposite each other across a desk. He unfolded an old copy of *Osservatore Romano*, the Vatican newspaper.

"The starting point," he began, "should be the statement put out by the Vatican on the morning of the Pope's death, in which the truth has been said, but missing some particulars. You can find it here.

"They said in the newspaper, 'This morning September twenty-ninth, 1978, at around five-thirty the private secretary John Magee went into the bedroom of the Pope, because he had not seen him, as was his custom, in the chapel, and found him dead in his bed in a position taken by a person reading. The light in the bedroom was on.' Now, you notice they don't say the light was over the bed, on the roof, or anywhere; they didn't say anything about it. 'The doctor was immediately called and said that the Pope had died around eleven P.M., and that the cause of death was myocardial infarction,' and so and so on. . . .

"Now look," went on Don Diego, "this is the official statement. They don't say what the Holy Father was reading, and they mention Father Magee finding the body. We should start from this laconic statement. They don't say anything in detail, but they do say *something*, and they say the truth.

"Afterward the journalists mentioned what he was reading. ANSA news service said he had a sheet with names of appointments. Nonsense! Bloody lies! Excuse me . . . Rot! . . . You see? And it was not in the official statement . . . and somebody said he was reading the *Imitation of Christ*. Nonsense! The official statement doesn't say *what* he was reading.

"He was reading in a position like this one." Don Diego imitated a typical reading posture; he pushed his glasses slightly down his nose.

I said, "You saw him yourself?"

"Of course. He had two or three cushions behind the back. The light by the bed was on. You couldn't say he was dead. And the sheets of paper were quite upright. They had not slipped out of his hands and fallen on the floor. I myself took the sheets out of his hand. *I* did! And when I took them out I noticed that they had been taken from the special pamphlets in which bishops publish their sermons. All over the world bishops do that. I think that he was trying to get an idea for the small speech he was going to make the following Sunday to the people who used to come to the main square."

"What happened to the sheets?" I asked.

"I don't know. And I don't know what happened to his spectacles or to his bedroom slippers that went missing. All I know is that I put the sheets on the side table. They printed all sorts of things about the missing objects. They said he was buried in my shirt, which was bloody nonsense! None of these people were in a position to know, only myself and Magee. Now what I am telling you is the truth, because I do not think I am allowed to tell a lie. I don't believe in telling lies. I am a Christian, I am a priest. I have nothing to lose by the truth. What motive have I, the lowest curate in a big-city parish?"

He was gazing at me steadily, I felt embarrassed. He was protesting a trifle too much, I thought.

"Let's start with who in fact found the body, if we could," I said.

Don Diego shut his eyes and leaned back. He was breathing deeply, with emotion. He paused for almost half a minute.

"To my mind," he said, "Sister Vincenza. Mind you, people should find out something about this Sister Vincenza." He paused a moment. The statement seemed designed to arouse my suspicions. "She was in bad health to start with," he went on. "She had been having heart trouble from the end of 1977 all through 1978. All the sisters who stayed with her in Venice are still in Venice living with the patriarch, and they're almost over eighty. They will remember that Sister Vincenza had to sit and keep quiet without doing anything, somehow giving orders. But of course she didn't, because women are all day active in the kitchen. When we went to Rome she was supposed to come down and stay there only for a few weeks, because others—three nuns—had been sent to run the household.

"She never intended in a certain sense to leave the Pope alone. In Venice she used to say at the beginning of supper, 'Please! Take this medicine.' So she was concerned about his health. Although, mind you, Luciani was not altogether in bad health.

"So, being an old woman, she went on getting ready coffee in the morning, around five-thirty, five-forty . . . I've no idea . . . leaving the coffee on a trolley outside the door of the bedroom. This is what I suppose she had been doing in the Vatican. That morning of the twenty-ninth—I was not there—she put this trolley outside the door of the bedroom. And because he did not come out after a few minutes to take his coffee, probably she tried to get in. We could go into the bedroom from the door in the corridor or from another door leading from his private study, which connected with the secretaries' study.

"So, Sister Vincenza went through this door at the end of the corridor. His bedroom, which was very large, was divided by a heavy curtain, and in the corner of the first half of the bedroom, and this is quite interesting because hardly anybody knew about it, there was a low bed used by Pope Paul VI when at the end of his life he couldn't climb into the high bed on the other side of the curtain. The other bed was very large. On that bed died John XXIII, and probably Pius XI, probably Pius X.

"So Sister Vincenza, I think, moved the curtains. Probably she called him by name, *Santità* . . . I've no idea . . . *Eminenza*. Probably she gave him a shake, and realized he was dead, around five-thirty . . . five-forty, I've no idea.

"Father Magee had his bedroom upstairs. I was sleeping on the same floor as the Pope, the other side of his bathroom. Father Magee was probably still in the chapel, which is off the main corridor opposite the door to the secretaries' study. Then she came and knocked at my door and it was about five to six. I got a shock. I thought, either I'm late for Mass—we used to say Mass together at seven o'clock—or something has happened to the Holy Father. These two things struck me immediately. I put on my socks and cassock and came running out of my bedroom. So I don't know whether Sister Vincenza, when she realized that the Pope had died, called Father Magee immediately or what. All I know is that I went into the bedroom immediately and saw that the Pope had died. I noticed these sheets I was referring to and what he was reading. Then at five minutes to six I phoned one of the Pope's nieces, Pia. And I said, 'Look, Pia, you need a great deal of faith. I found him this morning, about ten minutes ago.' She knew immediately to what I was referring.

"Then I called Dr. Da Ros in Venice at five minutes past six. He got the communication. He couldn't believe what I was saying. He had seen the Pope the previous Sunday afternoon and he found him in very good health. And I thought that the doctor couldn't accept the truth. He found himself somehow defeated by this sudden death. He couldn't accept it, of course. I know that he tried to get a seat on a plane from Venice to Rome, but he couldn't. So he drove all the way from Veneto to Rome, and he arrived in the Vatican around three o'clock. So it is silly to say as some people do that the Pope the previous night had phoned his doctor. In the meantime Father Magee had come along through the doors of the secretaries' study, and the doors of the Pope's study, and into the bedroom from the opposite direction to Sister Vincenza, and found the body independently of her. Now, when people came along and asked whether the body had been found by Sister Vincenza or Father Magee, they didn't know. And when I say 'they,' I don't know the people I have in mind. Because the Vatican doesn't exist"—he lowered his voice to a whisper—"doesn't exist. People say, the Vatican do this, the Vatican do that, but they don't know what they mean when they say the Vatican. On the morning of the Pope's death the Vatican was Villot. But he couldn't comprehend all the facts and the problems. How could he? Now, as far as this official statement is concerned, it's as simple as that.

"Just recently I said something in a television interview which had never been said before. I referred to the symptoms of a heart attack which the Pope had experienced on September twenty-eighth, 1978. At about quarter to eight, or ten to eight, he came to the door of his study and he said that he had had a dreadful pain, but that it had passed. And I said to him that we should call a doctor, but he absolutely forbade me to do this. And I obeyed, because one should obey the Pope. It was for this reason that I said to him when he went to bed, 'Now, if you have any problems, just press this alarm button and I will come at once!'

"I remember these symptoms, but I didn't connect them with a round-the-corner heart attack, because I'd never studied these things. I never made a link between the symptoms and his death until November—thirty-three days after his death. In Padua I have a friend who is a doctor dealing with heart problems. I had supper with him at the beginning of November 1978. And he said to me, 'Didn't you notice anything on that night when he was going to die? Didn't he say anything about depression, or trouble, or pains in the chest?' I realized what he was asking me, and I linked them with the symptoms I now talk about.

"In January 1979 I went to Naples, and on the way back I called Father Magee, who was now the new Pope's secretary, and I said, 'Look, John, you remember when the Pope told us at ten to eight that he had a pain?' And he said, 'Yes, I do.' Then I said, 'Don't you think that we had not done enough of certain things in order to save his life?'

" 'Oh,' he said, 'forget all about it.' I was not very pleased with this answer he gave me. I didn't like it. Anyway, he had not forgotten. The problem was that the Pope would not let us call anybody. He kept saying he was now feeling okay.

"After I spoke in public this October about the Pope's pain the night before he died, a journalist called me from Rome and he said, 'Why didn't you say that three or four years ago? Because if you had said that, there might never have been a suspicion that the Pope was murdered.' But I'm not so sure. You see, these writers look at things from a different point of view. They are misled through all the inquiries they make. They don't care about the holiness of the Pope, they see only money, people involved in dealing with money. Luciani was the last man in the world to worry about money and financial problems. The Holy Spirit doesn't choose a Rockefeller."

All this time Don Diego had been swiveling to and fro in his office chair, wringing his hands and arching back his body, talking in his remarkable combination of Liverpudlian- and Italian-English. There were long pauses in which he seemed overcome by emotion, on the verge of tears.

I asked him if there was anything else he wanted to tell me about the evening of the Pope's death.

"Around quarter to nine he called the archbishop of Milan, Cardinal Giovanni Colombo. I came to know what he said through other people. The only truth is this: the Pope was concerned about his successor in Venice, because over a month had passed since he vacated the see and he was trying to put in there a Salesian who was the provincial of the order. And this man had refused to accept the job, and to my mind Luciani was trying to get in touch once again, through the cardinal of Milan, with this man in order to get him to accept. I got the cardinal on the line from my bedroom and I passed through the line to Luciani's bedroom. And after he had made the call, Father Magee and myself went into his bedroom and said, 'Now look, if anything should happen tonight, if you have need of any of us, just push the button and we will hear the bell and we'll rush through to help you.' We had not forgotten the symptoms he had told us about that evening. But he never did call us."

"Don't you feel in retrospect that you should have called the doctor?"

"Yes."

"Have you ever really asked yourself why you didn't?"

"Because he said under no circumstances should I call the doctor."

"When did he say that?"

"That evening at ten to eight, at the door between his study and our study. And he said everything was all right."

"Did he look ill?"

"No. He had recovered immediately."

"Had he been overworked before he came to the conclave?"

"He didn't have many commitments in the month of July. And in the last week of July and the first week of August he had been having a complete rest with sisters at the Venice Lido. Cardinal Oddi gave an interview recently in which he said that Luciani had been overworked before he became Pope. This is not true. And from the tenth of August, when Pope Paul VI died, until the twenty-sixth he had no official engagements. And I am sorry that Cardinal Oddi said that after the death of the Pope he summoned together Father Magee and myself and Sister Vincenza, because he never did. He didn't summon anybody."

We sat for a long time in silence. Don Diego's chin sunk on his breast, his face suffused with tearful depression.

Eventually I asked, "What is it, Father?"

"I'm thinking . . . The poor man did not even receive the Last Rites. Of course he had plenty of prayers over him later. But when I found him parts of his body were still warm, his back and his feet. I could have given conditional absolution or something, but somehow we just didn't think. Surrounded by priests and bishops and cardinals and nobody to do that for him. . . . And I am remembering, now. In August 1978 a priest died in Venice on a Saturday and Luciani said to me, 'Look, imagine a priest who dies without the last sacraments.' He was very worried about priests who died like that, and he died in the same way. I had never thought about a pope dying without receiving the last sacraments. . . . But he had been living with God, mind you. I think he went straight to heaven."

"How friendly are you now with Father Magee?" I asked him, mainly to divert him from his melancholy regrets.

"Father Magee kept silence with everybody. Probably because he was concerned about Church organization."

"Are you surprised that you haven't been made a bishop?"

Don Diego sat for a while in stunned silence, then he started to laugh almost hysterically in a high-pitched wheeze.

Eventually he said, "We'll talk about something else. Life has taught me many, many, many things . . . and I am happy as I am. I try not to think and to talk about these things. The trouble is that people who come to talk to me have heard too many lies. And when I try to tell the truth, they're trying to trip me up all the time."

"What are you thinking of particularly?"

"So many things. Let me give you one example. The idea that somebody should be able to walk into the papal apartments to doctor medicine with poison or do anything. There are only two entrances into the apartments and they are guarded both day and night. I mean, these things must be said. There is one way through a very small elevator, a lift, but it is also guarded day and night. Then there is the entrance through the third loggia, guarded, again, day and night. So nobody comes in without being allowed."

He stared at me for a while. He started to giggle. "Unless, of course, somebody managed to jump from Saint Peter's Square straight into the bedroom."

"Who visited the papal apartment the day he died?"

"Nobody came. The only person allowed to come into the papal apartment, and he had to be summoned beforehand, was Cardinal Villot, Secretary of State Villot, and Casaroli, who came up three times, always summoned. Villot was always summoned. He couldn't say, 'May I come in?' In his private apartment the Pope could have worked in the nude if he had wanted, and nobody could come in to say, 'Oh, look!' He had private audiences in the morning on the second floor. In the afternoon he was almost always praying. So he used to spend that time in his private study or on the garden roof. He used to go up there every day almost, for an hour, walking, reading, studying and praying, because he was in need of fresh air. It's like a cage in there."

"What did *you* feel like, working in the Vatican?"

"In a sense I was the only friend the Pope had, and we had always respected each other. We had many things in common. Both of us came from mountain villages. We could understand each other without much useless talking. And he liked me and he loved me because I had been doing those few things as he told me when we first met."

"But how did you feel when you lived there with the Pope?"

"I didn't change my way of life. I wouldn't let them change *his* way of life. I told them when we got there. I said—now look, this man goes to bed quite early, and he gets up quite early, and he receives people from nine until twelve o'clock. So please don't make a revolution in his timetable. Give him a chance to have lunch at twelve-thirty, give him a chance to sleep for a short time in the afternoon and don't oblige him to receive people until after two o'clock in the afternoon, because he is not accustomed to it. The man will collapse. They would have liked to change him. Just one instance. He had an old windup wristwatch and his cross from Venice. One day Monsignor Macchi came along and said, 'You should have a better watch and nicer cross,' and Luciani—instead of telling him, 'Go to hell!'—just gave in and accepted them.

"I tried to keep his life as much as possible as it had been in Venice. I got up myself at six o'clock, but he used to get up at four-thirty. We said Mass together at seven and had breakfast at seven-forty, say."

"Was he overworked as Pope?"

"What should *I* say? I think that Cardinal Villot got hold of him immediately, putting before him many huge Church problems, which the late Pope had not faced because of his old age. Villot thought he had a man who was quite young. Through the various synods Luciani had come to know many of the problems of the universal Church, and although he had always said he had nothing to do directly with these problems, after he was elected he said, now it is up to me to do something, to discuss them and to find a way out. And from the secretary of state, twice a day, comes a suitcase full of papers, and on each paper there is a problem the Pope has to face, for which he has got to give a solution. It is an unbearable job. Villot spent many hours with him—walking in the Vatican Gardens and downstairs on the second floor discussing Church affairs. They met together like this on the evening of his death.

"Let me tell you what I think. I think that this man was elected by God's will, because God wanted to reward his humility. But, in a sense, at the end of 1977 and the beginning of 1978, Luciani was fed up with this world. He wanted only one thing—to die and to enjoy the presence and the goodness of God. He told me once— we had come home from a pastoral visit, and we were at the table, and he said—'Sometimes I ask the Good Lord to come along and take me away.' And this is my interpretation. God wanted to answer his prayer, but before calling him to heaven said, 'I want all mankind to have a good reason to enjoy life, to be for a short while in a good mood, to smile, to forget all the problems.' So God said, 'I want you to become Pope for a short while, and I give you time to teach lessons of faith, hope, love and meekness, because the world is in extreme need of these virtues.' And after Luciani had taught the world this lesson, the Good Lord said, 'Now come along, the lesson has been taught.'

"And I think that this prayer of his—'God, please take me away'—was said thousands of times during that month of his Papacy. Although, mind you, he told us many times, 'I am enjoying a deep peace of mind. I am light as a feather. I am not overburdened.

I am not unhappy.' And I think that if this man was mourned so much after his death, it is because all mankind fell in love with him, because he imitated Christ above all with meekness."

"Did you get any indication that Marcinkus was under a cloud and about to be sacked?"

"I remember many years ago the Catholic Bank was linked with the local hierarchy in the north. The profits of this bank were shared among the bishops. It is interesting to see how this bank was linked with all the other banks of the Calvi group. The only thing I know is this: that Luciani years ago wanted to get this word 'Catholic' out."

"Was Luciani interested in finance?"

"Nah! He very rarely accepted invitations to attend their meetings on these matters. He wasn't at all keen on these problems. A holy man worries about holiness."

"How did the story about him reading the *Imitation of Christ* at his death come into being?"

"The previous week he had been preparing a discourse for the Wednesday audience. And he had to quote the *Imitation of Christ* and tried to find the book and couldn't. The books had not yet been emptied from their boxes in his library on the second floor. I went out and borrowed one from my confreres who work in the Vatican Post Office. The Pope was already at the lunch table, and he wanted me to find a particular quotation. I went through the book myself, leaving my soup, and I found it. So he took the book to his office, wrote down the quote and then returned it to me. And I gave it back to my confreres. This is the story of the *Imitation of Christ*. The idea that he was reading it when he died was an invention. They could have said he was reading the [London] *Daily Telegraph*, or *Ulysses* by Joyce, or a magazine of naked women . . . you see? Or homosexuals. The only ones who know were Father Magee, myself and the sisters. There was another story that he was reading an address to be given to the Jesuits. Nonsense!"

"Where did that come from?"

"I don't know."

"Can you confirm what time the Pope said Mass?"

"Always at seven o'clock. We said it together."

"Tell me about the doctor who came on the morning of the Pope's death."

"Dr. Buzzonetti. He came very soon after I got up. When he came up, being a good doctor, not criticizing him, he should have said, 'Now, gentlemen, did you notice anything last night?' He should have been open to all possibilities. He's not a simple man. You would have thought that a doctor in the Vatican would have made some sort of inquiry. Why didn't he? Well, he didn't, and as a result I am being driven . . . mad! He could have said that. He could have asked us, 'Didn't you notice anything?' when the two of us were there."

"Are you still upset about the Pope's death?"

"After all things that have been said and written, I think the official statement of the death was written down too quickly."

"What about the morticians, the Signoracci brothers? Can it be true that they were called at dawn and brought to the Vatican at five o'clock?"

"No. They never came into the apartment at any time that morning. First came Villot. And as he walked into the room he wrung his hands above his head and cried out loud. He was deeply shocked and horrified. Then came the doctor. The doctor and Magee and I laid out the body. We did not have to wash it, and it was not incontinent. There was no difficult rigor mortis except with his hands. He had died in his pajama bottoms and he was still wearing his day shirt. I remember feeling his back was warm and also his feet. We dressed him in his white cassock. Buzzonetti tied a piece of silk around his head to keep up his jaw. Then Villot and the doctor stood together and wrote out the first bulletin. Buzzonetti held the pen. At first we put Sister Vincenza in the bulletin, and Buzzonetti said it was long-winded and unnecessary. So it was cut out. He put his pen through it.

"The Signoracci brothers, as far as I know, were not on the scene until the evening. Every day during the lying in state they came with other specialists and put up screens and locked the doors. On the first day they took away parts of the body, possibly bowels and so on. But after two or three days he was unrecognizable. The reason they embalmed him on the first evening was because of Paul VI, who had begun to swell up and smell unpleasantly. They wanted to prevent this."

Don Diego looked at his watch and leaped up. "My God, I've got to be somewhere else."

He dashed from the room and out into the corridor. I followed him, putting my notebooks and tape recorders into my bag as I went.

Out in the parking lot near the entrance ramp was a maroon Fiat 500. "Get in!" he ordered. "I'll take you to the station."

The car lurched with screeching tires out into the Sunday afternoon traffic on the Piazza Tripoli. He drove slumped over the wheel, peering forward as if uncertain of what lay ahead.

As we progressed through the suburbs of Milan, he said, "You know, Cardinal Villot told me that he thought he had killed Papa Luciani. It is strange that Villot himself died mysteriously just six months later. I believe that he died of a broken heart because he thought that he had destroyed John Paul I."

"But how did he think he had killed him?" I asked.

Don Diego nodded his head sadly. "I guess he thought he had overburdened him. You see, Villot was an old man himself. He'd had enough; he wanted to get out. So he thought he would clear the desks. He broke poor Luciani. It was all unnecessary. All that great *mountain* of paperwork. He could have done without it. Why should a pope have to spend his time on all that? Papa Luciani was a man of prayer; they should have left him to be quiet and he would have been effective."

We drove for some twenty minutes, and it seemed to me that we were driving in circles.

"Oh God!" cried Don Diego. "I don't know where the hell I am. I don't know the bloody way to the station."

Suddenly he pulled up. It was a five-way traffic junction. "Look! You've got to get out. Come on, out!" With this he opened the door and pushed me out into the road with cars narrowly missing me. Before I could protest he had driven off helter-skelter into the traffic.

On the long train journey back to Rome, I mulled over the encounter with Don Diego. I was deeply affected by his comments on the lack of the Last Rites, and I sensed an element of true tragedy in John Paul's evident humility, his holiness, and yet his unsuitability to play the part of spiritual ruler of the Catholic Church.

Don Diego had displayed an ingenuous exterior, but I suspected that he was clever, highly emotional and under stress. He had gone out of his way at the beginning of our meeting to justify the first bulletins by appealing to casuistry: they were "laconic," he had said, they said "little," but what they had said was the "truth." It was a classic example of "economy" of the truth, characteristic of Scholastic hairsplitting. I realized that I needed to refresh my memory about some of those strange mental cobwebs that had festooned the clerical mind in my youth and had remained despite the brooms of the Second Vatican Council.

His testimony, however, had raised some fascinating details. He had depicted Luciani as unequal to the "unbearable" job of Pope, and hinted that Villot was a tyrant who had overworked John Paul in an attempt to clear his desk.

It was clear from Don Diego's remarks that all had not been well in the papal household: his remarks about Magee smacked of rivalry and enmity, and he had clearly not hit it off with Sister Vincenza.

Above all I was shocked to learn the important role of the Pope's Venetian doctor, Da Ros, so far into the reign. According to Lorenzi, Da Ros had still been paying medical visits as recently as the Sunday before the Pope died, and it was Da Ros whom Lorenzi called immediately on learning of the Pope's death, rather than one of the papal doctors in the Vatican's own Health Service facility just a hundred yards from the Papal apartment. Da Ros, I had noted, took nine hours to reach the Vatican on September 29.

11

On my return from Milan I collided with Monsignor Paul, the military-style Vatican bureaucrat, in the *salone* and he asked me how I was getting on.

We sat for a while over a bottle of whisky and I told him about my visit to Don Diego.

"What I find most astonishing," I said, "is the apparent unsuitability of John Paul I to the task of being pope."

Monsignor Paul shook his head. "It's an *impossible* job."

"You know, I'm not at all sure what a pope actually does," I went on. "We all know he's busy and hardworking and weighed down with responsibilities, but when John Paul I woke up on that morning in 1978 and contemplated his agenda, what was the job description?"

Monsignor Paul thought for a moment; he took a deep breath; he raised a forefinger backward, as if about to cast a rod. "Well, in the first place you have to realize that the Pope maintains contact in a very real way with all the hierarchies in something like a hundred and ten countries of the world—each one with its own specific crises and problems. The flow of information that comes in for his scrutiny is simply torrential and unremitting. And in addition to that, all the bishops, from every corner of the globe, come into Rome for their *ad limina* visits, three thousand of them once every five years, all to have personal audiences with the Pope.

"Everywhere you look in the universal Church—this vast congregation of nearly a billion people—there is a major crisis and the buck stops with the Pope. In Latin America you've got the huge forces inspired by modern political and economic thought challenging traditional teaching in the midst of poverty, war, injustice, overpopulation. In Africa and Asia you've got strong cultural forces threatening a disintegration of the traditional Catholic mold of belief and worship. In North America you have the crisis of authority and conscience. Wherever you look in the world the Catholic Church, and thus the Pope personally, is being challenged, pulled this way and that way. In Europe you have the crisis of reaction with Lefebvre, the quest for Christian unity, the problems of the persecuted Church in Eastern Europe, the pleas from the laity for greater participation; crises with priests, with nuns, with celibacy; questions about Anglican orders, Orthodox orders; crises over the Church's teaching on sexuality and marriage, annulments, birth control, abortion . . . All this floods across the Pope's desk.

"Now Paul VI was a workaholic, capable of doing an eighteen-hour day, slaving over papers every night into the small hours. And yet they said he was *indecisive*! Do you know that during the period when tens of thousands of priests were seeking laicization, Paul VI was deciding personally on every single case? This was the legacy inherited by John Paul I! Now, the Pope has to take the strain of all this in a very real and personal way, while at the same time dealing with the bureaucracies here in Rome, the local situation, which is huge and unwieldy and problematic enough in itself, the congregations, tribunals, commissions, the secretariats, the major offices concerned with Christian teaching, liturgy, discipline of the clergy, education and so forth."

Monsignor Paul took another deep breath and sipped his whisky.

"Now!" Up came the finger once more. "This is the role of the Pope as a *reactive* manager. Then you have to consider the positive contribution he is required to make in the light of his own special gifts, his own inspiration at any point in the history of the Church. Every week he is churning out a prodigious quantity of writings:

addresses, encyclicals, homilies, sermons . . . Just consider the number of addresses he makes on one foreign trip. And in the midst of this he must demonstrate to the world, to his clergy here in Rome, the most exemplary life of prayer and devotion. He must spend many hours in prayer, for himself, for the Church.

"And on top of that he must find time to play the role of head of state to world leaders and important visitors; to offer hospitality, pay an interest in all the worthwhile activities and initiatives going on in the secular world. . . . It is an IMPOSSIBLE job!"

"So what was the prevailing feeling inside the Vatican a week or two into John Paul I's reign?" I asked.

"The general feeling was that he was absolutely *overwhelmed*. And you know, even though there was a great sense of joy at his election, there were many who felt on the very first day that he had done nothing in his career to qualify him to take over the running of the universal Church. He had done a bit of catechetics, that sort of thing, but he was a fairly simple, devout pastor, a good man, but a small and simple man."

"So was it a mistake?" I said.

"Well . . . the Holy Spirit has to work within the laws of man's condition. You can't expect to leave the airplane door open and be protected from disaster."

"So how on earth did he slip through?"

"I imagine it was because of the capable people who were being kept out, particularly by the foreign cardinals. They didn't want Benelli because they thought he would be dictatorial. And they didn't want Siri because they thought he would be too rigid. They didn't want Pignedoli because they thought he was past it. So they said, 'All right, we'll choose an Italian who will be a *pastoral* Pope.' They looked at Luciani and thought. 'Venice, ah, like John XXIII'; they thought that he looked like a *holy* man. Then they chose him. He turned it down once, but they chose him again, and he was obliged to accept. Poor chap!"

12

At lunch on the day after my return from Milan, I told the rector that John Paul I had not received the rite of Extreme Unction.

He looked at me, baffled. "There's no such thing; it went out with the council."

Canon Harry, the college tutor for pastoral theology, said, "There are special prayers for the dead, that's what Don Diego means. I'm surprised they didn't do that. They should have at least done that for a pope."

Within moments all the staff were making contributions.

Father Pat, who had worked for many years in a large city parish, said, "People still expect something like the old extreme unction rite, especially the old-timers. There's no harm in dabbing a little oil on a body to give a bit of consolation to the relatives."

"But they shouldn't have given the Pope conditional absolution, especially if they were uncertain as to when he died," said Canon Harry.

Another priest said, "What would we do if the rector here croaked?"

When the laughter had died down, he went on: "We'd certainly say the special rite of the dead over his body, but you see we've all worked as pastoral priests—the Vatican is just an office full of bureaucrats."

As I was drinking coffee in the students' common room after lunch, I was called to the telephone. It was Marjorie Weeke.

"Can you get yourself over to the Vatican? You're invited to take tea with Cardinal Deskur, the Pope's best friend. It won't do any harm to make a good impression."

The prospect of meeting Deskur seemed to me a great stroke of luck. Cardinal André Deskur, a Pole, had been in a position of extraordinary power in the world of Vatican information on the day of Pope John Paul I's death. He had been president of the Communications Commission. He was now in retirement after suffering a stroke on the very day Wojtyla had been elected. All the same, he was the most influential man in the Vatican. He met with the Pope several times a week and it was said they shared many confidences. The Pope was in the habit of saying, "Deskur does my suffering for me."

A meeting with Deskur might pave the way to a meeting with the Pope, and I might at least get some indication as to the Pope's attitude toward Marcinkus.

When I arrived at the office of the Commission for Social Communications, Marjorie Weeke met me in the lobby. She appeared on edge.

"All set?" she said. "The cardinal lives on the third floor here. We'll take the elevator."

As we were going up, she said, "I warn you, he looks a bit debilitated, but this is a pretty smart guy; he's got three doctorates and speaks six languages."

A nun in white answered the door of the apartment. She was a real nun, covered from head to toe with only her face showing; there were more nuns in the background, popping their heads out of doors and smiling demurely. The polished surfaces of the floors and furniture gleamed and sparkled. There were vases of flowers on every available surface.

The cardinal was in his study sitting by a battery of buttons and telephones. He asked me to sit close to him. His hands and face were smooth and hairless, his nose pinched and glossy. His hair was thick, furlike.

He was wearing an expensive-looking suit down the front of which were several items of decaying food. He eyed me fishily through horn-rimmed, schoolboy spectacles. The nuns ran in and out, bobbing and bowing as he rapped out orders.

The tea trolley was brought in: an elaborate ritual of teapots and china and lemon and silver milk jugs. There was a cake stand heaped high with cakes, nutty and fruity and rich in butter and glazed jams. He started to fill my plate, using a silver trowel.

"I am trying to clear up the conflicting stories surrounding the death of Papa Luciani," I began, a little diffidently.

"Yes!" he said. "Eat up! You are an Englishman? Yes? Do you have such a thing as a count in your social hierarchy?"

"Count? I think not," I said.

"We had counts in Poland . . . they have *Monsieur le Comte* in France, and *Il Conte* in Italy."

"We don't have counts in England."

"Yes! But why do you have countesses? You have the countess, no?"

"I'm not sure."

"And you have a county, like county of Kent. Eat up! Would you like some Polish bread? The Pope and I share the same bread maker and cake maker, a Polish bread maker. He lives in a gilded cage." The last sentence was said with a little sigh.

I looked at him curiously.

"The Pope, the Pope . . . in a gilded cage."

"Do you remember, Your Eminence," I asked, "the day the last Pope died?"

"Yes! This is Earl Grey tea. How many cups of tea do you drink a day?"

"I'm not sure."

"I have an Englishman friend in the English College in Rome drinks seventeen cups a day. A Polishman can drink seventeen cups an hour." He shoveled cakes on my plate. "I apologize for my strong Irish accent."

I looked bemused.

"My English teacher was Irish," he elucidated. "Do you like my cuff links?"

He sported handsome Maltese Cross cuff links in his snowy starched cuffs.

"They're splendid."

"Yes! Very discreet. I do not like precious stones: that's indiscreet. I am chaplain to the Knights of Malta."

I helped myself to milk from one of the jugs. He eyed the action with fascination. "Englishman!" he said, and helped himself to lemon.

"When the Holy Father and Cardinal Casaroli were in Poland," he went on, "the cardinal only drank coffee and wine. I was very surprised."

"John Cornwell has spent some time with Archbishop Marcinkus," said Marjorie helpfully.

"Pliss?"

"The Chink," I said, using Marcinkus's Vatican nickname.

It was a mistake. I could see Marjorie grimacing and looking up at the ceiling.

"The Chink?"

"I believe that's what his friends call him," I said.

"His name is Paul, I think," he said shortly.

We sat in silence for a while.

"Have another cake!" he said. "This cake comes from a certain forest in Poland. Nuts and dates . . ."

Time passed. I tried this way and that to elicit a comment about John Paul I, Archbishop Marcinkus, poison plots, the Pope's attitude toward Archbishop Marcinkus, but all my ploys and gambits were gobbled up along with glittering shovelsful of little buttery, sugary cakes, until there was nothing left. And all the time his large suffering eyes behind the schoolboy spectacles never left my face for a moment.

When an hour had passed and a nun came to take away the trolley, it finally dawned on me that the purpose of the tea party was to allow the cardinal to observe *me*. And he had managed to do this without giving me the slightest clue to his reactions.

As I went down in the lift, bloated and queasy, I wondered what report of me he might pass on to His Holiness the Pope.

13

Had Archbishop Marcinkus a motive for murder because John Paul I was about to expose the involvement of the Vatican Bank in the Banco Ambrosiano scandal? To what extent was Marcinkus guilty of malfeasance in his business dealings?

By the time I arrived in Italy I had collected a considerable dossier of printed sources on the involved story of the Banco Ambrosiano and the Vatican Bank. Much of this material was in the public domain, and was well known to those with an interest in financial journalism. As a layman in these matters the very sight of the fat file in which it was contained made my head reel, but I consoled myself with the thought that Touche Ross, the London liquidators of the Banco Ambrosiano, had engaged more than fifty companies of legal advisers throughout the world and had input more than a million documents in the task of disentangling the mess of the bank's collapse.

What could one journalist, by no means a financial specialist, do to make an original contribution to the already huge volume of information available? Nevertheless, I flirted for just a few hours with the idea of doing some original sleuthing of my own.

The day following my first interview with Marcinkus, I had called on Prince Carlo Caracciolo, whom I had met at a lunch in London in 1976. Caracciolo was the proprietor of both *La Repubblica*, the newspaper with the largest circulation in Italy, and *Espresso*, an influential current-affairs weekly. His reputation as a journalist and publisher was unrivaled, and he had formidable contacts at every level in Italian society.

I was ushered into his odd little office under the slanting ceilings of an attic of the *Espresso* building on Via Po near the Villa Borghese. He rose, smiling affably, a cigarette between his fingers. He had gaunt good looks, a thatch of wavy iron-gray hair and was elegantly dressed in a well-cut gray suit.

I asked a little sheepishly if he could suggest a contact who might introduce me to the Italian magistrates in Milan who were attempting to bring Marcinkus to court. It would be helpful, I said, even to get a flavor of what they had against him.

"The man you want," said the prince in his Oxford-English accent, "is a lawyer named Salvatore Gatti. This man has excellent links with the Vatican and all that Ambrosiano business." He winked at me, a deeply knowing Roman wink. "He will have much inside information on this Archbishop Marcinkus. His son works for me here. He is the economics editor, Roberto Gatti, and he works downstairs in this building. I'm sure that he will be very sympathetic, and what better person could introduce you to Avvocato Gatti than his own son? Maybe he will invite you to drinks at his house and you can bring up the subject in a casual way. You know the sort of thing." His face was wreathed in affable mobile smiles.

Armed with this tip I went down three floors to pay my respects to Signor Gatti Junior.

He was sitting behind his desk sipping a cup of coffee, a neatly dressed young man with a serious expression. He invited me to sit down.

"And why do you want to speak to my father?" he asked unsmilingly.

"I was hoping," I said, "that he would introduce me to these Milan magistrates who are trying to bring Marcinkus to book."

"And why would my father want to do such a thing?"

I was perplexed at his seeming obtuseness. "Well, to be frank, I was hoping to dig up a bit of dirt on Marcinkus."

There was a silence. He was looking at me as if I were utterly insane. Then: "And why would my father help you dig up a bit of dirt, as you say, against His Excellency Archbishop Marcinkus?"

"Well, why not?" I asked feebly.

"Because," he said with icy indignation, "because my father happens to be the personal lawyer of Archbishop Marcinkus."

As I stumbled nervously down the stairs of the *Espresso*'s office, marveling at the brilliance of Caracciolo's practical joke, I decided to stick to more available sources.

In the two days leading up to my second interview with Marcinkus I set about drafting an aide-mémoire, pulling together the essential facts on the Ambrosiano scandal as far as they were available to me at that time. My dossier included notes of conversations with Lorana Sullivan of the *Business Observer* (London), an authoritative series of articles by Charles Raw and Tania de Zuluetta of the *Sunday Times* (London), an impressive investigation in the *Wall Street Journal* by Laura Colby in April 1987 and a major cover story by Shawn Tully in the December 1987 issue of *Fortune* magazine. There was also an abundance of material from Italian newspapers and periodicals.

I had applied for information from a number of institutions, such as the liquidators, Touche Ross, in London, and I had acquired from an official at the Banco d'Italia in Rome two highly authoritative memorandums giving the results of the bank's own independent investigation into the affair. In addition there were three books: Rupert Cornwell's *God's Banker*, Larry Gurwin's *The Calvi Affair* and Richard Hammer's *The Vatican Connection*.

This was my draft.

The IOR, or Vatican Bank, is officially in the personal ownership of the Pope, as opposed to the Vatican or the Holy See, and for this reason has been able to operate under a cloak of secrecy. It is situated in a former dungeon in the Cortile di Sisto Quinto, immediately below the papal Palace; its entrance adjoins a service lift

that rises directly into the Pope's apartment. Its staff numbers just
a dozen employees under the presidency of Paul Marcinkus.

It is important at the outset to distinguish the Vatican Bank from
the considerable finances of the great religious orders—the Jesuits,
the Franciscans, the larger missionary societies—which are finan-
cially independent of the Vatican, and of APSA, the Administration
of the Patrimony of the Holy See.

APSA is both the Vatican treasury and a financial investment
operation run by twenty-six lay professionals, including four traders,
under the direction of Benedetto Argentieri, formerly of the Banque
Européenne d'Investissement in Brussels. Excluding its art treasures, the Vatican claims to be worth some $500 million in invest-
ments, a relatively modest figure compared with some of the
American charitable foundations. The APSA staff manages more
than $100 million in government and corporate bonds, while a $50
million balance is spread across a portfolio of more than a hundred
stocks, including blue chips like Fiat and Generale Assicurazione.

The days of adventurous investment activities are over following
losses sustained by APSA through involvement with the building
conglomerate Immobiliare, in which APSA was said to have had a
majority stake. Nowadays the strategy is conservative and concen-
trates on gold and bonds.

On the other hand, the IOR, the Vatican Bank, is basically a
savings-and-loan house. Its depositors are principally Vatican employees and religious orders enjoying modest interest. Money is lent
out at paltry rates to missionary projects, dioceses and religious
societies throughout the world. It makes money by depositing rev-
enues in government bonds and securities, and accounts in other
banks. It was not established to get into the business of high-risk
investment—at least, that was its policy until in the early 1970s
the IOR bought shares in Banco Ambrosiano and made large deposits at high interest rates.

Banco Ambrosiano also had a staid and venerable image until
its subsequent scandal came to light. It had been closely associated
throughout the century with the Catholic Church and particularly
the diocese of Milan, where two previous popes had been arch-
bishops. Before the Second World War depositors were required to
produce baptismal certificates.

In 1971, Marcinkus had already taken over at the Vatican Bank when Roberto Calvi became managing director of the Ambrosiano. Calvi, born in 1920, had worked at the Ambrosiano since 1947 and was consumed by two ambitions: to extend the bank's activities into the international arena and ultimately to acquire a personal controlling interest in the business. The methods he employed were far from staid, involving the setting up of shell companies, the laundering of money, the rigging of the Milan stock market. His close associates included the convicted criminal financier, Michele Sindona (once a financial adviser to the Vatican), and Liceo Gelli, the grandmaster of P2, the unofficial Italian Freemasons' Lodge.

The Vatican also figured largely in Calvi's schemes. In addition to the substantial investments and deposits made in the Ambrosiano, the Vatican Bank acquired a stake in Banco Ambrosiano Overseas, in Nassau, and Marcinkus joined its board. There were stories of close relationships between Marcinkus and Calvi and his family, including exotic interludes in the Bahamas. There were allegations of large financial kickbacks from Calvi.

Calvi's criminal activities were not to come to light publicly until he was convicted of currency offenses in 1981, when he was fined $10 million, and spent four months of a four-year sentence in jail. Marcinkus continued to do business with him after he was convicted.

The nub of the Ambrosiano scandal and the Vatican's part in it involved the setting up of ten shell companies in Panama by the bank's Luxembourg subsidiary, itself a shell holding company. It appeared that the Vatican Bank nominally controlled these companies; Marcinkus insists that they were collateral for loans made to Banco Ambrosiano. Both Calvi and Marcinkus ran them during different periods, but the legal and responsible ownership remains an enigma.

Calvi lent $1.3 billion to the shell companies ($600 million of it borrowed from 120 foreign banks), and this money, it appears, went to manipulate the stock of Banco Ambrosiano and push up its price during a period of rapid expansion when Calvi was buying larger stakes in other companies. The Banco Ambrosiano stock eventually fell, revealing a hole of $1.3 billion, mostly owed by the ten shell companies.

Marcinkus claims that the Vatican Bank knew nothing about the setting up of these companies, nor of their objectives. Yet a year before the collapse he had issued "letters of comfort" or "patronage," indicating that the Vatican "directly or indirectly controlled" the ten companies. In return, Calvi wrote a letter acknowledging that the debts were owed by the Banco Ambrosiano and not the Vatican Bank.

Calvi's fortunes, however, were beyond redemption. In June of 1982, with his empire collapsing around him, he fled the country. On June 18 he was found hanging by the neck from a builders' scaffold below Blackfriars Bridge in London. After two inquests conducted by Scotland Yard it is still unclear whether he committed suicide or was murdered. A half-brick was stuffed down his trouser pocket. It is pointed out that Blackfriars, *fratelli neri*, is an Italian nickname for the Freemasons, and that the Masonic oath acknowledges that a traitor to the brotherhood should be roped down in the proximity of the rising tide. The brick could be taken as an item of "Masonry." It is likely that Calvi acquiesced in a ritualistic "suicide" for fear of something worse: threats perhaps to his wife and children. But was this gruesome charade a Masonic retribution, or did it mask a more inscrutable executioner? If it was not suicide, Calvi's death remains one of the most intriguing murder mysteries of our time.

Calvi's bank crashed on June 30 and its creditors began to look for restitution and a scapegoat. The international banks joined forces and started proceedings to secure inclusion among the creditors of the Banco Ambrosiano for their $600 million. The status of the "letters of comfort" was at the center of the debate over the Vatican Bank's involvement and liability. The Vatican Bank claimed that it was merely a trustee of the Panamanian companies, and that therefore it was not liable for their debts.

As far as Italy was concerned the issue of liability was officially settled in May 1984 following a special joint commission of inquiry, described as "international," but exclusively comprising representatives of the Holy See and the Italian government. The Vatican Bank allowed the commission scrutiny of its documents. In a carefully worded formula the Bank of Italy stated in October 1984 that "though the commission did not arrive at unanimous conclusions, it did demonstrate the objective involvement of IOR, thus establishing the premise for the negotiation of a contribution from the IOR." The contribution from IOR, the Vatican Bank, to the creditors was a sum of $250 million. The decision was taken by a higher authority than Marcinkus, officially by Casaroli, the secretary of state. The money was paid on the understanding that this was a full and final settlement against all future claims, and that it in no way indicated admission of culpability.

The Vatican's contribution appeared to close the matter. Marcinkus continued as president of the bank and an unhappy chapter seemed to have closed. By the summer of 1986 the liquidators Touche Ross had recovered most of Ambrosiano's missing assets, an operation that had cost them some $25 million by that point and the maintenance of forty of the company's staff in Luxembourg, along with a team of ten lawyers. Taken together with the $250 million paid by IOR, deemed in banking circles to be the amount owed by IOR to Ambrosiano at the time of the crash, the recoveries made by the liquidators amounted to just some $40 million short of the losses. It is commonly assumed that this figure had been embezzled by Calvi.

Allegations about the Vatican Bank's complicity in Calvi's murky dealings continue to be aired, and the $250-million payment has given rise to speculations about the IOR's guilt, by critics and friends alike. Magistrates in Milan are still attempting to pin down the element of criminality in the Ambrosiano episode, and this led to warrants being issued in April 1987 for the arrest of Marcinkus and his two senior bank officers. The warrants were later rescinded as a result of technical and political considerations.

Meanwhile the media continue to harp on the letters of patronage and other evidence. Much was made by Rupert Cornwell and Larry Gurwin of statements made by Clara Calvi, Calvi's widow. When in prison in 1981 Calvi had told her that Marcinkus had information that would get him out of jail by admitting the IOR's involvement—the illegal currency transfers that put him in jail, Calvi claimed, had been made in the interests of the Vatican Bank. In a much quoted account, when Clara and her daughter Anna emerged from Lodi Prison after taking notes of a conversation with Calvi, they were met by Alessandro Mennini, an employee of Banco Ambrosiano, and son of Mennini of the Vatican Bank. He tried to snatch the notes from Anna's hand but she foiled him. He apparently shouted after them as they drove away, "You must not mention the name IOR, not even in the confessional."

In Laura Colby's *Wall Street Journal* article, "Vatican Bank Played a Central Role in Fall of Banco Ambrosiano" (see Appendix, p. 348), another example of incriminating involvement is alleged. On October 16, 1979, the IOR received two deposits, one for $65 million and the other for Swiss francs 101 million ($69 million) from Banco Andino of Peru. IOR then lent identical amounts to United Trading, its Panamanian affiliate. When in 1982 the deposits matured, the Banco Andino asked for its money back, but the IOR refused, saying that United Trading now owned the money and IOR had no control over it. Since the IOR owned the entire share capital of United Trading this was plainly false, concludes Colby.

My draft omitted much speculation about a larger web that included Liceo Gelli, Michele Sindona and Marcinkus, and matters as diverse as the financing of Exocet missiles in Argentina and the collapse of Sindona's own bank. I also decided to postpone scrutiny of allegations that Marcinkus had been involved in a billion-dollar U.S. counterfeit-bond fraud in 1972.

My principal objective was to conduct a useful encounter with Marcinkus on the central issues that had already absorbed scores of competent experts and hundreds of journalists for years on end. I felt that I had enough information to probe quietly the central matters, so that I could reflect on the style of his answers as much as their content.

Yet whatever the involvement or otherwise of Marcinkus in the complicated affair of the Ambrosiano, I reminded myself that the principal objective of my inquiry was to ascertain the extent to which John Paul I had been apprised of the state of affairs of these murky relationships and dealings, and their likely outcome, in September 1978 after a Papacy of just thirty-three days. Furthermore, what evidence was there that the Pope intended sacking Marcinkus on the basis of his information up to the night of his death on September 28, 1978?

14

J entered the dark quadrangle of the Cortile di Sisto Quinto and walked along the arched and vaulted cloister to the entrance of the Vatican Bank. As I passed through the frosted-glass doors two clerics passed me carrying large black briefcases. I found the archbishop in the carpeted corridor, bending down to reach for a pack of Marlboros from a display case against the wall.

"Hi there," he called out breezily, "come right on in."

He seemed more relaxed this afternoon. He settled back into his executive chair and set about stoking up his usual smoke storm.

"You know," he said affably, between long, rattling drags on the pipestem, "if you want information here, you've gotta know how to set about it. These people come in like a district attorney. . . . Bang! Bang! Bang! Bang! The old inquisition. You won't get any help from anybody like that."

I was thinking of the busy-looking clerics who had passed me at the revolving doors. "What I really want to know," I said, "is how a man can be a priest, a man of God, and at the same time a good banker. Isn't there a kind of contradiction there?"

His face clouded at the abruptness of the question. There was a pause, as if he were deciding whether to take offense.

"I'm not a banker in the strict sense," he said at last. His voice was cautious, a little indignant. "We've got technical people who do that." He paused again. "I work out the policy. And my policy has always been that money is a tool in the service of the Church, it's not a goal in itself. And we're not supposed to do anything that would be illegal, or speculative.

"I'm not ashamed really for anything I've done." He was speaking more confidently now. "I've nothing to apologize for because we didn't do anything. I might be ashamed of one thing, if you want to call it that: that I trusted Calvi, maybe, too much. But it wasn't hard to do because he had a tremendous reputation in the banking community. He brought that bank, the Ambrosiano, from just an ordinary bank to an important bank. And maybe as a human being, in my limited relationship with him, I felt he was a decent fellow. But my relationship with him was purely on a level of business. But not any *particular* business."

His voice slowed down to a slow, gravelly funeral march. He was picking his words ponderously, carefully.

"I never did *one* bit of business with Calvi." He paused, as if to allow me to digest the curiously syllogistic advance of his argument. "But my office did," he added. "Deposits with his bank, made loans to his bank. And maybe we were too trustful. But everything else led for us to do that. We got tremendous recommendations from Milan, from people around here." He made a sweeping gesture as if to implicate the entire Vatican. "He had great rapport with governmental officials. Maybe I should have known the man personally. I would suspect that many people have excellent relationships on a business level and know nothing about them as persons, because business is their contact point. But there was no reason for us to question his honesty, his integrity."

I felt confused. Hadn't Calvi spent time in jail for fraud? And hadn't the Vatican Bank continued to do business with Calvi for a year or so after that?

"The relationship we had with the bank were things that all banks do," he went on. "If I put a deposit in the bank, the banker may say, 'You know we have this particular project: if you give that money and I'll earmark it for that project and we'll get you a higher percentage.' And I say, well that's *your* business. I don't want to know what you're doing."

He paused again, as if to consider whether he had said too much. And I was wondering, what if the money were put into contraceptive devices or armaments?

"The thing that people should ask is this," he said. "All these companies that had dealings with Calvi, banks and so on. They lent money to Calvi: was it for *us* or the Ambrosiano? If they give it to Calvi for us, they've got to have a piece of paper that says he's my representative. Where's that piece of paper?" He looked at me with glazed, bemused eyes. He shook his head. "It don't exist."

He stopped and gazed at me steadily for almost a minute. Then he said gravely, "Now, I fell into the same trap with *you*."

My blood ran cold for an instant. There was menace in his voice.

"Father Foley, Bishop Hume," he went on in his most macabre tone yet, "wrote me a note and talked to me. Father Jack Kennedy talked to me. You present yourself. Now, in normal circumstances if I were to follow what all these people tell me, I should have gotten a whole dossier on you and so forth."

He paused. I was giggling, partly with relief, but mostly at his unconscious verbal demotion of all the aforesaid persons. He looked at me, baffled.

"Is that right?" he growled severely. I pulled myself together.

"Can a man live like that all his life?" he went on. "Every time you meet somebody you've got to have a dossier? So—Calvi's *word* is his bond—if they give the money to Calvi for the Vatican Bank, they've gotta get it out of him, not out of me."

He was now, for the first time, pausing for a lot longer than he was speaking—as if he no longer trusted his ability to control his tongue.

"Take Sindona," he said, opting for another tack. "I met him about twelve times, sometimes for a minute, sometimes at a baptism, once or twice at lunch, at a reception, a ceremony . . . dropped in here once or twice. The whole twelve times might have been six hours. Never had a dealing with him. The ones that had a dealing were APSA. They sold him the shares for Immobiliare. So they said Immobiliare is sold to Sindona by the Vatican. So immediately everybody said it was me. I had nothing to do with it. Sindona himself said he never had dealings with me. I remember saying before Sindona went to the States, I said, 'Hey! You operate over there like you operate here in Italy, you'll end up in jail.' See? Different laws, different standards. The only thing I can think is that Sindona and Calvi got carried away with their own sense of importance. Anyway, so when Sindona left, the natural candidate for advising the Vatican on financial matters was Calvi and the Banco Ambrosiano. But these dealings, these companies and stuff, I never even heard of them. One or the other of them may have been given to us as guarantees for a loan, and that sort of thing. But that's all. I say that with all honesty."

He put his hand dramatically on his breast pocket.

"I didn't even know where Calvi lived." He went on more brightly. "If I ever asked him, say about his house or something, he'd say, 'I just go out there at the weekend and rest.' That was it. That was the extent of my knowledge. I never sought him out. I met his wife and kids on one or two occasions, I think, in the Bahamas back in 1974. I met her again, went back for a meeting, never saw her again in my life. I could be very upset about what she has said, and so on and so forth."

His face assumed a bleak, hurt expression, as if he were contemplating a list of injuries.

"She called me all kinds of names and accused me of a lot of things. That's something *she'll* have to answer for, not me. I thought she was an ordinary housewife. She wasn't interested in a lot of different things, at least she didn't impress me as such. . . ." His voice faded away vaguely.

"Everybody was calling Sindona a very close friend at the Banco d'Italia. But it's strange that I'm now the only one who has ever known Sindona in Italy. It's like they said right after the war, 'There's not a Fascist in Italy.' Where do they all go?" His eyes smiled glassily. "I never set foot in the Ambrosiano Bank. I was down in the Bahamas on, I think, two occasions. When we had board meetings it was in an office building in Zurich."

I raised my hand. I said, "I'm still genuinely puzzled, Monsignor, about the companies that owed Banco Ambrosiano the money that caused the collapse. Did you not issue letters of comfort relating to those companies, thus indicating some degree of responsibility for them?"

"No, not at all!" he roared. He looked at me, as if with disappointment at my slow progress. He stoked his pipe some more, fiddled with the papers on the desk. "Look! Here's Calvi comes out of jail in 1981, and he says, 'I'm having trouble and I've got to get this thing all set up, and I can't get around in different places, so would you kind of oversee these things, look after them.' He didn't say they were ours. In the letter I asked him to write for us—a condition letter, where he said they're not yours and they never had been yours. And I insisted everything has to be done to decrease indebtedness, and that in one year and a half everything has to be settled and we're out. It's like a trustee. I didn't give any guarantees or anything like that. We knew what their indebtedness was, that's all."

"Do you know where the money went?" I asked.

Marcinkus shrugged and grimaced. "The reports we had from the company—they had more assets than debits—I think where a lot of the money went, myself, and I think they realize this too, at least I hope they do. . . . He was trying to get money to pay high interest rates. You break it down. He was expanding at that time. If you're borrowing money at twenty percent, and you can't put it out, it's a heck of a nut to crack. All the loans that I saw were sufficiently guaranteed according to the audit. I always asked them, I said, 'You're not making any loans to anybody, I should hope, unless you have sufficient collateral.' And the administrator at the bank always assured me that they'd got this or that in guarantee. And this was just us asking them what they'd done. They weren't asking us for approval.

"Now. When he asked us to take over and control those things under these conditions—that's where I might have been too trusting." He had fallen back again into a slow drawl. "But there was no indebtedness on our part, no commitment on our part, or anything. If he'd maintained his word to us, it was that they should have done nothing but decrease their debt. But what he did I had no idea."

"But, Monsignor," I said, "we're talking about one and a third billion dollars."

"Well, it's coming out in the liquidation process. I understand some of the money he used was in expansion—they owned the Banco Gottardo fifty-some percent, which the liquidators have sold and got some two hundred fifty million bucks back. So that brings it down, nonetheless. They tell me, I don't know . . . the holding company in Luxembourg has recouped about six hundred million bucks or so. And other stuff you've got there—they had Centrale, insurance companies, that they kind of sold off. They were worth a lot of money, I suppose the money went into those things. Other money I suppose he put in his pocket."

"What of rumors that the money went into P2, or into the Argentine war effort?"

"If it did, I never saw it. You know, as I said to you before, it would be a very sad state if every time you met somebody you had to get a dossier on 'em. People you like, people who when they present themselves . . . people who've got a good reputation."

"But, Monsignor," I said with some exasperation, "Calvi went to jail and you continued to do business with him. You hardly needed a dossier to tell that he was a crook."

He smiled at me blandly, as if to say, who's being naive *now*?

"When Calvi was in jail," he said, "I *asked* somebody—'Hey! What's going on?' And the fellow says, 'Nah, if you're not caught, you're not worth anything.' "

We sat in silence for a while as the statement sank into the deep-pile carpets and the heavy leather furniture.

"So, putting aside the personalities and their trustworthiness," I continued, "can the Vatican nevertheless take an altogether neutral attitude toward what others are doing with its money?"

"Look, I was accused once of owning a big share in Cyntex—birth-control stuff, pharmaceuticals. And I checked. Yes, we did have ONE share, that somebody had left in a will. Since I've been here . . . First of all we don't have many investments . . . and I gave orders—no pharmaceuticals, no armaments, no luxury buildings of any sort."

"What about the Watergate complex?"

"The Watergate wasn't . . . There it is again, see!" he growled testily. "*That* was Immobiliare. Apparently right after the war the Vatican had a major interest in it. For the simple reason that nobody had money. So the Vatican invested, APSA primarily. When I came here in 1969, APSA—that's not this bank, you remember, it's another Vatican section over which I have no jurisdiction—had seventeen percent of Immobiliare: seventeen percent doesn't control the company. But when they were building Watergate, they asked our nuncio in the States there at the time to put in a good word for them—so everybody thought it was the Vatican. I remember talking to the administrator of Immobiliare, I said, 'Listen, every time I turn around the Vatican owns Immobiliare.' I said, 'I wish we *did* own it!'

"We were involved in a bank in Switzerland where somebody from the Council of Churches made a statement that we were involved in financing things in South Africa, *our* bank. The bank answered and said, 'It's not true. The bank as such has no exposure in South Africa, but some of our clients do.' I mean, if you have an agreement with the bank, and you say to them, I want you to buy me five hundred shares of some big company in South Africa, that's yours, it's not the bank's. The bank made this statement publicly to all the newspapers, but they don't pick it up. They don't want to pick it up." Once more Marcinkus was looking hurt.

"These people jump the gun, and accuse. I always said, it's more difficult to prove innocence than to prove guilt." He stirred his frame, picked up my list of questions, gave all the appearance of moving on to less sticky matters.

"You could go through our stuff," he said, shrugging. "I think we've got a pretty honest, clean record. All these accusations they made are completely without foundation. All these companies that were established in Panama, who established them? In whose name were they established? Certainly not in our name. Who gave you orders to establish it?"

The last rhetorical question was rapped out to an unseen audience in the far corner of the room.

"Now. If you want to establish something in my name," he went on a little more calmly, "if you want to buy a car in my name, you've got to get the authorization. No?"

"Absolutely."

"Now, if unknown to us somebody sets it up in our name, he's responsible for it—we're not. Now, you imagine if what Calvi says is true—they're all mine that he was handling for me—why did Calvi have to commit suicide? All he'd have to do is come with a piece of paper and say, these are yours. I want my money."

The archbishop sat staring into space a little above my head for a while, his jaw set, his eyes half shut. Was it possible that we were thinking the same thing: what, after all, if Calvi had died, not by suicide—but by homicide?

I broke the silence: "Is it true, Monsignor, what Calvi said, that he sent fifty million dollars to Solidarity in Poland on behalf of this Pope?"

Marcinkus shook his head vigorously. "I had no idea. He never talked to me about Solidarity. Our conversations as a rule were talking about generic things. As I said to you before, I never sat down and talked specifics with him in any sense. He never mentioned Solidarity to me at all. If he gave something to Solidarity, okay, but I didn't know anything about it."

He began to laugh hoarsely and extended his hands in an Italianate gesture of innocence. "Somebody said he gave six million bucks to me, too," he went on. "I never saw it. I never got from him, personally, one lira. I did receive from the board of directors meeting every time I participated a certain sum to cover our costs. Like they do. Everybody gets it. Even at Christmastime I would never get one lira. I wouldn't want to have received it, but I hadn't."

The time had come, I decided, to tackle the implications of the "goodwill gesture" made by the Vatican for its part in the collapse of the Banco Ambrosiano.

"Now, the Vatican was asked to pay two hundred fifty million dollars in compensation for its involvement in the Ambrosiano debacle. Why did the Vatican pay that figure if, as you say, you didn't do anything?"

"You're talking to the wrong man," he cried out, looking up at the ceiling. "Oh, you're talking to the wrong *man*. I told them right from the beginning, 'You're *crazy*! Don't even open up that conversation,' I said. 'If we're not guilty, we don't pay. And we're not guilty.' But these guys were smart enough to put pressure on the Vatican by a threat of lawsuits. See? I said, 'This is *business*! Don't be afraid of a lawsuit.' I said, 'If you're preaching the truth, you've got to fight for it.' And now they've got two problems. I said, 'How is it you're telling everybody you've got no money with the deficit, and you're paying out money that you don't owe?' I said, 'My whole goal was to help you guys in building up this stuff so that we could help you with all your problems. And when times are heavy you're just throwing it out the window.' And the way they came out with the thing—'For *moral* considerations,' they said. I said, 'What d'you *mean* for *moral* considerations? If there are moral considerations, then we must be guilty.' Then they got those so-called wise men into it. But they don't solve no problems at all. They create another problem. Because with that payment the stigma is there.

"If they said . . . If they said . . ." The archbishop was worked up to a point where he was speechless. At last he blurted out: "They could've gotten away with it! They could've gotten away with it! See? You might have worked it out by fighting it, the cost of lawyers and so on—you might just as well settle and come to the same thing. . . . But *say* it that way. *Don't* say for moral considerations. You've just destroyed everything you've just built up. And it's a heck of a lot of money. You'd better believe it. Here we are trying to get nickels and dimes from people to build a church, then suddenly—BOOM! You've blown it all away. . . ."

He was pensive for a while, chin resting on his huge fists. "Mind you, it didn't come from the faithful's money. It didn't come out of any Peter's pence or anything like that. This was money that was created here with good investments and properties and things that we took advantage of at the right time. We didn't get a dime from the Vatican; we gave more to the Vatican than they ever gave us. In fact, the figure was two hundred forty-one million dollars, not two hundred fifty million. I negotiated a discount. So we *made* nine million bucks! When I think, behind the lines, some of these guys figured if I couldn't pay it they'd have to come up with it and they could get rid of me, see? Then that killed them when they found out that I didn't have to go *anywhere* to get it. It didn't kind of clear us out completely; we had to kind of lower our capital level. But it kills me, because of the problems of tomorrow. I'm not thinking of the covering up of the deficit—that's secondary. It's tomorrow, your pensions and stuff. And once you're trying to run everything out of *ordinary* administration, that's when you get killed. If your company had used over the years the money for the pension fund, then they'd go broke. You've got to have the pension fund set aside . . ."

I looked at him blandly, although I felt like laughing nervously at the insanity of it.

"What sort of financial dealings," I asked, "did you have with John Paul I before he became Pope? People say you had a brush with him over diocesan financial policy when he was patriarch of Venice."

"There was a bank in Venice called the Banco San Marco that was having a lot of difficulties," said the archbishop promptly. "We owned by that time majority shares of Banca Cattolica. And these people said to me, 'Why don't you buy the San Marco?' See? I said, 'We're not in business to buy it.' And I said, 'From what I understand, it's in very bad shape and there's no use getting involved in anything like that.' I said I don't know how important it is to the bishops up in that area, but I said it would be a bad purchase. But I never said this to Luciani or anything like that. And I never throw anyone out of this office. Even if I'd like to. And especially a cardinal. . . . You never brush him off. . . . Then later, he thanked me . . . *they* thanked me. Said it was a good thing we didn't get involved. Because it was absorbed by the Banca Cattolica. See? So indirectly these guys said, 'You were right.'

"But when I saw Pope Luciani that time after he became Pope . . . I went up there for that meeting. If I had brushed him off, it would have meant he'd remembered me, in a bad light, see. When he walked into the room, I stood up and he looked me up and down, big smile on his lips, you know, and he said, 'Are all Americans big like you?' And I said, 'Your Holiness, I'm just on the second team, you should meet the first team.' He laughed! And it was the most cordial meeting I could have had. He thanked me for giving him all the information. He said, 'I'll be seeing you again,' and all that stuff, see, about forty-five minutes to an hour. He was most gracious.

"Now, one of the reasons I went up to see Luciani was that there were certain funds, foundation moneys of certain kinds, and I tried to explain what was available to him. But he couldn't care less! *'Grazie, grazie, grazie . . . va bene, va bene, va bene . . .* ' He didn't

want to know. And he talked a lot about the Secretariat of State
reports that they bring him, and what a burden it was. And I
reminded him that Paul VI was in the Curia for thirty-five years
and it took him six months to get adjusted to it. And I said it's not
necessary to go through all that. You could just get a résumé of all
the problems, I told him. It couldn't have been more cordial. And
with regard to the finances, he didn't show any interest at all. Paul
VI was very cordial and gracious, but he didn't have that . . .
country style of Luciani. Luciani was like a country pastor."

"Did you ever consider suing these authors who portrayed you
as a murderer?" I asked him suddenly.

"I did," he said emphatically. "I said to somebody to go and
check it out. He dealt with a big outfit in London, and the guy said,
'You've got a chance, a good chance. However, the way the libel
laws and everything are written, *you* would have to prove . . . not
that he proves that he's right. So you'd have to open up *all* your
archives to him. There's nothing that you have that's sacred.' And
he says, 'You have to spend two or three million bucks, and take
two or three years, and even then you're not too sure.'

"Then, people say, I fixed the Holiday Inn deal in Rome! I wasn't
involved in it at all. In Chicago the Holiday Inn people were looking
around and wanted to build one in Rome, and they said, 'Do you
know anyone in Rome?' So they gave the name of Dr. What's-his-
name, who these guys knew. And we were in problems building
the house for the American clergy in Rome, Villa Stritch. We'd
just finished building Villa Stritch, and this guy was the builder.
So when this guy, what's-his-name, the head of Holiday Inn, came,
I said, 'I don't know what you guys want to build, I don't know
what kind of design you want. Why don't you look at our building,
Villa Stritch? Give you some ideas of construction. This is what it
cost.' Anyway, they came up to the building we had, and they
wanted to know who the architect was. So the guy who did our
building designed their building according to what they wanted,
and stuff like that. I had nothing to do with it at all. Absolutely
nothing."

I found myself for a moment considering the style of his answers.
He might well be innocent of all the allegations that had been hurled

at him, but his street language, his muddleheaded nominal aphasia, his baffling confabulations, made him *sound* distinctly evasive. It struck me that he might not have fared well in a libel court.

"Have you *ever* been a businessman in your own right, Monsignor, apart from your presidency of the bank? I mean, made money for yourself?"

"People are always coming here asking me to do all sorts of stuff. But I tell 'em we don't get involved in that stuff. They come in saying they're scared stiff, want to get their money out, I say, 'Sorry, this is the wrong place.' Then people come and say, 'So much will be for charity.' Now that thing gets me griped. It gets me *very* griped, because it's an excuse."

"There are people, Monsignor, who say you set up a travel business, a sort of pilgrim business on your own account."

"No, I didn't do any. During the Vatican Council I didn't want to see all our cardinals and bishops getting fleeced by all these airlines, so I got ahold of this friend who ran pilgrim deals, and I said, 'How can we arrange a charter flight for these guys?' You can imagine the money we saved. We used to have two charters coming, and two charters going. I didn't make anything out of it. If there was any money made it went back to the bishops' conference. But I invented the charter idea because I said if the Church has to pay for the guys all over . . . You see, the airlines were against the idea. But I got all the conditions necessary; I said these bishops are a regular club, aren't they, and they were a genuine association before the council was ever called, in-house thing, see? The Propagation of the Faith was paying a lot of bills for these guys, so we had charters coming in from the Far East, from Africa, from South America. *I* never ran a tourist agency. I've *never* been involved in a tourist agency. I *used* people that were involved. I needed a guy who knew how to handle the logistics, tickets, the baggage; we never lost a bag. Same with the Pope's trips.

"You might say, 'How come all these stories about Marcinkus and not anybody else?' The only thing I can say is, maybe because I'm American and I've been successful in doing certain things, and maybe I've used people in whom I have confidence who've been involved in different things, and therefore I get washed with the same brush. I provided a lot of services for American bishops, did a lot of favors, got to know a lot of people around town. If I didn't do anything, I wouldn't be involved with these people."

"Why weren't you made a cardinal last time round?" I asked. "People say that this indicates you're being punished in some way."

"Number one! Nobody has a right to be made a cardinal," he said defiantly. "In fact, when they made me a bishop, I told them, 'You're out of your minds.' Because it gives you authority without a matching responsibility. You become a bishop, you know, everybody bows and scrapes to you and all that stuff, especially here. It didn't change my job. I still climb ladders, scramble around on the roof, all that stuff—being in charge of the buildings. If I became a cardinal I'd go on doing the same thing, which they wouldn't like."

"Don't you ever become stir-crazy, trapped in the Vatican . . . living in this small, enclosed society?"

"I go out!" he said indignantly. "The myth about me before this trouble was that I was running around everywhere. It's a myth! I have a reputation of attending all these *salones*. I don't know how they can say that. I never go to receptions. I *hate* them! The reverse is true. If I went to somebody, they'd say, 'How come he's here?' '*Why* is he here?'

"I'm not afraid to go out. It doesn't bother me if the police pick me up. But I wouldn't want to give them the satisfaction. You know, putting a pair of handcuffs on me or something like that, for the newspapers. And I think I have a certain responsibility. Now I live by choice at the Governor's Palace. I'm six hundred yards away from this office, and forty yards from the other one."

He sat musing for a while, sucking on his pipe. Then, out of the blue, he said, "You know, Christ is such an admirable figure that even if you don't believe in him and come in contact with him, you're taken up with him. And if you believe, imagine what can happen. I began to realize that when material things take possession of you, you're no longer free. If you've got nice things in your house you hide them."

It was a bit below the belt, but I could not resist. "So what do you think," I intervened, "of the great treasures of the Vatican? Isn't it time to get rid of them? Sell them off to give to the cause?"

"Okay, the only answer I can give is this. You sell 'em off. Let's say you sell the *Pietà* and we get a hundred fifty million bucks, and we give everybody a dime, we haven't resolved their problems and we haven't resolved our problems. The problem's still there."

It struck me as a crude answer in view of the pretensions of the preceding statement, but it was getting late to pursue that particular polemic, even if I had thought it profitable to press him on the matter. Suddenly he had embarked on another homiletic ramble on the question of charity, charity in the sense of speaking well of one's neighbor. Was he, again, touching on the attitude toward him of his priestly colleagues in the Vatican?

In a pause in his monologue I said, "There's a lot of gossip around here, isn't there, Monsignor?"

"If you can't find charity here in the Vatican, where will you find it?" he said quietly. "It's supposed to be a place where you find joy. You get three or four priests gathered together and they're criticizing other people. You're going to say, 'What *is* this! I thought this was a place of love?' *This* is the reason why I don't mix in a lot of these places, because somebody *gives* you stories, you've got to *tell* stories back. I don't want to work like a Hoover, pick up dirt—pass it on. I guess it sounds as if I'm trying to excuse *myself*, but that's a basic fact. In this place, of all places . . . You can get caught up in this exaggerated bureaucracy where all the bad elements of being a person can come out."

He rose and went over to stand by his door. He seemed to be searching for his keys; he was making it clear that our meeting had come to an end.

"This is what happens in this place," he went on, "and that's the whole problem of this investigation you're doing. You get a little bit here, a little bit there: that's what creates confusion. This is a village, excuse me if I say this, a village of washerwomen. You know, they get down in the river, wash clothes, punch 'em, dance on 'em, squeezing all the old dirt out. In normal life people get away and have other interests, but here—what else is there to talk about? I used to have a great secretary at the tribunal in Chicago, she looked like this Phyllis Diller, she wasn't the greatest mover, not like Mavi, but anyway, at five o'clock she was finished with the office. She put on her lipstick, took her purse, went home and forgot the office. But when you're in an enclosed place like this there's nothing else to do, nowhere to go, nothing else to talk about. . . ."

He was standing with the door open, inviting me through. He shut it behind him and locked it. He put on a black raincoat and a brown corduroy flat cap, which had been hanging on the coat stand in the corridor. With his pipe between his teeth, he turned to me and said, "I'll tell you something. You ask me about ambition. I'll tell you something: perhaps I haven't been nearly ambitious enough. If I had, perhaps I wouldn't be in the mess I'm in now."

I followed him out into the courtyard to an aging silver Peugeot. "Get in," he said, "I'll take you part of the way."

We backed up, turned, and he sped forward through the arch and into the Cortile di San Damaso, Swiss Guards saluting on all sides. He gave a brief John Wayne–style salute in return.

"See that?" he said. "There are people here get promotion and wonder why they don't get polite treatment from these people. These guys give a salute and they ignore it. I say to them, 'It costs nothing to acknowledge and salute, and it pays off, see?' "

We were speeding breakneck through tunnels and archways. The Vatican City was deserted and barely lit. The cobbles were glistening in a fine rain.

"Today," he said, "the Vatican car pool had a new car, Peugeot, and asked me to try it out. This one's thirteen years old; they all think I should get a new one, see. But this one's fine. Anyway, I drove the new model different places in the Vatican, checking it out. A guy comes over and pokes his head in: 'Congratulations on the new car, Excellency!' See? So this afternoon—all over the Vatican—Marcinkus has given himself a new car! Next thing I pick up my old car again, drive out. The guy's all confused: got his information wrong. 'What's goin' on here!' he says. See?" The archbishop chortled around his pipestem.

He was now barreling the wrong way down a *senso unico* and emerged from the Arco delle Campane and out onto Saint Peter's Square, where he made a loop and stopped by the fountain on the left-hand side. We sat for a while in silence, watching the traffic passing on the outer perimeter of the square. He puffed at his pipe, looking straight ahead, his eyes smiling. He was still on Vatican territory.

"Is there such a thing as Freemasonry in the Vatican, Monsignor?"

He looked at me narrowly.

"There was a list of names and I was on it," he said promptly. "I was supposed to have been a Mason since 1963 or something, with a special code name. How would you identify a Mason? If he's got a Mason's badge or something, you might; but how do you identify him?"

I said, "I suppose that that's the whole point. It's a secret, and you're only known to the lodge."

"Yeah," he said, "but I don't belong to a lodge. I don't even know what a lodge looks like. I was at the golf house the other day and somebody said to me, 'Monsignor, can a Mason go to Communion with the new rules?' And I said, 'No, the Mason's still in mortal sin.' And I'm a canon lawyer, see. I gave him a very frank answer."

He turned to me sideways on.

"I presume and I say with utter conviction," he said roundly, "that inside the Vatican there is no such thing as Masonry. I swear it. I have no doubts in my whole mind about it. They said Baggio was one, Villot was one, Benelli was one, Casaroli was one, but I could swear . . . " He raised his right hand as if in the dock. "I take an OATH, to say that all those people mentioned are not Masons!"

He leaned across and opened the door for me, the pipe still clenched between his teeth.

"Take care!" he said.

He burned rubber as he started away. He made a wide loop across the cobbles of Saint Peter's Square and headed back the way we had come.

15

After dinner in the English College, I was sitting at "recreation" in a circle of staff and students taking coffee; my neighbor was an earnest-looking young priest who described himself as a specialist in moral theology.

After a while I steered the subject of our conversation to the Roman Catholic Church's teaching on lying. I was recalling the heated nineteenth-century debate between John Henry Newman and Charles Kingsley, the Anglican author and clergyman, who alleged that the Roman clergy encouraged lying "on a system." It had occurred to me that some of my clerical witnesses might well believe that it was moral to tell a lie in order to avoid scandal. If this were seen as legitimate behavior, where did it end? Could I take the word of any one of my clerical informants who might have a motive to avoid scandalizing the faithful?

"Are there any circumstances," I asked the young moral scholar, "in which one can tell a lie?"

"Aha," he began with a twinkle in his eye, "well, you might find some of the older generation, brought up on the old moral handbooks, who would give you some fairly involved answers to that question." He wrung his hands and leaned forward. "But even by the standards of the old Scholastic textbooks a lie is *always* held to be intrinsically evil, and it can never be justified for any reason whatsoever."

"But can there be such a thing as a subdivision of the lie?" I asked, groping in my memory for some of the lost formulae of my seminary training.

"Indeed. Lies can be *profitable*, as they say, or *harmful*, depending on whether they benefit the liar without harm to another, or whether they cause injury. A moral theologian of the old school would say that the first sort—you know, boasting and so forth— are venial sins, and the second sort are grievous sins. Under the heading of venial you can have lies that are merely jocose, or a type of insincerity, or a kind of hypocrisy—like if you pretend to be virtuous or holy when you're nothing of the kind." He smiled at me self-consciously. "But they're all wrong, because a lie is a voluntary utterance contrary to intellectual conviction."

"But what about a white lie, or what I seem to remember we called 'economy of the truth,' or the good old Jesuit equivocation?"

"Ah, now! That's not exactly lying you see. That comes under the heading of mental reservation and the principle of amphibology."

"Amphibology?"

"That's it. It means a statement with several meanings. If I say, 'Peter is *at home* this evening,' I could mean either that he was giving a dinner party later on, or that he was literally physically present in his house right now. You're allowed to have recourse to broad mental restriction of this kind, where a prudent man could gather the intended meaning from the surrounding circumstances; but you couldn't engage in strict mental reservation, intending deliberately to mislead, because that's an odious lie. I mean, even Christ himself indulged in amphibology on occasion. . . ."

"Let's take the example of the Vatican telling the world that Magee found the body of the Pope, when in fact it was the nun. They say they did this to avoid scandal."

"Aha! That could be the principle of double effect. That's when an action has two results; one may be good and the other bad, like when an abortion would save the mother's life and you permit it for that reason, despite the other consequences. But I don't think it applies in this case. There are various sorts of scandal: you have active scandal, passive scandal, formal or diabolical scandal. But the interesting one here is *passive* scandal. That's where scandal results not from an evil action, but from a good action which is accepted by another through ignorance or through malice as an occasion of sin. This would apply to an action that leads people to believe that the Pope slept with the nun if you announce that this nun woke him with coffee in the morning. There is no moral obligation to avoid the scandal that arises from pure maliciousness, although you must avoid it if you can when it arises through people's weakness or natural inclinations. But you shouldn't tell a lie to avoid it, anyway."

"Okay," I said, "here's another question. Say the Church had got itself mixed up in fraudulent or criminal financial deals likely to cause grave scandal to both Catholics and non-Catholics. I suppose they can just keep quiet about it, but would it be permissible for the Vatican to tell a deliberate lie, or deliberately mislead through amphibology, or whatever you like to call it, in order to make people think that they were in no sense guilty?"

"There's only one answer to that," said the moral theologian, "and it's *no!*"

16

Don Diego Lorenzi had brought to my attention a quarterly newsletter on the life of John Paul I, published from a convent in Giustina, Belluno. It was called, simply, *Papa Luciani—Humilitas*, and was evidently intended as a starting point for the process of John Paul I's canonization. I received in the post at the English College the edition for the second quarter, for May 1986; it was a cheaply produced, small-circulation pamphlet, of the sort one finds at the backs of churches. The front page announced that the issue contained "remarks collected from Sister Vincenza by a confidante" in the year before Vincenza's death on June 28, 1983. The confidante was one Sister Irma Dametto of the Holy Sisters of Bordeaux, who, according to the publication, had been personally granted this interview by Sister Vincenza, who for twelve years had been the permanent housekeeper in Venice and in Rome of Albino Luciani, later John Paul I.

This is the text of the interview:

"Papa Luciani was a saint! He left us an example of great human and evangelical virtue. He had great piety and faith and an abandonment in God. He was very charitable, especially toward the humble, the poor, the deprived. He was an example of a true Christian, of a priest and a bishop. He was an example as a spiritual father.

"I can tell some stories which show his qualities. He prayed often and at length. He rose at five in the morning. At five-thirty he came into the kitchen for a cup of coffee, then he spent a long time with the Lord to have 'light and strength,' he used to say. Often, when his duties permitted, he would come to the *guardaroba* to recite the Rosary with us sisters.

"He was very good and paternal with us sisters. He wanted us to get proper rest, and when one of us was ill he had someone accompany him to visit us, encourage us and give us his blessing. He was always very discreet. I don't recall his ever being angry. Once when he was patriarch he sent us all on a pilgrimage. When we returned in the evening we found a hot meal all prepared by him.

"He used to say, 'Everyone has a *toket*,' which is Venetian dialect for a talent. 'At the right moment we must bring it out.'

"He usually spoke in dialect, even in Rome. Two words were commonplace with him: 'Sister' and 'Thank you.' He would say to us, 'Remember, you are part of the family.'

"We took care of his wardrobe and shoes, which he never wanted with buckles. We had to take care of everything. He was not difficult, but he was very well-groomed. Yes, very.

"Once during the summer I put a few drops of eau de cologne on his cassock. He noticed it immediately and asked me with great courtesy not to do it again.

"He was also very easy about food, even though he had very delicate health. He found everything good. I don't remember once in twelve years his ever sending a dish back or complaining. Only once he said, 'The soup is a little salty tonight.' But if there were guests, whoever it was, he wanted the best and served on the best dishes.

"At night he went to bed early, at nine o'clock. He watched the TV news and that was that. He only made an exception for the comedies of Goldoni.

"Once he had to go on a parish visit near Mestre. It was the period of the petrol shortage and there were restrictions. The patriarchate could have had a dispensation, but he didn't want to use it. He went from Venice to Mestre by train, then he borrowed a bicycle and cycled into the parish in his scarlet robe, to the joy of the parishioners. On another occasion, I remember, his little car was parked at the side of the road all covered in dust and somebody wrote with his finger: 'This is poverty.'

"Whenever he went around the city he dressed as a simple priest, not as a cardinal. He would put his red *zucchetto* in one pocket and his cross and chain in the other and go among his people. Everybody knew him and saluted him with respect and love. He was a friend of the *gondolieri,* and all who needed comfort and help, not just spiritual and moral. People were knocking at the door of the patriarchate at all hours of the day for all sorts of things, and he gave orders that the door must always be answered.

"The street outside the house was a constant procession. And nobody went away empty-handed. He often went out with his pockets full of money in envelopes he gave personally to people he was helping. And there were a great many of them.

"They called him the 'smiling Pope.' He was full of affability, of good nature, but he also suffered, both in Venice and in Rome. He often said to us sisters: 'Remember that your road is difficult. You will meet tigers, and lions, and panthers that want to tear you to pieces. And at the best of times there will be flies and mosquitoes, biting and attacking you . . . so many, so many. . . .'

"In the Vatican I was in the habit of cleaning his room at around eight o'clock, when I thought there would be nobody there. One morning I went in as usual; I realized, too late, that Papa Luciani was in there at the other end of the room. He was standing in a depressed and hunched posture, with the secretary standing over him.

"I made my excuses and retired in a hurry, but I could not help hearing the secretary saying to him, 'Holy Father, be Saint Peter! You have the authority! Don't let them bully you and intimidate you!' He kept saying this insistently, over and over again.

"He often spoke with great admiration and affection of Paul VI. 'He was a great pope,' he would say. 'He suffered much and was misunderstood. . . .' He would say, 'Watch out for the crowd that applauds you; what will they do tomorrow!'

"He would say, 'You see that the crowd cries out "Hosanna" at the beginning, and before long they are calling, "Crucify him!" Only trust in God and put your faith in *Him*.'

"When things were quiet in the Vatican at about ten o'clock in the morning, I used to take him in a little cup of coffee. He said to me many times, 'Look, Sister, I should not be sitting here in this seat. The Foreign Pope is coming to take my place. I have *begged* Our Lord!'

"And Our Lord heard him."

Some essential characteristics of John Paul's personality shone through the nunnish pietism, making the disturbing implications of the final paragraphs all the more poignant. The detail about the secretary pleading with him confirmed the consistent evidence that the men around him considered him a poor pope and that he was unequal to the task. But I was disappointed not to have been given more information about the morning the Pope had been found dead. I decided that I would take steps to track down the "confidante," Sister Irma.

17

Two days before I was due to return to London I called on Dr. Navarro-Valls at the Press Office to see what progress had been made in getting me appointments with Dr. Buzzonetti—the Pope's doctor—and the morticians.

Sister Giovanna had a dubious expression. She said, "I'll see if he can talk with you." And she went away for five minutes.

When she returned she was biting her lower lip. "Dr. Navarro-Valls is extremely busy right now. He can't talk with you and sends his apologies. He says that Dr. Buzzonetti is unable to talk to you because he says he only knew the patient for a short time and so is not in a position to say anything. Also, that everything is secret."

The patient! I uttered a soundless oath. "Can I have some paper?" I asked her.

I sat down in the secretaries' office and wrote a note:

To: Dr. Navarro-Valls
From: John Cornwell

It is impossible for me to establish the truth of the various published claims about Dr. Buzzonetti's actions and statements and those of the Signoracci brothers unless I can speak to

them. In view of their inaccessibility I intend to abandon this
project and return to England.

Sister Giovanna took the note away. She was back within half a
minute.

"The director is waiting for you."

She led the way.

He was standing in his room amid the familiar reek of antiseptic.
He had his hands open wide and wore an apologetic grin.

"I am sorry. I spoke with Dr. Buzzonetti this morning," he said.
"He will not talk. He is adamant. He says that the information is
secret."

"But I don't want any secret information. I want to know when
he instructed the Signoraccis to embalm the body. Why should that
be a secret?"

"I don't know."

"May I speak to the Signoracci brothers?"

"I don't know."

"There's no point in continuing here if I can't see key living
witnesses. You're a press officer; do you realize that ANSA reported
that the Signoracci brothers left for the Vatican before the body was
found? Don't you think we should check that out for the sake of
the historical record? This is basic!"

Navarro-Valls shrugged and smiled with his big, fulsome teeth.
"My hands are tied. I run this Press Office. I can't tell the Pope's
doctor what to do."

"You're not bothered, then, if I drop the project?"

He shrugged again. "What can I do?"

I turned on my heel and walked from the office. I was enraged. In
the lobby of the Press Office they were building a crèche. I felt
considerable ill will in my heart at that moment for the exponents
of the Christian message.

I went out into the misty dusk on the Via della Conciliazione and
straight into the Santo Spirito bar to make a call to Marjorie Weeke.

"Is it Navarro-Valls or Buzzonetti?" she asked.

"What do you mean?"

"What I mean is, did you get a sense that Navarro-Valls has been told to lay off and not to help you by somebody higher up? Because if that's the case, you're finished."

"How would I be expected to grasp something like that?"

"I don't know. Just a feeling, an instinct. They usually find a way of letting you know."

"If it's a question of instinct," I said, "I think it's Buzzonetti who's holding out. Is there anything you can do?"

"Nothing," she said.

"Then the thing has run out of steam."

"It could be." Her voice was at least sympathetic.

I put the phone down and was surprised to find my hand shaking with anger.

I looked up my contact book and called the Vatican Bank.

Vittoria Marigonda answered.

"Oh, it's you!" she said. "I was trying to get in touch with you. I can't talk now. Can you come in here later on, after the bank is shut? I want to see you. I'll be waiting at six-thirty."

18

The Cortile di Sisto Quinto was in virtual darkness when I arrived for my meeting with Marcinkus's secretary, Vittoria Marigonda. The bank was silent and deserted. The archbishop had retired to his isolated quarters in the Governor's Palace. She was sitting at her desk with a cup of coffee.

"Come and sit here," she said.

I drew up a chair.

"I hope you're on the level. I want to help you . . . so long as you're on the level. He's been hurt too much already."

Her accent and inflection were American, with just an edge of Italian. She was dressed in a smart, well-fitting suit.

"Don't worry," I said, "I'm going to drop the project if I can't talk to Buzzonetti. He's refused to talk to me, you know."

"Marjorie told me. News travels fast in this place. Let me see what we can do. I'll see if the archbishop can fix it. But it's a tough one. Buzzonetti is answerable only to the secretary of state and the Pope, and if he doesn't want to meet you he won't, unless he's been told to by the Holy Father. But I just wanted to show you something. Listen, you call me Mavi, that's what people call me.

Here, this letter was written by the sergeant of the Swiss Guard who appears in Yallop's book giving incriminating evidence against the archbishop. You know, you should see Roggen."

She handed me the letter.

The Most Rev. Paul Marcinkus
Pro Presidente dello Stato della Città del Vaticano
Stato Della Città Del Vaticano   22 June 1984

Your Excellency:

Last week on the evening news a report was given by the Rome correspondent of a new book which implies that Pope John Paul I's death may have been induced by outside forces. In this book [*In God's Name*] I was quoted as describing the events of the morning after an encounter with you as you reported to your office at your usual hour.

I recall having spoken about the affair in innocence to a few friends and how shocking and unexpected it was and of how you yourself were so surprised over the suddenness and un-expectedness of it all. I never intended in any way to give an interview or speak with any authority.

I am very angry and upset over the book and over the abuse of the author in using my name. I don't even remember ever meeting the person. I am especially concerned over the in-convenience this may cause you. I want to apologize and ex-press my dismay over the publication of such trash. I would also express my denial of any part in the publication of this book.

I take the occasion to express my appreciation for your friendship and kindness to me over these years, and I assure you of my continued support and loyalty to you and to our Holy Father.

With every best wish, I remain,
    Yours respectfully in Christ,
        Hans Roggen

Scribbled at the bottom of the letter was:

Just a note of reply—assuring him that I have confidence in him. I'll see him when he returns to Rome! PCM. 1.7.84.

It was an interesting document for it appeared to claim that Hans Roggen had only ever spoken to "friends." I was by no means convinced of the truth of this. At the same time, Mavi clearly intended that I should note the bland and friendly reaction of the archbishop. It seemed to me that a meeting with Sergeant Roggen would be worthwhile.

I looked up at her.

"You know," she said, "the archbishop has suffered so much because ever since the trouble began, even some of his best friends have treated him badly, and . . . well, the authorities here have never lifted a finger to clear his name. He's been really hurt. People he knew well, people he'd helped—they cut him dead, as if he never existed."

"Mavi, can I ask *you* some questions?"

She lit a menthol cigarette. "Sure, go ahead."

"Tell me about the morning the Pope died? What sort of time did you get up?"

"I was getting dressed, about half-past seven and a neighbor knocked at the door and told me. So I came straight here at about eight o'clock; everything in the Vatican had been upside down anyway, because they had been taking down everything from the consistory and now they were having to think about putting it all back again. The archbishop was here, but he always got in here early. Always. He was an early riser. He would say his Mass at the crack of dawn, get in and read the papers."

She ventured a wry smile. "I'm just remembering. After the archbishop had his only audience with Luciani, he came back down here and said, 'He looks so small and tired!' And I remember looking at the archbishop and thinking, And you look so big and strong!"

"What's your relationship with him?" I asked. She flashed a look, and I immediately realized that I had asked an impertinent question. I added, "You're very devoted to him, yes?"

"I've worked with him for seventeen years. I'm devoted because he is a very good man. He's got a heart of gold. The best. There have been all sorts of stupid rumors . . . I don't care. Look, I was the first woman secretary in the history of the Vatican. When he came into the bank he said he didn't want some little priest, he wanted a properly trained secretary from the world of commerce.

These people were terrible to me when I first came; they wouldn't talk to me, even on the phone. There were priests and monsignori who would come and stand at the door and just stare at me in silence. Even the lay staff was difficult; after the first day they had me banned from the canteen. Later on, big deal, they changed their minds and said I would be welcome. I never set foot in there again. Things are difficult: you go out with a man for a cup of coffee at lunchtime and it's all over the Vatican."

"Do you socialize with the archbishop? I mean, do you ever meet him outside the office?"

She laughed. "You can't be serious! This is a goldfish bowl. I wouldn't even be able to play a round of tennis with him without it causing scandal. Socialize? No. I've helped him out a bit with entertaining at the Governor's Palace. There were some raised eyebrows over *that*! He won't have a little team of nuns living there, even though he's entitled to it. He's actually extremely frugal and hates wasting money. I have to beg him to buy a suit. He'll wear a suit until the elbows and knees are out and it's falling off him. I tell you, the only thing he treats himself to is a round of golf. So what! Anyway, he asked me once or twice to come and help cook and serve when he had guests at the Governor's Palace. But I really resented it. I'd go in and serve and find these priests looking me up and down. They were astonished to see me there. And I didn't like it. It wasn't right. I mean, I'm a senior secretary, it was demeaning. In the end I told him that I'd do a buffet and that they'd have to help with the clearing away and washing up. But he was okay about that. He leads a lonely life. I know the whole of it. There are no sinister secrets. I know all his friends . . . mostly priests. He takes his priestly life seriously. He's always told me *obedience* is the first thing. He'll always do what the Pope asks him to do. You know, he saved the Pope's life twice. He went on these trips because they were dangerous and he was determined the Pope would get the best protection. Nobody had a clue. None of them has their feet properly on the ground. When Paul VI started to travel around, only the archbishop knew the score. If it hadn't been for him they would have got Paul and they would have got this one. He would have cherished Pope Luciani just as much had he lived. He's the Pope's man, any pope! To suggest he'd kill a pope . . ."

Mavi stopped for a moment. "But he knows, and he's always known, that he's not popular and people would like to get rid of him."

"Has he a bad temper? Does he get rough?"

"Oh, he can shout but it's all over in five minutes. He can't stand gossip and backbiting . . . stories. He gets mad; marches out and slams doors, all that. I say to him, 'Take it easy. Listen and just switch off. Change the subject.' But he can't stand it. That's another reason why he's not liked around here. You know, they tell you something so that you'll tell them something back. He can't stand that."

"Where did you work before you came here?" I asked.

"I worked for an investment company. I was in the same building as Sindona, so I saw all that from the other side."

"Do you understand this Ambrosiano business?"

"Are you kidding? I've been with it every inch of the way."

"Tell me, honestly," I said, "has he anything to be ashamed of?"

She was silent for a while. She looked at me intently and drew on her cigarette. She shook her head.

"He only knew about Church policy. He's never *ever* technically run the bank. The bank has been run by Luigi Mennini for nearly forty years. The archbishop has always taken responsibility for everything at the end of the day, and stood by him and everybody else. There's nothing to be exposed—except naïveté, and the archbishop wasn't responsible for that."

"Does he have money?"

She laughed. "I know every last cent that man has," she said. "He's going to be in real trouble when he retires, because he has absolutely nothing. He's given away what little he ever gets. People are always coming to him for help and he'll give his last dime. They probably think it comes from the bank, but it comes straight out of his own pocket. They rarely think of paying him back. He's never taken anything out of the bank. He can't. He refuses all stipends, payments for confirmations and ordinations and so on."

"Steady on," I said, "you're making him sound like a walking saint. Is that realistic?"

"He's no saint, but he's a great guy. Why did I stay working here for seventeen years on my pay surrounded by all this? I can tell you, I wouldn't do it for a jerk or a crook. Who needs it? Anyway,

I know what you're thinking. . . . You're going to have to decide what he's like for yourself."

I got up to go.

"I really do want to get to Buzzonetti, Mavi," I said. "If I can't make headway I'm dropping the whole thing."

She showed me to the frosted doors. "Look, just forget about Buzzonetti for twenty-four hours, will you? Put it right out of your mind. I'll talk to the archbishop in the morning."

I bade her good night and crossed the Cortile. The carabiniere, huddled in his shelter, grinned and gave a gloved salute. My face was beginning to be familiar. As I walked down the cold, echoing grandeur of the staircase, I wondered how I could capture the character of Marcinkus properly, in the round. A snatch of Browning came to me as I plodded down the steps:

> What needs a bishop to be fool or knave,
> When there are a thousand diamond weights between?

The deepest irony was that the strongest ally in my Vatican inquiries had become the office of Archbishop Marcinkus himself.

On August 26, 1978, Albino Luciani was elected Pope and took the name John Paul I. He was known universally as the "smiling Pope." Thirty-three days later he was dead from a heart attack, the Vatican announced.

Even as the Pope's body lay in state in the Vatican that September 1978, there were rumors that he had been murdered. Was a secret autopsy performed?

Archbishop Paul Marcinkus, from Cicero, Illinois, was banker to three Popes. Twice he saved a Pope's life on foreign trips. Though a man of great power and charm, he had had brushes with past scandals and was a target for gossip in connection with the Pope's death.

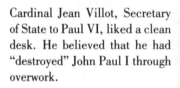

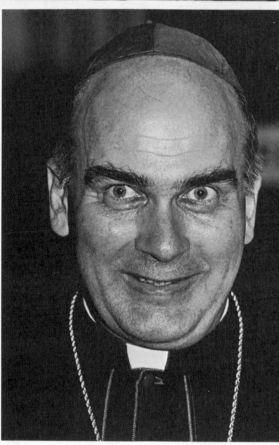

Cardinal Jean Villot, Secretary of State to Paul VI, liked a clean desk. He believed that he had "destroyed" John Paul I through overwork.

Archbishop John Foley, President of the Vatican Commission for Social Communications, was a former Diocesan newspaper editor in Philadelphia. He sought a new investigation into John Paul I's death.

Sister Vincenza, who had cared for Albino Luciani for twelve years, claimed she was the first to discover him dead in bed when she brought him a cup of coffee early on the morning of September 28, 1978.

Dr. Renato Buzzonetti, deputy director-general of the Vatican Health Services in 1978, signed John Paul I's death certificate without reference to the patient's medical history and without knowledge of the medicines he was taking.

The two papal secretaries, Don Diego Lorenzi and John Magee (above), whose task was to look over the Pope at all times. They both dined with the Pope on the evening before he died but then, at certain crucial points, their accounts of that night diverge. Was Lorenzi in the Papal apartments? Did Magee see the Pope to his bedroom?

Ernesto and Arnaldo Signoracci, papal morticians, were summoned out of retirement to embalm the body of John Paul I. Were they called to the Vatican before the Pope's body was found?

Behind the murder theories lay Vatican links to the Banco Ambrosiano scandal. Among those rumored to be involved were Roberto Calvi, president of the Banco Ambrosiano, who was found hanged under Blackfriars Bridge in London in June 1982; his associate, Michele Sindona, poisoned in jail in March, 1986 and Liceo Gelli, head of the illegal P2 lodge.

19

The following day I hung around the English College waiting for a call from Vittoria Marigonda.

She rang at six in the evening. "We're there!" she said. "It's been a hell of a nut to crack, but it's going to be okay. Will you be in later this evening?"

"Yes."

"You'll get a call. I can't tell you now, but everything's going to work out fine. Come and see me in the morning."

"What time? I'm going back to England tomorrow."

"You'll already be in the Vatican. I can't explain now. Just trust me." And she hung up.

I had supper in college and sat in the *salone* chatting with Monsignor Paul over a glass of scotch. I was consumed with curiosity about Mavi's call and I kept listening for my telephone throughout the evening until the lateness of the hour made me abandon hope.

At half-past ten, the rector appeared in the *salone*.

"There's been a call from the Vatican," he said. "Be there to-morrow morning. Six-fifteen, Bronze Door!" His face was bright with pleasure.

"What do you mean?" I said, rising from my chair.

"The Pope's secretary, Father Stanislav, has just rung through. You're to attend the Pope's private Mass in the morning and see him straight afterward."

"Him? Who? The secretary?"

"No, you're a bit slow this evening. His nibs! The POPE!"

"Mass? But I don't go to Communion."

"Don't worry about that. Just be there. It's the only way you're going to meet him. And wear a tie. You *can't* be late."

It was a long night. I had lain listening to the quarters from the clock tower until I rose at 4:30 and dressed in a dark, pin-striped suit and a sober tie.

It was still night and the moon shone brightly through an aureole of frost as I let myself out by the side gate into the Via di Monserrato and headed down the narrow lanes of the old city toward the Vatican. Halfway to my destination, on the Corso Vittorio, I stopped for coffee in a bar filled with silent early workers.

Saint Peter's Square at 5:30 was still dark and misty. The Bronze Doors were shut fast and several people were walking up and down nearby. There was a tall monsignor in cassock and magenta sash, three nuns, three pious ladies in black with mantillas and clumpy shoes carrying large prayer books. None of us strayed too far from the doors.

I looked up at the papal apartment: there were lights in all the windows. I was filled with excited anticipation, associated with a sense of awe at the very idea of the Papacy. Since my childhood, the Pope had seemed somebody totally remote from experience, and yet all-powerful—a Roman emperor. I had grown up on curious anecdotes about Pius XII; photographs of that emaciated, large-eyed demigod had hung in all the corridors of my youth. He always ate alone, we were told. When Vatican officials received a telephone call from him, they instantly fell to their knees. He had experienced visions of Christ, seen colored spinning suns and had died of hiccups. All this had somehow to do with the *idea* of being pope.

At 6:30 the doors were opened to reveal the misty lengths of the Scala Reggia. A valet came forward to check our names at the door. I gave mine and it was ticked off on the sheet on his clipboard.

We were escorted now up the great marble staircase to the Cortile di San Damaso. The glass panels of the loggias were lit up. Swiss Guards were all about us with smoky breath, saluting and calling out, *Buon giorno!*

We ascended by lift to the third loggia with its glowing Raphael frescoes, grand doorways and architraves. It was no more than thirty yards' walk to the papal front door.

In a vestibule there were two valets in black suits, snowy white shirts and black ties. Once again they checked our names one by one, then we entered a reception room lit by brilliant crystal chandeliers. On the walls were modern paintings: the Assumption of the Virgin Mary, Mary Queen of Heaven, Christ healing the blind, a bronze plaque of the Nativity . . .

Then there was another, larger chamber, with bookcases and a long, modern oak table in the center with boardroom-style chairs. There was an impression of polished white marble and institutional modernity. A decorated Christmas tree stood in one corner. The room was lit by chandeliers of modern design and there was discreet lighting above the pelmets of the sumptuous gold curtains.

We were taken on into a final corridor, the scene of the early-morning activities surrounding the death of John Paul I. At the end was the door to the Pope's bedroom. To my right was the secretaries' room. The door was open and I could see their desks and files.

To my left was the door of a small private chapel, and there on his own knelt the familiar figure of Pope John Paul II. It struck me as a peculiarly ugly room: modern in design, a clutter of undistinguished bronzes depicting the Evangelists, mosaics of early Christian symbols, a reproduction of the Black Madonna of Czestochowa on the right of the altar, and lighted panels depicting gospel scenes. There was something overdone about it.

A priest, whom I recognized from photographs as Father Stanislav, placed us in the chapel with reverential gestures. He seemed to be observing us all closely, and especially me, I thought. I was so close to the Pope that I could have reached out and touched him. I was struck by the hugeness of his shoulders; his cassock was not, as I had expected, snowy white, but a curiously yellowing off-white, like ancient cricket flannels. His head was bowed as if in concentration, and occasionally he looked up at the bronze crucifix above the altar. After we were settled, there was a commotion as a nun in black, with a strange Victorian headgear, came limping in late; she was muttering and fussing, but the Pope did not flinch. As I looked back I saw that the Pope's household nuns had come to kneel in the corridor outside, looking into the chapel. They were dressed in black with red heart-shapes embroidered on their breasts. Like Deskur's nuns, they were covered from head to toe and peered out from starchy wimples.

As the bells of Saint Peter's struck seven, he stood up and turned. His face looked worn and tired, his eyes half-shut. He managed a weak paternal smile, his head to one side. *"Buon giorno!"* he said, his voice deep and quavering. Then he walked to the altar and began vesting. Every gesture was slow and deliberate, but I noticed that when he took off his pectoral cross, which involved raising the long chain above his head, it was a swift, almost petulant movement.

Then the Mass began.

When Mass was ended, Father Stanislav led us out into the large chamber. He placed the pious ladies in one group, the nuns in another, and myself standing alone.

The Pope appeared. We clapped politely. I noticed that his cassock was a little short and a considerable length of white-socked ankle was clearly visible. He was wearing a pair of rather sharp, brown casual shoes. My eyes fixed on them, as they seemed to me utterly incongruous. I had expected him to be wearing the traditional red slippers, peeping modestly from beneath a cassock that reached his toes. These fashionable, highly polished tans were a surprise.

He engaged the pious ladies in conversation for a while; like the very elderly, he stood with feet apart as if steadying himself. He was deeply stooped. He had a way of shutting his eyes fast, bowing his head deeply. . . . Then he would nail you with a sudden upward, penetrating beady eye—crafty, peasantlike.

He spent a little time with the nuns. He grabbed one little one by the head in an action reminiscent of a football game—this is *my* ball!

Then he approached me, slightly pigeon-toed, dragging his feet a little.

Father Stanislav whispered in his ear and he nodded. Then he was next to me, short in stature. His face looked drained, exhausted, his flesh a little slack, almost feminine. He studied me with narrowed eyes, as if wary, as if attempting to discern any evil in me. I was surprised by an overwhelming sense of anticlimax. One of the most charismatic figures in the world from a distance, he seemed deflated at close quarters.

He stood sideways to me, and seemed to be inclining an ear, inviting me to speak. His hand went out; as I grasped it and wondered whether I should kiss his ring, he managed to clutch and push away my hand at the same time, leaving my pouting lips stranded in midair. He now held on to my arm with a strong, firm hand. His great square head went down until his chin was buried in his chest; then the eye opened, a pale-blue, knowing eye, scrutinizing me. There was a silence between us. He was waiting for me to say something.

"I'm writing a book about John Paul I, Holy Father," I said, speaking slowly. "I hope to discover the truth about the way in which he died."

"Yes," he said with slow emphasis, "I know. I have heard of this initiative of yours." Then in the famous slower Polish delivery: "I . . . WANT . . . YOU . . . TO . . . KNOW . . . THAT . . . YOU . . . HAVE . . . MY . . . SUPPORT . . . AND . . . BLESSING . . . IN . . . THIS . . . WORK . . . OF . . . YOURS!"

He lowered his head and seemed to cock his huge, bloodless Slavonic ear toward me, as if to invite some further comment. In that moment I could have said anything, or asked for anything. I had, quite literally, for the first and only time in my life, the Pope's ear. In fact, I was looking straight at it, and I had a sudden appalling impression of the sheer torrent of verbiage that flowed into it, hour after hour, day after day—all the arguments, pleas, demands, homage, sycophancy. I had not the slightest desire to add one drop to that Niagara.

He turned and faced me full on. He seemed amused, a smile played about his lips. He appeared relieved that I had kept my mouth shut. He pointed his finger at me, wagged it a little.

"You are Englishman!" he said, and his eyes twinkled. I wondered for a moment if he found Englishmen funny. Then I remembered my tea party with Cardinal Deskur and felt that I had

understood something about the conduct of this peculiar Polish
Papacy.

"Yes, Holy Father," I said, "Englishman!" I tried to look proud.

"Englishman!" he said again, and he nodded deeply, still smiling
to himself as he moved away slowly, almost reluctantly, I thought.

He approached the tall monsignor who was one of the party that
morning, then Father Stanislav was at my side. The priest took me
by the arm and shook my hand. He said to me quietly, "We have
heard all about the book you are writing. I want to wish you the
best of luck. Everything will be all right now."

We were being led out of the grand chamber, out of the vestibule,
onto the loggia. The elderly nun who had come late took hold of
my arm. She appeared dazed. "Let me hold on to you," she said
in a startling American accent. "I've got an arthritic hip."

We were not invited to ride the lift; we were directed to a staircase.
As we clambered down the long flights to the Cortile di San Damaso,
she told me that her name was Sister Assumpta and that she worked
as a clerk in the Governatorato Palace. Her boss was Archbishop
Marcinkus.

"I've waited thirty-seven years for this audience," she said.

She had a beaten-up car parked in the Cortile di Sisto Quinto
next to the bank, and I walked her to it. Archbishop Marcinkus
was standing under the arches near the door of his bank wearing a
gray cardigan and smoking his pipe. He waved cheerily.

In farewell, Sister Assumpta grabbed me by the arms and kissed
me straight on the mouth.

"Hey!" roared Marcinkus. "*I* don't get that!"

The archbishop led me through the familiar frosted revolving
doors. Mavi was by her desk pouring coffee.

"Do you want a bun?" she said to me. Then, turning to Marcinkus,
she nodded at me and said, "Look at him, he's walking on air."

"Come in for a minute," said Marcinkus. "I'm flying to Chicago
this morning."

I sat opposite him.

"You don't know the problems I've had getting Buzzonetti," he
said, shaking his head. "I had to go straight to the top. I went to
the secretary of state, then to Father Stanislav and the Holy Father.

I said, 'You've gotta quit blocking this guy. He's trying to do a *job*!' So *now*, you're clear. The Holy Father is signing a directive today. But he wanted to get a look at you this morning. You're gonna be okay. This is how this place works. See?"

As we spoke I looked up to see the extraordinary figure of Mennini, the managing director of the bank; he was coming and going with undulant step, clutching a file. He looked crestfallen and ancient in an old-fashioned, baggy suit. He was trying to catch the archbishop's eye. "I've gotta go now," said Marcinkus, rising. "Get in touch with Buzzonetti right away and make an appointment to see him after Christmas."

With this he clutched me by the hand and propelled me out of the office.

Mennini scuttled in.

20

J n my efforts to get to the bottom of Marcinkus's part in the 1972 counterfeit-bonds case, I had come across the name of the FBI agent in charge of the case in Italy, Tom Biamonte. I discovered that he had left the bureau and was now working as director of investigations into consumer fraud in the state of New Jersey. When I spoke to Biamonte on the phone he told me that he could "fill me in" on many aspects of Marcinkus and the Vatican. "I conducted a complete file on the man," he said. I realized that I had little alternative but to travel to the United States.

Biamonte's office was in Newark, where I arrived late one dismal winter afternoon shortly after Christmas. The State Department of Consumer Affairs was on the fourth floor of a gray, boxlike building a quarter of a mile from the station. When I went in, the workers were streaming out onto the dark windy street.

I found Tom Biamonte, former special agent of the FBI in Rome, in an empty office, sitting at the head of a conference table. I guessed he was in his early sixties; he was short and dapper, with a strong aquiline nose, deep lines under gray eyes and gray thinning hair. He was dressed in a brown tweed suit and a yellow button-down shirt.

He shook my hand with a hard, dry grip, settled himself back and said, "Listen, I'm not sure what I can tell you, but what are the rules? Anybody who writes a book, I'm suspicious of."

"How do you mean?"

"I prefer all this to be unattributable."

"In that case," I said, "I'd rather not go any further."

"What's the problem?" he said sharply. He spoke in a gravelly Bronx accent.

"I'd rather you told me nothing that I can't use with your name against it," I said.

Biamonte rubbed his chin, showing off a chunky signet ring. He looked at me thoughtfully. "I guess the archbishop needs a break . . ."

"What do you mean?"

"I believe he got a bad deal back there. The record should be set straight. I'm convinced of Marcinkus's innocence."

He lit a cigarette and made himself comfortable in his chair.

"After nine years of service, the FBI assigned me to Italy in the beginning of September 1962," he began. "I also covered leads during that time in Cyprus, Greece, Israel, Lebanon. Officially I was legal attaché at the Rome embassy, but I was in fact an FBI agent and known as such by police and intelligence contacts throughout Italy. I learned a great deal about Church bureaucracy, a lot about Italy and the political scene. I became acquainted with Archbishop Marcinkus when he was just a monsignor, in 1963. If the embassy needed someone to call on at the Vatican for assistance—someone wanted an audience with the Pope—Marcinkus was your man to arrange for the tickets; he kind of liked helping people out. . . . So I knew him from all that time back. You couldn't miss him. And he had a name as a golfer in the American community in Rome; he was a tremendous athlete.

"What I want to lead up to in relation to Marcinkus is a series of events known as the counterfeit-bonds case. I personally handled that case in Italy, I was in charge of it. It's a long time ago, but I still remember all the players. But let me tell you how that began. . . ." Biamonte stopped and rubbed his chin.

He started again. "Marcinkus's problems all started in my view because he had a bit of an association with Michele Sindona; it

wasn't a business association, it was an association based on Marcinkus's friendship with another fellow, named Antinucci. Mark
Antinucci. Sindona and Antinucci were entrepreneurs, extremely
intelligent and aggressive. Sindona was Sicilian, and in Italy all
Sicilians are suspect, because if they have any kind of money or
power—ergo they must be connected with the Mafia. In 1971 to
1972 Sindona did something unique. He made an effort to take
control of a large company in Italy called Ital Cimenti, owned by
a guy called Carlo Pesenti. In the United States mergers and takeovers, hostile and otherwise, take place every day; but when Sindona
made his move, such a takeover was unheard of in Italian business.
People were aghast that an individual would acquire the stock of
another company and take it over. In his attempt to buy in, naturally
the stock went up; and Pesenti, who was very powerful in the
Christian Democrat party incidentally, had to buy back his stock
at a highly inflated price. In the meantime Sindona sold, but it cost
Pesenti a lot of money, and as a result, with that hostile takeover
bid, Michele Sindona's troubles began in Italy. If you were an astute
observer of the political scene in Italy, you would have gradually
seen articles in newspapers commenting about Sindona. Is he involved in drugs? Is he involved with the Sicilian Mafia? I remember
one night they had a documentary on TV about Sindona, and they
showed the dimly lit paths of the old Sicilian village of Patti where
he came from, and the inferences were obvious. . . .

"Pesenti was very, very close to the Vatican, and he was very
familiar with a cardinal who is now dead: I mean Cardinal Benelli
of the Secretariat of State, who was intensely ambitious and autocratic and who resented and disliked Marcinkus. Marcinkus, you
see, had a lot of independence as director of the Vatican Bank and
had direct access to the Pope. Cardinal Benelli was vicious, he was
tough, he was ambitious; he wanted to be pope, he wanted control
of the Vatican. He was like the chief executive officer, the shaker
and the mover, and this interloper Marcinkus, who wasn't even a
cardinal, had a straight reporting line to the Pope. I'm telling you
this, because I was told that Marcinkus refused a loan to Pesenti
on Benelli's recommendation. Benelli naturally saw this as an attempt on Marcinkus's part to favor Sindona. This didn't come from

Marcinkus himself, who has never disparaged the Church or its
bureaucracy in my presence. Anyway, you've got to grasp that
Benelli did *not* like Marcinkus. My view is he hated him.

"Now, why am I telling you all this? One day an individual comes
into my office in Rome by the name of Mario Foligni, the key role-
player: he's the one who set it all in motion.

"He said he had fifteen million dollars worth of securities, American stuff—certificates from Coca-Cola, Occidental Petroleum and
so on, that were given to him by certain people, and he gave me
the names. He said that he went to the Handels Bank in Switzerland
in order to get a loan on these securities on behalf of these people.
But then what happened, he presented the certificates to the bank,
he went to his hotel that night congratulating himself on a tremendous deal, goes back to the bank the next day and the officials had
by now checked and found that the certificates were phony. They
immediately got an arrest warrant out against Foligni; he flees Switzerland and runs to me because he had given the people on whose
behalf he was doing the deal fifteen thousand as front money, because they wanted his good faith in respect of carrying off those
securities. So he was out by fifteen thousand.

"He reports all this to me, and I took down all the information.
Then next thing I personally took him to the Italian police, the
Interpol representative, and he swore out an affidavit against X, Y
and Z: there were two Italians and one Austrian. Then he tells me
he believes there is also a link with the Vatican, and Marcinkus
in particular. He comes to *me*, by the way, because they were
American securities, because he trusts the FBI, because he thinks
he's going to get quick action. The typical Italian way.

"What happened next? Eventually a case began in New York on
the counterfeit securities; it appeared that it was a chain of people,
starting in New York and working right down to Foligni who attempted to use them as collateral in Switzerland.

"Over a period of seven months or so the FBI in the United States
established the connection with the Vatican, citing an incriminating
statement under a Vatican letterhead signed by a monsignor. I
checked this so-called evidence out and discovered that the letterhead is phony and the monsignor is a defrocked priest and a fraud.

So I finally, in one sum-up cable, warned them in Washington not to swallow this bullshit about the Vatican connection, because it couldn't be substantiated.

"In Washington there was an assistant attorney general by the name of [William] Lynch, and there was an attorney, name of [William] Arronwald, representing the FBI, and they announced they were coming to Italy with agent [Dick] Tommaro to cross-examine Marcinkus. I was aghast.

"When they arrived I gave them a tongue-lashing; I taught them a little bit about geography, you know—they thought the Vatican was part of Italy. I was angry. But anyway I approached Marcinkus direct and asked him if he would submit to cross-questioning by us: something that he had no need to do. In fact, we had no right whatsoever to enter the Vatican unless specifically invited. But out of courtesy to us at the embassy, he agreed to answer any questions they wanted to throw at him.

"We went on over to Marcinkus's office. Marcinkus is kind of a tough guy; he doesn't give the impression of being an archbishop, but he has a degree in canon law and he's very well educated, but if he didn't have his black smock on, or whatever you call it, you'd swear he was a big Chicago truck driver.

"So he doesn't come over the smooth Italian monsignor; he presents himself as devastatingly direct and open, right down the line. We had a conversation of over an hour and a half. They were pumping him questions—what about this, what about that? He answered every question we threw at him, more than satisfactorily. Finally we said, 'Have you these certificates in the Vatican vault?' Then Marcinkus says, 'Look, I don't have to tell you anything! But I will, because I want to cooperate with the FBI, and I will have a list of the securities in the Vatican in your possession within the next hour.' That list was put into our hands before we left.

"Essentially, that is the story of how the Vatican got implicated. But that was the beginning of Marcinkus's downfall. Because what happened was that over the years the press gets a hold of it, and the Italians love to attack the Church; and the Italian magistrates when they have an opportunity to attack the Church, especially if they're Communists, they make every effort to do so."

Biamonte lit another cigarette and made himself comfortable again.

"I'm going to tell you something else, because it's an allegation that raises its ugly head inevitably with Marcinkus, and I made a point of checking it out for the simple reason that I think a guy's life is all of one piece, and it seemed very relevant to me in a man who sets himself up as a priest, a man of God, and kind of claims special immunity as a result. I'm a very suspicious individual and I would wish to know just how justified I was in trusting his special status. Let me explain.

"To the Italians, every archbishop, every priest, has a *woman*. And it was very true in the small villages years ago; they had to satisfy their sexual urges and there was always a housekeeper, and it was common knowledge. What's wrong with a priest having sex? But in the United States that attitude was unheard of. Do you want me to be very frank?"

He stopped again and rubbed his jowls. Looked up at the ceiling. "You be careful how you quote me, see. There was a fellow by the name of Steve Barclay. He was an American movie actor who in the early fifties had quite a success. When his success waned he came to live in Italy and he married this very lovely lady, Lisa, who had once been Miss France. And they had a child. Steve Barclay was a wonderful, warmhearted guy, never really had a proper job after he worked on the screen. I knew him because he lived in the same compound where I lived; I'm talking 1962 right into the seventies. The Barclays were Roman Catholics and very friendly with Marcinkus, and they were also friendly with Mark Antinucci; they were buddies; Marcinkus would go to their home for dinner maybe twice a week, and invariably Antinucci was there too; Steve was a very personable, gregarious, nice guy. Nice wife and little daughter, and he loved to entertain people. I don't know how the friendship began but there it was; Marcinkus was a very close friend of that family, he was a friend of both of them, but he became Lisa's sort of confidant and it was a friendship that was protected from any kind of rumor of impropriety by Steve's marriage. Steve was always there. And you've got to remember that for Marcinkus it meant a bit of home life, and he was devoted to their kid. If you're a bishop or a priest and you get a regular home-cooked meal, it's not a bad deal. A great many priests have a family where they can feel at home. Normally a priest back in the States would spend time back home with his mother; so for Marcinkus, who was an expatriate in that setting, it meant a great deal.

"Of course in the Vatican, with all the vindictive gossip there, quite a different interpretation was put on that relationship. She was French, very beautiful, Miss France. You see? That was a terrific opportunity for all those people who hated Marcinkus in the Vatican to run off at the mouth about him. I checked out that relationship this way and that through people who knew them well, and there was never anything in it beyond pure friendship. I never saw Marcinkus and Lisa alone, and nobody else ever saw them alone to my best knowledge. But I've heard that the rumors and innuendos cost Marcinkus his cardinal's hat. He should have made cardinal around 1974; Pope Paul loved him, respected him, but such were the rumors about this so-called liaison . . . Let me be frank with you, Mr. Cornwell. I observed Archbishop Marcinkus over a number of years, and in my view he was a priest of the strict old-fashioned sort. And what got people was that when they looked at him he didn't *look* the part of the priest, because of his size and athletic build, huge shoulders, huge hands. . . . You should see him hitting a ball on the golf course. To this day I dream of hitting a ball that far! He smoked cigars! Had a close friendship with ex-Miss France. See? And he told things the way they were! Rubbed people the wrong way in that Vatican. You see, Italians are very diplomatic; they have that way of seeming to say yes when all along they're telling you no . . . they lie! I tell you there's a great bureaucracy in the Vatican; there's more politics, they make more deals . . . You've no idea! And it still goes on. But unfortunately for them Marcinkus is like the mayor of Vatican City, *and* he runs the bank; that's a lot of power. Those priests in there are just like any other bureaucrats or politicians. They want the right office, they want their cars, and so Marcinkus has a difficult job, and he's not *Italian*. He has to say *no* to them.

"Now. The so-called murder conspiracy against John Paul I, the Pope of the thirty-three days. I was working in Rome from 1962 for seventeen years. I was close observer of Vatican affairs. My personal view is that if there had been a conspiracy involving priests inside the Vatican it would have leaked all over the place. To me it's inconceivable that out of the thousands of priests who work in the Vatican there wasn't just one who would say, 'Hey, I'm not going to be part of this cover-up.' No such priest has ever come forward to this day. No, it's complete crap. When these books came out, I know that Marcinkus was in touch with lawyers here in New York. He was furious, but they gave him the same advice as I would—don't *dignify* it. I had FBI agents call me when that book hit the stands. They said, 'Hey, Tom, boy! Did you read that book? Jeez, you were over there, what's the score?' I said, 'I can't believe this, you're grown intelligent men. . . .'

"Now let me give it to you for the record. This is my makeup: I'd put my mother in jail if the evidence was there. I handled the Getty kidnap case in Italy, I personally conducted the negotiations over the phone with the kidnappers. I did the Italian leads into the Warren investigation of President Kennedy. I have a reputation for scrupulous honesty. Every cop in Italy knew me and the kind of guy I was, the kind of guy that I am. See this job I have here? Director of consumer fraud for the State of New Jersey. I'm a very, very suspicious guy. You'd better believe it. And at the time I left the FBI in Rome, 1978, there was nothing in the files of the Federal Bureau of Investigation that would even create a scintilla of evidence that Archbishop Marcinkus had any connection with any wrongdoing."

"But excuse me, Mr. Biamonte," I interrupted. "*Had* he been involved in any wrongdoing, would you necessarily have had evidence of it? I mean, was he under close surveillance?"

"I'm *telling* you," his voice fell to a macabre whisper, "I reported back to Washington every single accusation ever made against him. But we always look at the source, and if the source stinks, and it always did in his case, you want independent evidence. It was never forthcoming. You know what I honestly believe? I got the distinct impression in the latter years that there are a lot of people out to get Marcinkus, because if they can discredit him they can discredit this Pope [John Paul II]. That's very sad, but that was the impression I got finally."

Biamonte sat looking at me in a bemused fashion for a while.

"Come on," he said, "I've got to get out of here sometime." He started to put documents into his briefcase.

He sat as if ready to go. "What else did I want to tell you?" he said. "I could go on and on about Italy. You would have to live in Italy six months to a year with the goal of doing nothing but prying and investigating and being inquisitive about a specific subject, and you would gather up as much information as I could gain in one morning because I eventually became part of the fabric."

"Okay," I interrupted, "let me ask you a question. Did you have any evidence whatsoever that there were Freemasons in the Vatican?"

"No!" he said bluntly. "Never, ever. I knew some of the players in the P2 organization who ended up in jail. If there were any inside the Vatican they were unknown to me."

He rose from his chair and went to put his coat on.

I asked him what he knew of the Ambrosiano collapse.

"I was out of Italy by the time that happened, but I studied it closely and made my own discreet inquiries. My reading of it is this: the only thing they had on Marcinkus were those so-called letters of comfort. They were written with the intention of helping Calvi get straight, but they created an inference in the minds of people that Marcinkus was in fact behind the whole thing. And I don't know whether Marcinkus actually agreed to it; his signature wasn't even on the documents. Now, as I'm told, as a result of all the scandal, the Vatican Bank had no alternative but to pay. I think it was a simple dumb mistake. Then this guy killed himself in London under the Blackfriars Bridge, connection with P2, and again the illogical inferences going back . . ."

"Who do you think killed Calvi?" I asked him.

"I don't think it was murder; I think it was suicide. But again I don't have that kind of mind. . . ." He said finally: "Scotland Yard has never come up with one shred of evidence in two investigations that it was murder."

He walked me down the long deserted corridors back to the main lobby. We stood for a moment saying our farewells in the street in freezing gusts of wind and snow.

As I walked back gingerly along the icy sidewalk to the railway station, I felt that I had at last heard a formidable case for the defense. It seemed ironic to me, however, that it had come not from a religious source, eager to provide an apologia for one of its senior prelates; it had come not from within the Vatican, nor even from Marcinkus's priestly acquaintances on the outside. It had come from the gray files of J. Edgar Hoover's international inquisition. But did I believe it? In the absence of an indictment, Marcinkus appeared innocent in the counterfeit-bonds case. And yet, conspiracies are hydra-headed. . . . Perhaps the FBI had been shielding Marcinkus for another deeper purpose? What had my conversation with Biamonte proved? One was left with the testimony, the tone of a living voice, one piece in the jigsaw puzzle.

PART

II

If there is one thing more than another which prejudices Englishmen against the Catholic Church, it is the doctrine of great authorities on the subject of equivocation. For myself, I can fancy myself thinking it was allowable in extreme cases for me to lie, but never to equivocate . . . I think evasion . . . to be perfectly allowable; indeed, I do not know, who does not use it under circumstances; but that a good deal of moral danger is attended to its use; and that, the cleverer a man is, the more likely he is to pass the line of Christian duty.

— JOHN HENRY NEWMAN,
Apologia pro Vita Sua

21

On a bright blustery morning in January I traveled to north London to meet David Yallop, the author of *In God's Name*. When I made the appointment on the phone, he had informed me with a knowing chuckle that it would be the Feast of the Epiphany.

The principal purpose of my visit was to assess the strength of several items of crucial evidence that were unique to his book, above all an interview with Sister Vincenza, which he had quoted with decisive effect. Sister Vincenza had died on June 28, 1983.

Yallop was a fit-looking man with a ruddy complexion and gray eyes. He was dressed in cream-colored slacks and an electric-blue cardigan. He grew his thick iron-gray hair long to one side, brushing it across the top of his head. His strong Irish features were wreathed with ready avuncular smiles, but every so often his jaw tightened with sudden sternness.

He invited me up to his study in a quiet part of the house, where he sat at a king-sized desk on which we placed our tape recorders side by side.

"One of your most damning pieces of evidence," I started, "concerns the Signoracci brothers and the fact that they were evidently summoned before the body was officially found. . . ."

"I thought it was very important," he said, "and I had my researcher Philip Willan go back to them twice more to attempt again and again to crystallize precisely what time the call had come through." There was a faint Cockney twang in his voice that could have been mistaken for an Australian accent. "We went all manner of ways. I've got the transcripts of the interviews and the report that Willan did for me. After a number of conversations the best they could do was to say 'dawn'; we then worked out the distance they came from, bearing in mind I was dealing with brothers who were confused about which exactly of them had gone; there were three of them and they weren't certain which combination of the two had gone; it was a bit like an Italian opera. It was the genuine inability of people to remember things, but also this kind of Italian element of confusion that runs riot in their thinking very often. . . ."

"Let's look at the text, shall we?" I said. "What did they actually say?"

Yallop had fetched down a copy of his book and was flicking through to find the appropriate page.

"Here it is," he went on, " . . . 'a dawn telephone call and a Vatican car arrived at five A.M.' Well, the Vatican car was to take them to the Vatican. I've got a feeling that on their way they stopped at the Institute of Medicine to get their equipment, but when they talked to Professor Gerin he was very laconic. He said, 'Bring some new equipment, another pope's dead.' A tossed-off line like this, which they recalled to Willan for us."

I was perplexed. Yallop's book clearly intended the reader to understand that the Signoraccis went straight to the Vatican; yet he now understood that they went to the Institute of Medicine. Was I hearing him right?

"So let's get it straight," I said. "They told Willan they went to the Vatican at five o'clock, or what . . . ?"

"I went at this a number of ways because I knew how important it was. I was asking them precisely where they lived, about times and things, and where they examined the body. I worked forward, when dawn was, but at the end of the day that was the best that one could do in terms of a specific time; it was certainly within that area of time. I mean, if I'm adrift it's by minutes not hours."

"Is it possible," I said, "that there was a mistake made about the time? Could it be that there was an error in translation?"

"No," said Yallop emphatically. "I mean, the fact that they were interviewed more than once was precisely this point. The fact that they were interviewed three times was *precisely* this point. It was *very* important to me, because it shows something quite extraordinary. That's why I know which two of the three were involved on this particular embalming; one of them was out of Rome, and what time did the car come, again and again and again. Willan is a very meticulous, very careful, very cautious man, totally fluent in Italian."

"If it was morning, then, what do you think they did when they first got to the Vatican?" I asked.

"I think they would have helped," he went on, "and I'm not basing this just on what *they* told me, but what *Lorenzi* told me: they helped lay out the body."

"Don Diego told you this?" I asked him.

"Yes, he *did*," said Yallop; his voice was cold, definite. "So did Sister Vincenza. You can't get to her now, but you can get to Lorenzi. He wouldn't lie about a moment like that unless he saw a significance in it. If you broach it in an insignificant way you may get the truth." He fell silent for a few moments, before continuing in a fading voice. " . . . But yes, he *did*. There is what I call a classic kind of rationalization, a secondary source becomes a primary source."

It was a casual, passing remark, but important. And Sister Vincenza, the dead nun, was being cited to settle a crucial contradiction.

"The fact is," I said, "I've spoken to Don Diego and he says nothing of the kind. I pressed him very closely on it because it's a central point. Don Diego said that he, Magee and the doctor laid out the body. Now I said to him specifically, 'The Signoracci brothers?' And he said, 'No! They didn't come near the place.' He said they didn't get access to the body until the evening."

"What about Professor Gerin? Professor Gerin sent for the Signoraccis. See if you can get to him!"

Had Yallop got to Gerin? I wondered. There had been no quoted testimony from that quarter in his book.

I changed tack again. "Do you think the Vatican lied?"

"Why did they lie about who found the body?" he said. "Why did they lie about what papers were in the Pope's hand? Some lies will be significant. When people lie, some of the lies will be logical, others are totally illogical, and I think total panic ran riot through the Vatican.

"I don't know what happened to my researcher Philip Willan," he went on, "but I know that the Signoracci brothers got a coating and a half from the powers that be in the Vatican for talking to me, as did a great many people. I just wish that at the end of the day I'd revealed no sources except the dead ones, like Benelli and Vincenza. . . ."

I was intrigued by the reference to Benelli. Benelli, who had died in 1982, had formerly been *sostituto* secretary of state, and latterly cardinal-archbishop of Florence. Benelli, according to Biamonte, the FBI agent, had been a formidable adversary of Marcinkus.

". . . because they're very vindictive in there," he went on. "And the only reason they've talked to you is because somebody's picked up a phone from the Vatican. That should tell you something instinctively, that these people you are being led to have been given orders as to what to say and what not to say."

I let the comment pass, but I savored the irony of the assumption that I had been *led* to Buzzonetti, or the Signoraccis, or Magee.

I thought I would move on to the evidence of the sergeant of the Swiss Guard, who had been cited in the single and extremely damning item of circumstantial evidence against Marcinkus.

"There's Marcinkus, in your book," I said, "lurking around suspiciously at an unearthly hour on the morning of the Pope's death, and your reporting of this episode puts the finger on Marcinkus in a very definite and dramatic kind of way. The Marcinkus-Roggen story as it's related to me is that Roggen met Marcinkus, who was getting out of his car, having just driven into the Vatican. In your account the car is missing, and Marcinkus is wandering aimlessly, suspiciously, no car in sight. It makes a huge difference."

"Didn't Roggen have a bad night sleeping when he was on duty

the night the Pope died?" insisted Yallop. "Doesn't he remember
any of that now?"

"Wasn't Marcinkus just parking his car, having driven in from
Villa Stritch?" I said, deliberately ignoring his question. "Marcinkus gets out of the car at his normal time—he is an infamously
early riser. Roggen tells him that the Pope has died; they have a
brief conversation at complete cross-purposes, because Marcinkus
thinks he said, 'I dreamed the Pope had died.' "

"He makes no mention of Marcinkus staring at him transfixed?"
asked Yallop. "And Marcinkus explaining to him days later, 'I
thought you'd gone mad,' or something to that effect? Well, let's
see what we can find you in the transcripts. What that tells you, I
don't know. But I think I can confirm my version. They can't confirm
theirs. In fact, I can disprove what they are alleging they said to
me. Because I assume they're telling you that they've told us both
the same thing, and I've turned it round and distorted it."

Eventually I said, "The other thing is Sister Vincenza. As the
poor woman is dead, almost anything you might have would be of
enormous help. The point is that as I can't interview her whatever
she may have given you is terribly important."

"Well, she gave me a lot of things," said Yallop, "but over and
above what I've already revealed in the book . . . I don't know that
there's anything else that I want to add to that, because it might
compromise other nuns."

"You can only give me what you can," I said. Although I was
wondering what the elderly nun Vincenza might have confided in
Yallop about her fellow sisters.

We began to talk about other matters: about Don Diego and the
subject of who found the body; about the story of the *Imitation of
Christ,* about the exact time the Pope normally said Mass, about
the hour at which Sister Vincenza found the body and roused the
secretaries.

ANSA news service had claimed in a dispatch headlined VATICAN
RUMORS on October 5, 1978, that, according to "indiscretions"
inside the Vatican, Sister Vincenza had found the body at 4:30.
Yallop maintained in his own book that in his personal interview
with her, Sister Vincenza had confirmed the 4:30 timing.

The effect of this evidence was not simply that it contradicted all the other Vatican household personnel (after all, they had lied already about *who* found the body), but that it revealed a lost hour. What had the Vatican been up to during that critical period between 4:30 and 7:30, when the death was announced? According to Yallop, it had been spent in tidying away incriminating evidence.

It seemed to me that I could not ignore the Yallop interview with Sister Vincenza; its implications were vital. But as the nun was now dead, was I prepared to accept Yallop's report as incontestable without actually hearing the tape?

For the time being, I decided, I would shelve the dilemma and see if I could approach the problem from another direction.

"What time did you say Sister Vincenza found the body of the Pope?" I asked.

"Four-thirty, quarter to five. If you go through the man's routine, and he was a man of routine, you'll get some of the answers independently of me."

"But the schedule you're working on is based on what Sister Vincenza told you?"

"And others, like his former secretaries Monsignor Da Rif, and Monsignor Senigaglia in Venice. . . ."

"But they were not in the Vatican. I'm talking about the timetable on the morning of the Pope's death."

"But I'm talking about rituals of a lifetime. There's the business of the English tapes that he used to listen to in his room—at five-thirty, not in the chapel."

So what was the Pope supposed to be doing between 4:30 and 5:30? I wondered. It seemed an unconscionable amount of time to spend on morning ablutions.

"Da Rif, his former secretary, will tell you about his rituals, but of course they're all going to be got at; they're all going to say that black is white now," he said.

"My main problem is the exact time at which Sister Vincenza found the body. Everybody says about five-thirty, and you say four-thirty because the nun herself told you this. But unfortunately she's dead."

"It also comes from Lorenzi," said Yallop.

"That's not what he's saying to me."

"But you're dealing with people who are lying to you," insisted Yallop. "That's your problem, not mine. I'm not going to be involved in an exercise whereby I rejustify myself and prove that they've lied. I've already proved that they've lied to the satisfaction not only of myself, but my publishers' lawyers and several million readers. Now they want to rerun the ball game. I don't choose to rerun the ball game. What I choose to do with you, where it's humanly possible, is give you my raw research which led me to demonstrate that they are lying in their teeth. I would have thought once or twice would have sufficed. I could go on and on and on, but they are duplicitous men you're dealing with. They are not men of God, by what you and I mean by that phrase."

"Okay," I said.

"She used to go into his room in Venice with coffee at four-thirty, but Vatican protocol was so outraged they thought it better if she put the coffee outside the door. Nevertheless, it was still put out at the same time and a knock was given on the door. That pattern goes back twenty years, to Vittorio Veneto. . . . And suddenly we're now being asked to believe by these duplicitous men that in the last thirty-three days of his life he varied this habit. I'm patient with you, but I'm impatient with them because they are masking something very evil, and still waiting desperately for the cavalry to come."

He glared at me bright-eyed for a few moments. "You are the cavalry, by the way!"

I shifted in my seat, smiling uncomfortably.

"You are John Wayne . . ." he said.

"That could misfire," I said faintly.

"Well, if there's a God up there, you can only pray that it does."

As I prepared to depart, I asked him if he had been a member of the Roman Catholic Church.

"I left the Church when I was fifteen," he said. "There were two specific moments. There was the Assumption—the dogma on that insulted my intelligence, I thought. And the other was a very small incident."

His voice was quiet and steady. He was looking down at his desk.

"I went to Benediction one Sunday," he went on. "I came straight from Clapham Common where I'd been playing football with my friends. I had shoes on not dissimilar to these—plimsolls—and the Redemptorist brother in charge of the altar boys ordered me out of the church. I never went back. That was it."

It seemed to me that the incident still rankled, more than thirty-five years later.

He saw me to the front door, and I drove off into the darkening January afternoon to join the heavy traffic bound for the city.

As I mulled over our conversation I judged that he genuinely believed in the conspiracy case he had made out. I could give his conviction the benefit of the doubt, but his circumstantial evidence seemed to me negligible except for the three items I had raised that afternoon. There were the Signoracci brothers and their extraordinary dawn ride, the precise circumstances of Marcinkus's presence in the Vatican early on the morning of September 29, and the exact time at which Sister Vincenza had found the body. I had not demolished those items of evidence, but, more significantly, Yallop had by no means convinced me that they were incontrovertible.

22

The next day I telephoned Bishop Magee in Cobh, County Cork. A secretary announced himself as Father Sheehan and I explained my project and asked for an interview. Father Sheehan sounded doubtful; he asked me to hold on.

Three minutes later he was back on the line. "Mr. Cornwell?" he said. "I've talked with the bishop and he says that he cannot be available to see you. He feels that he does not want to go on record any further in the matter. You'll understand, I'm sure."

I put the receiver down with intense disappointment; without Magee my investigation would be lame.

My disappointment gave way to anger. I had the backing of the Pope, of Casaroli, of the Commission for Social Communications. How dare he refuse me? His refusal surely indicated that he had something to hide. His rebuff encouraged me to dwell upon the criticisms I had heard. I wondered at his refusal to see me, which, it seemed to me, could only be part of a stratagem of evasion.

I felt defeated, and yet I did not want to concede, having come this far. I pondered the idea of depicting him in my inquiries as a shadowy figure, guiltily lurking in his Irish diocese. I would travel to Cobh and doorstep him. I would stalk him in his cathedral and study him in the pulpit.

When I had calmed down a little I realized that the best plan was to take the problem back to Rome. If nothing else, it would be an interesting test of the power of the Vatican to control its bishops, even in far-flung regions.

Later that day I made a call to Poland to talk with an Australian journalist called Kay Withers, who had covered the conclave and death of John Paul I from Rome for the *Chicago Tribune*. Kay Withers's reports had been the most extensive and impressive of any journalism I had read in my initial research, and only after Christmas had I managed to track her down. She was now working as a stringer in Warsaw, covering East European affairs.

"I don't know what I can tell you," she said in a distinct Australian accent. "I researched a biography of Papa Luciani for a couple of years, but I got disheartened. I talked to people all over Italy, everybody who ever knew him. I got into the Vatican, too. You see, I was tackling a complete life. But you know I got a bit disillusioned with him in the end. At the outset I was immensely impressed. But he was no saint and no hero; he wasn't even particularly likable. In the end I decided he was an extremely anxious, nervous little man. His Papacy looked good for a month, but it ended in the nick of time—it would have gone to pieces.

"He could be stubborn and haywire. Once he rushed to Rome when he had a problem and found the Curial offices all shut because it was a holiday. They told him to go away and stop worrying. Marcinkus, I gathered, didn't like him."

"Did you meet Sister Vincenza?"

"I did. I went to see her with his niece Pia, and I discovered that everybody was completely wrong about the slippers and spectacles and things going missing. Pia's mother had all those things as mementos. She used to wear both of Papa Luciani's sets of spectacles."

"What about Villot? Did you find anything interesting about him?" I asked her.

"I've got it on excellent authority that Villot was absolutely furious the morning the Pope died. I imagine it was because it was the last thing he wanted. He was hoping to get out, and he was thrust back into the middle of it all again."

"How well received were you as you went around?"

"I guess I shocked one or two of the priests with my lack of ceremony. I found his old seminary rector still alive up in the Veneto. I said to him, 'When Luciani was a student, how was he?' And he said, 'Oh, a nice boy just like all the rest.' So I said, 'Well, tell me something about him—I mean, was he interested in girls?' And he said, 'Oh dear, no, no, no, no. . . .' As if this was the worst crime you could imagine, you know—old-fashioned seminary rector. Then I said, 'Well, was he interested in *boys*?' and he nearly fell off his chair with fright!"

23

Before returning to Rome I applied among my medical acquaintances for a suitable consultant to advise me on the specialist questions that were arising in my research. I was eventually put in touch with a visiting doctor from the United States—C. Francis Roe—who was on sabbatical in London. Francis Roe's background was very specifically appropriate for the case of John Paul I: his field was vascular surgery. Trained at Aberdeen he had become a research fellow and instructor at Harvard in the late sixties, followed by a professorship in surgery at Yale. He had contributed some thirty written papers during his career. He was still in his forties and had been chief of surgery at New London Hospital in Connecticut.

I asked him first of all to explain to me in layman's language exactly what was meant by a myocardial infarction.

"What in fact happens," said Roe, "is that a main branch of the arteries that nourish the heart, the coronary arteries, gets shut off. These arteries provide the muscle of the heart with oxygen and nutrients, and if there's no blood getting through, the muscle will die. Infarction simply means death of the muscle—the nutrients being blocked off."

"Pope John Paul," I said, "was found sitting up in bed, his eyes still open, wearing his spectacles as if reading the document he held in his hands, a faint smile on his face. Does that sound to you like myocardial infarction?"

"There is something very suspicious about the posture you describe, whatever the cause of death. Dead bodies do not sit up smiling and reading in death. People have been known to die in their sleep, but I have never known, or seen, anybody die in this way in the middle of an activity like reading. I find it really hard to believe that he would be reading one moment and dead the next. I would have thought that he'd had enough time to sense that something was happening—he would probably have had pain, and he'd probably have made some sort of effort to get his breath, or to get out of bed, to get help. There would have been a few moments at least . . . I've seen many deaths of this sort, but I've never known anybody die unresponsive to what was happening to them. Life, in my experience anyway, doesn't just *stop*. And somebody with a massive heart attack, or a massive brain hemorrhage, moves around or makes *some* reaction, because they would be in mortal discomfort if not severe pain. The smile also sounds suspicious. People don't smile when they're dead: smiling involves controlled activity of facial muscles; this is lost in death and the face reverts back to a resting position. It's normal too for the jaw to drop."

"In fact, Don Diego Lorenzi commented that the jaw had to be shut with a ribbon," I said.

"Well, that indicates the point I'm making. It's hard to imagine somebody with a dropped jaw maintaining a smile at the same time."

"There's an alternative theory from another source," I said, "suggesting that perhaps he suffered a pulmonary embolism. Dr. Navarro-Valls in the Vatican spoke of the Pope having an embolism in the eye, and of having had massively swollen legs after he got to the Vatican. He deduces that the eye embolism anticipated the pulmonary embolism. Can you describe exactly what a pulmonary embolism is in layman's language?"

"All right. Putting it very simply: inside the fluid of the blood there is a clot. The clot goes along through blood channels until it reaches one that it plugs. You can get that kind of plug in the arteries of the body, and it's not uncommon in the leg. A pulmonary embolus is in the venous system rather than the arterial system. The commonest cause of pulmonary embolus is clotting in the deep veins of the leg. What that causes initially is swelling and pain in the leg. The clot is jellylike.

"Just as the arteries get smaller as they go out into the extremity, so the veins get larger as they come back up in the circulation. The clot will start, say, in the deep veins of the calf and it will extend at the top end like a finger projecting into a larger vein, and it waves around. What happens is that a piece of this loosely waving clot—this is the embolus itself—will become detached and get caught up into the circulation, going up through the large veins of the abdomen into the chest and then into the heart—the right side of the heart, which carries blood destined to be pumped into the lung to be reoxygenated. If this clot is big enough it will travel up through the circulation as I have described and jam somewhere in the circulation of the lungs. If it's a big embolus—and they can be *very* big, I've seen some that are a foot long and as wide as my thumb—then you get complete arrest of the circulation through the lungs. Death occurs within a matter of a minute or two. The patient experiences terrible constricting discomfort in the chest, a feeling of asphyxiation. The fastest one I ever saw was when I was an intern in Aberdeen. There was a nineteen-year-old girl who'd had her appendix out; she'd had some problems with it and stayed in bed for about seven or eight days. The first day that she got up, and it was just when we were doing rounds, she got this massive pulmonary embolus and dropped dead in front of our eyes. You could see that she was horrified, that she knew that something absolutely dreadful was happening to her. But not for very long.

"You read about people being *poleaxed* when they drop dead. Well, in all my years practicing medicine I've never seen that in the middle of an activity. There is always, unless they are already unconscious, some reaction to, or awareness of, what's happening to them. The same would go for any of these poison theories; had he been poisoned he would be conscious of some terrible, mortal trauma going on.

"Incidentally," he continued, "your Navarro-Valls talks of the embolus in the eye leading to a possible pulmonary embolism. Many physicians make the common mistake of linking emboli in this way, but they come from two quite distinct causes and are quite unrelated. The eye type comes from the carotid artery in the region of the neck; the pulmonary embolism is the result of venous clotting in the lower part of the body."

As a result of my talk with Dr. Roe I immediately renewed my attempt to make contact with John Paul I's ocular specialist in Mestre, Professor Giovanni Rama, in order to gain further information about the Pope's reported embolism in the eye in 1975. I also tried to make an appointment to meet his physician—Dr. Da Ros—in the Veneto.

Professor Rama's office told me firmly that he would answer only written questions addressed to him via the Vatican. Dr. Da Ros, despite my attempts to approach him through a go-between, absolutely and finally refused to meet me or to make any comment whatsoever.

I agreed with Dr. Roe that we would talk again when I had gathered more medical information in Italy, and especially some indication as to John Paul I's medication.

24

A week later I was back in Rome, once again comfortably ensconced in the English College. I immediately fell in with the smooth routine of the community, as if I had never departed.

In the middle of the morning I walked to the Vatican Press Office on Via della Conciliazione and wandered in to the Sala Stampa where the "Vaticanologists" were sitting around in their familiar fug of tobacco smoke. I went up to an old man who was sucking on a pipe in the corner.

"I'm Max Bergère of Agence France Presse," he said pleasantly, extending his hand. "I'm the dean of the corps, so to speak. Can I help you?"

"Do you remember the day the last Pope died?"

"Will I ever forget it?" he replied.

"A story was put out on Vatican Radio at about half-past two saying that he had been reading the *Imitation of Christ*."

Bergère began to chuckle. "Of course I remember. That story was made up in this room as a joke; it got onto the wires almost immediately and Vatican Radio picked it up by lunchtime."

I looked at him amazed.

"You're certain of that?" I said.

Bergère pointed across the room to a man smoking a cigarette over a newspaper at the central table. "Look! There's the fellow who made it up. It was a joke; then all these crazy people started to use it."

"Would you introduce me?"

"Certainly." He called the man by his Christian name.

The colleague came over; he had bags under his eyes and an anxious expression.

"*You* were the one who made up that story about the *Imitation of Christ* the day the Pope died, weren't you?"

He looked me up and down. "No! It wasn't just me!" he snapped. Then pointing at my chest, cigarette still smoking between his fingers, he said, "And don't you print that, see! It was all of us here. Nobody in particular. We were just laughing and joking and it kind of came out. And you don't use my name, see!" He walked away grumbling "*pazzo*"—madman—under his breath.

Bergère shook his head and laughed. "Journalists! They're a funny lot. He was the guy, all right. Is there anything else I can do for you?"

"Is there anybody here from ANSA news service?"

"Certainly. You want Mandillo. There he is, come on over." I followed him across the room to where a middle-aged man in a tweed jacket sat hunched over a typewriter.

Bergère introduced me. "This Englishman is asking questions about the death of the last Pope."

Mandillo looked up at me sharply.

"Do you remember the report put out by your news service on the evening of the Pope's death?" I asked. "It said that the Signoracci brothers were called at dawn and picked up by a Vatican car."

"I remember," he said abruptly. "It was a mistake."

"How do you mean?"

"It was an error."

"But it was never corrected."

He shrugged.

"Who wrote that report?" asked Bergère.

"It was somebody . . . He doesn't work for us anymore," said Mandillo.

"What's his name?" I said.

He shook his head and turned back to his typewriter. "I can't tell you his name. It's got nothing to do with me."

"Signor Mandillo," I said again, with some insistence, "*come* on, tell me his name."

There was a tense pause. He was not looking at me. He said petulantly, "His name is Mario di Francesco. He works on *Messaggero*. Now leave me in peace."

Max Bergère smiled benevolently. He had a soft spot for the English, I thought. "Anything else I can do?" he said.

"Yes. Could you give me the name of somebody at Vatican Radio who would know how the newscasts are put together?"

"Sure. You could try Father Arregui, he's a Spaniard—a Basque, in fact." He wrote the name on a piece of paper.

As we walked to the lobby of the Sala Stampa, he promised to send a brief memoir he would write for me about Cardinal Villot and the circumstances of John Paul I's death.

"I knew Cardinal Villot very well, over a great many years," he said.

25

J walked the length of the Via della Conciliazione and turned into the Piazza Pia, a spacious square on the banks of the Tiber opposite the Castel Sant' Angelo. At number one, in a barracklike building, I found Vatican Radio. The functional lobby, painted gray, had no hint of religious auspices. There was a crudely worked piece of sculpture entitled *Onde di Pace*—Waves of Peace—and a bust of Marconi.

A chirpy girl took my inquiry at the reception desk and made some calls while I sat in a utilitarian chair in the waiting area and picked up a copy of *Radio Vaticana,* the station's magazine.

In the center pages I found a map indicating that the Vatican's powerful antennae penetrate every continent on earth. On the program schedule the language transmissions included Japanese, Chinese, Arabic, Vietnamese; under the East European section there was Armenian, Ukrainian, Lithuanian, Byelorussian, Latvian and Russian. The programs in English featured such titles as: "With Heart and Mind," "The Pope, the Church and the World," "Vatican Week," "Rosary and News" and "A Many-Splendored Thing." I felt a sense of languor creeping over me.

At length a layman arrived, introducing himself as Dottore Giovanni Bosco. He shook my hand and listened carefully to my inquiry about the authorship of the story of John Paul I and the *Imitation of Christ*. "Yes, you must come with me to meet with Father Ignacio Arregui, the director of information."

As we ascended in the lift to the third floor he told me that the station was run by some four hundred staff under the direction of thirty Jesuit priests; seventy programs were put out each day in thirty-six languages, including Latin.

We ran into Father Arregui in the corridor, a sallow-complexioned cleric comfortable in a soft gray cardigan; a Roman collar was barely discernible above a tartan scarf cast studentlike around his neck. He inclined an ear as I spoke. "Ah, yes," he said, "I know exactly who wrote that story on the morning the Pope died, but you must come with me and meet with Father Querecchi, head of programming."

We turned a corner and entered a spacious office where a small man rose to meet us. He looked to be in his early forties, with gray hair and steel-blue eyes. He wore a baggy black suit flecked with herringbone gray. He shook my hand with a strong grip and I recited my inquiry yet again.

Arregui and Querecchi exchanged looks. These Jesuits were not typical of the soft-jowled, white-cuffed Vatican monsignori at the other end of the Via della Conciliazione; they were lean and observant, and they looked very smart.

Querecchi winked at his colleague: "I was in Formosa at the time."

"So you were," said Arregui with a grin. "We can hardly put the blame on *you*." Then, turning to me, he said, "That story was written by one Father Francesco Farusi, who was head of Radiogiornale. He wrote it personally in his own fair hand and it would have been put out in seven languages. I don't think it emanated from Vatican sources, but you'll have to ask Farusi himself; he's now the head of the information services of the Jesuit order down on Borgo Santo Spirito."

Turning to the layman, he said, "Dottore, would you kindly call Father Farusi and see if he's willing to talk with this gentleman?"

As Dr. Bosco disappeared on his errand, I talked with the Jesuits about the official status of Vatican Radio.

"Is it possible," I asked, "that the story was taken off the wires?"

"Yes," said Arregui, "but he would have wanted to check it out. You have to live with a story like that."

"Perhaps it would have been difficult to check with the papal household before noon on that morning?" I said, offering a plausible excuse for the mistake.

"No," said Querecchi flatly, "Father Farusi was not just *anybody*; the Vatican would have taken a call from him without delay."

Querecchi, it seemed, was a stickler for accuracy, however uncomfortable. I was impressed.

"So how official is a Vatican Radio news broadcast on the morning of the death of a pope?"

We started to walk back down the corridor toward the lifts. Father Arregui spread his hands. "We're independent, but we have direct lines into the Vatican; if we get a story wrong there's little excuse. But we're not a mouthpiece; they don't tell us what to say. A news broadcast doesn't have the status of an official bulletin."

Dr. Bosco met us halfway down the corridor. "Mr. Cornwell, Father Farusi says that he is at your disposal to see you now. You'll find him at number five Borgo Santo Spirito. It's the street that runs parallel with the Via della Conciliazione on the left side facing Saint Peter's.

"Incidentally," he added, "he tells me that he got the story about the *Imitation* personally from Don Diego Lorenzi."

I stopped in my tracks and looked with amazement at the Jesuits. They exchanged looks again, but their faces gave nothing away.

Querecchi put out his hand. "Best of luck, Mr. Cornwell. Father Farusi will clear the whole thing up for you, I'm sure."

26

Number five Borgo Santo Spirito is the entrance to the huge complex of austere nineteenth-century office buildings that house the international headquarters of the Jesuit order, the Society of Jesus. It is situated on a one-way street two hundred yards from Saint Peter's Square. As I entered the portals of the gray central palazzo I somehow expected to see ascetic-looking men in black flitting along shadowy corridors. I was greeted at the porter's lodge by a sleepy-looking old buffer in a soutane. He asked me to wait in the lobby and he wandered off into the echoing interior of the building to look for Father Farusi.

Through open double doors I could see Mass in progress in a private chapel; I gathered that the service was being conducted in Japanese, and as I watched this unusual expression of the liturgy, I had a fleeting impression of the global ramifications of this society whose thirty thousand members are scattered throughout the length and breadth of the world on all manner of missions, some of them inscrutable. Although I knew at least two perfectly pleasant and normal members of the order, I still carried with me an ineradicable prejudice about the Jesuits as sinister mischief-makers. The Jesuit figment of anti-Catholic propaganda, powder glass in one pocket, a spiked discipline in the other, dies hard.

Somebody was tugging at my sleeve and I turned to find a small, gnomelike man myopically looking up at me through thick-lensed, horn-rimmed spectacles. Father Farusi was completely bald, with deep furrows in his scalp. His eyebrows were jet-black and shaggy, and his sallow face was creased with grubby wrinkles. His upper lip was nicotine-stained. He was dressed in black pants and a gray sweater with holes in the elbows.

"Come with me!" he said, and he trotted ahead down the corridor and entered a bare room with a simple table and two chairs.

He saw that I held in my hand a copy of a Vatican Radiogiornale broadcast transcript. Leaning across the table he grabbed the papers with gnarled brown fingers in a swift gesture: "Yes, yes . . . what's this?" he said.

I was rattled by his impatience. I sat down slowly and attempted to regain my composure. At length I said, "Good morning, Father. It's good of you to see me here today."

"Don't mention it," he said. "I'm at my desk here seven days a week. So what do you want to know?"

"Did you write the story about the Pope being found dead reading the *Imitation of Christ*?"

"Yes, yes. I did this. I wrote this," he said, fidgeting with the pages.

"But it was inaccurate, and it was retracted on October second. Where did you get the story originally?"

He was scrutinizing the appropriate page and looking up at me with swift, birdlike movements. "It was circulating throughout the mass media by the middle of the morning of September twenty-ninth," he said testily; his voice had a deep ragged edge. He squinnied at me as if he were looking into the sun.

"It wasn't a Vatican story?" I asked.

He tossed his head back a little. "Vatican story!" he said, as if with contempt. "I checked it out myself at some time between noon and twelve-thirty that day. I checked it personally with Don Diego Lorenzi. He told me it was true."

"Don Diego? Are you sure? He was the man who told the Vatican and the press that it *wasn't* true. This doesn't add up at all, Father."

Farusi peered at me through his thick lenses. "Don Diego! Listen, let's get something straight about Don Diego Lorenzi. It was my business to know what was going on around this place, you understand. I've been a specialist in Vatican information for twenty-nine years. The first reliable information I had on that day was that Don Diego was absent from the papal apartment when the Pope died. He had been *out* that evening. Yes, *out of the papal apartment* on the very evening the Pope died. He returned late in the night and went straight to bed. In the morning he overslept. . . ."

He clearly saw the amazement on my face; his voice died away as he let this item sink in. It seemed to me astonishing that it had been Don Diego all along who had told the story about the Pope reading the *Imitation*. Now, in addition, I was being told that he had gone absent the very night the Pope had died. Why had he not admitted this to me himself? "Everything I tell you is the complete truth. I have no motive to lie," I remembered him telling me sincerely in Milan. And was it possible that Marjorie Weeke, Navarro-Valls, Marcinkus and Vittoria Marigonda had never heard this before, not to mention my monsignorial friends? Was there no end to these discrepancies? These little evasions? I felt angry with Don Diego, with the whole of the Vatican. Whom could I trust in this strange little world where people seemed to play fast and loose with the truth? I looked at the Jesuit sitting before me. I should be equally on my guard with this man, I decided. Was it possible that his accusation against Don Diego was a diversionary tactic?

"What is the source of your story about Don Diego going missing, Father?"

The priest gave me a weak smile through nicotine-stained teeth.

"*Various* Vatican sources," he said. "But in the end I spoke to him myself and he confirmed that he went out that evening. Look, mister, you have to understand the Vatican. Everybody is making a big attempt to let it be known that they were doing their jobs properly."

The thought crossed my mind that this might be equally true of Father Farusi.

"Do you have any idea at what time Don Diego returned to the papal apartment?" I asked.

"Around midnight," he said. He sat looking at me for a while, wringing his walnut-brown hands, the hands of an old man. I guessed that he might be in his early seventies.

He bowed his head and rubbed his bald scalp, as if he were trying to drive away a headache. "I know that after a few days I was called to the Secretariat of State and they told me to be very careful when speaking to Don Diego," he went on. "Maybe Don Diego had said too much, and I suppose it was easy for him to talk a lot because he was a little in shock, and also he felt guilty and was trying to justify himself for what had happened. On the other hand, and I'm telling you this as something which is very interesting and something which I know with absolute certainty, they told me to be careful when speaking to Don Diego because not everything he said was exactly true. You see, he hadn't even gone to the Pope's room to make sure everything was okay when he got back."

He joined his hands again and looked at me directly. "Then it all came out about the nun finding the Pope first; that came from the Secretariat, and it was quite a different story from Don Diego's. So at that point I said to myself, 'Who's right, Don Diego, or the Secretariat? Is the Secretariat trying to give the lie to Don Diego's story because there's something else going on?' So there was quite a lot of uncertainty in my mind. They never actually said he was a liar; they just said he was speaking too freely—he wasn't being sufficiently discreet."

The squat little Father Farusi leaned across the table toward me and touched me on the arm. "Listen, mister," he said, "I don't know whether you know this, but let's start with the conclave. For me this was the key to everything, and it's what makes Don Diego's behavior a bit strange. I'm talking about the conclave at which John Paul I was elected. I was running Vatican Radio, and I was guessing who the leading candidates would be. At a certain point the rumors came to me that the cardinals were asking about the health of the patriarch of Venice. It was a large number of cardinals, and many of them were foreigners. This alerted me at once that he was the front-runner. I went to a colleague who had contacts in the police and I said I wanted a thorough dossier on this man Luciani's health. When the information came back I was shocked, because I learned that he was in very poor health. If the cardinals had known the true state of his health, they should never have elected him. But they elected him all the same. He turned it down the first time, but they elected him a second time and he was obliged to accept. The burden on a pope is enormous, but to shoulder all that and not be in good health is an added psychological weight, do you see?

"Don Diego knew all this. So how come he went out, and then comes back late and doesn't check on him? If I were a colleague I would want to ask him some questions about all this. I have information that on the day before he died Luciani telephoned his doctor in the Veneto because he was unwell and wanted advice; then we learn that Don Diego knew that he had a severe pain on the very evening of his death. But he goes out. What are we to make of all this? Eh? Why didn't he call the secretary of state?"

Father Farusi had surprised me with his information, and yet, something bothered me about the priest's dogged insistence on Don Diego's culpability. What did it prove? And wasn't Father Magee in the papal apartment? Was the priest nourishing a special grudge?

"How certain are you, Father, that Don Diego went out?" I asked.

"He *was* out," he said bluntly, looking away from me to the shuttered window.

"Why did you publish the retraction of the *Imitation* story on October second?"

"I did it at the suggestion of the Secretariat of State."

"Why did it take four days to put out a correction?"

"I don't know. It was a mystery to me, too, but they asked me to do it, so I said, 'Fair enough!' and I did it."

I said, "Do you think that John Paul I died because he was overworked?"

"It was not just the work," he said promptly. "He was frail all right, and overburdened, but he was also a spiritually intense man and deeply humble. He felt unworthy. He was worried about his election. When you take all this together, it adds up to huge psychological suffering, anxiety."

The priest fell silent and smiled to himself for a few moments. He said, "You know, the people loved his teaching at the audiences. But the Secretariat of State didn't. The Secretariat criticized him because he was speaking at too popular a level, too simplistic and so on. One morning I remember this phone call came, someone asking me, 'What does the Pope think he's doing during the audiences? He's blaspheming!' " Father Farusi chortled at the memory of it. "Why? One day during the Wednesday audience he said to the people, 'Pray for this poor Christ.' And he pointed to himself. And this person in the Vatican had taken it as an irreverent expression. So they didn't understand that in popular terms he was speaking of this poor Christ, crucified on all sides: on the cross, like Jesus Christ."

Here it was again, the little, incompetent Pope, so naive that he was capable of uttering blasphemy!

But I found myself wondering about Father Farusi. He seemed complex, perhaps subtle. Was he playing some clever Jesuitical game with me? I wondered. I felt he had certainly been extraordinarily indiscreet at the expense of the Vatican. But why? Was it in the interests of the unadorned truth?

I decided at last to confront him with the principal question.

"Was it possible, Father, that John Paul I was murdered? Do you rule it out completely?"

The priest shut his eyes and hunched his shoulders. He considered the question for a few moments.

"Listen, there's a fact which is beyond dispute as far as I am concerned. That Pope won enormous popular affection from ordinary people. He was being thought of as even more popular than John XXIII; he was even holier, more humble, more modest, more simple. His death appeared so inexplicable that the only possible explanation seemed that he had been poisoned. This idea would have been readily accepted by people.

"I can tell you something, and this isn't just hot air: there's a serious background to it. Good man that he was, there were rumors that John Paul I was going to clean up the Vatican. It was being said that he was going to fire Marcinkus and have him removed. Why? Behind all this there's a true story. A couple of years before Luciani became Pope, the Banco Ambrosiano was trying to take over the Banca Cattolica of the Veneto. It was funded by the Catholic associations in which the Church had great interest. At a certain point it was transferred to Banco Ambrosiano by Marcinkus. Luciani came to Rome as patriarch of Venice to discuss the matter with Paul VI, but he was sent over to Marcinkus to see what could be done to stop it. Marcinkus saw him and told him, quite crudely, that the patriarch of Venice should be concerned with his people and not with banking.

"Next thing, Luciani becomes Pope—and Marcinkus is frightened that he is going to be sacked. If you were able to quietly ask questions around the Vatican, everyone was saying this at the time: after the election Marcinkus changed completely. He was depressed and desperate. I am convinced that Luciani would have made them pay for taking away the funds of the Catholic movements of the Veneto: it was a whole banking system based on the gifts of the faithful.

"This is going off at a tangent. But given such a wonderful pope, the suddenness of death, unless there's a logical explanation, it's open to all sorts of suspicion. Next there's the impression that they were not clarifying things, for whatever reason. We've never known, or it has never been said, exactly what happened. So there's room for suspicion. Do I explain myself? One thing I've never understood, even if they give their reasons in the Vatican, is how come there was no autopsy?"

The priest fell silent, as if *I* might have the answer. At that moment I was reflecting on the irony of the situation. Here was an example of "sources inside the Vatican," or "impeccable sources close to the Curia"; with men talking like this on the inside, it occurred to me that the Vatican might well have got off lightly with books such as *Soutane Rouge* and *In God's Name*. I sat looking at Father Farusi in amazement. My clear and unambiguous question about the possibility of papal assassination had led immediately to insinuations about Marcinkus and a possible motive for the removal of an "interfering" pope.

"They say, on the inside," went on Father Farusi, "that to concede an autopsy would be to admit that there was the possibility that he had been poisoned. This was a pope's body. Fair enough! Stand by your decision and refuse an autopsy on that basis. But at least state precisely what was known."

Father Farusi cocked his head at me quizzically. "Am I making myself clear? The fact that he was elected indicated that he was considered to be in good health. So how come he died all of a sudden? Then they all say, 'But he was in *bad* health—everybody knows that!' So if that's true—how come they elected him? They want it both ways. The problem is that everyone is trying to save his own skin, and this has given rise to a whole host of complications and suspicions."

"The Banco Ambrosiano collapse, Father. Do you think that Archbishop Marcinkus was culpable?"

Father Farusi leaned across the table toward me again. "Marcinkus has kept silent about the real facts to protect the people who are really behind the big mistakes."

He fell silent. I waited with bated breath.

The priest shook his head and waved one hand a little, as if to tell me that he would talk no further on the matter.

"That is why," he went on, "the name of Paul VI is clean."

He smiled to himself and looked myopically up at the ceiling. "Let me give you a little example. Paul VI is always thought of as the great modern benefactor of the museums," he said, "but many things went on behind the scenes. There was the case of the modern religious-art museum he started. I know all this because the Jesuits were involved in getting a collection together. Many first-class, world-famous artists sent gifts of their work to start it off, and when they turned up for the opening the works weren't there. Somehow they had disappeared. Eh? You see?"

It was an intriguing snippet. But what on earth could it mean? That Paul VI was stealing paintings? I considered the implications for a moment, and decided to steer clear of them.

Father Farusi rose from his chair. "Look, I have to go for my lunch now. You could always come back. Or I could write some more answers for you." He led me to the door and started to walk with me down the corridor.

He stopped to say: "By the way, this business of Villot wishing to block *Humanae Vitae* is utter rubbish. Paul VI brought in Villot to represent the views of the Church in France. Villot believed profoundly in the French view of freedom of conscience; he was in *favor* of relaxation. Incidentally, it was Villot who wanted Lefebvre excommunicated."

The priest looked up at me defiantly. "Mind you, I think that a lot of what Lefebvre was saying was quite reasonable. Things had gone too far. . . . Mass on coffee tables!"

With this he shook my hand and began trotting down the corridor the way he had come.

Back at the English College I called Marjorie Weeke.

"Marjorie," I said, "have you ever heard a rumor that Don Diego was absent the evening the Pope died?"

"No!" she said flatly. "It's the first time I've ever heard it."

After lunch I called Mario di Francesco, formerly a journalist at ANSA news service, now working as a theater critic at *Il Messaggero*. I got straight through to him.

"Signor di Francesco," I said, "is it true that you wrote the story about the Pope's morticians leaving for the Vatican at five in the morning the day the Pope was found dead?"

"Yes," he said, "that is correct." His voice was slow, defensive.

"Could we meet to discuss how you put that story together? I know it's many years ago . . ."

"No problem. I remember it very well indeed, and I'll tell you what I've always said. I knew the Signoracci brothers well; I went back and confirmed the story with them. But unfortunately the brothers we are referring to are now dead."

I fell silent for a moment, stunned by this information.

"There might be a nephew alive," he said, "I don't know. But let's meet and I'll be glad to try to reconstruct how I wrote the report."

We agreed to meet at the English College the following afternoon.

27

A memorandum by Max Bergère, the dean of the Vaticanologists, arrived for me from the Sala Stampa:

I knew Cardinal Jean Villot from the time when he was completing his studies in Rome, and I was just starting out as a journalist. Thereafter I saw him on his regular visits to Rome. He used to let me know he was in town and I would go to visit him in the simple little room they kept for him at Saint Sulpice. He would be in his shirtsleeves and would sit and chat about things. Our relationship was in no way affected when he became bishop, then cardinal. He was always the same: simple and unaffected. When Paul VI nominated him secretary of state, he paid homage to Villot's great fidelity to the Church as well as his goodness of character and even temperament.

Cardinal Villot made a major contribution in the election of Luciani. After the third ballot on August 26, Villot addressed an exhortation to the conclave, urging them to wind the thing up quickly, as there was such an overwhelming support for Luciani. The agreement was stunning, according to the expressions on the faces of the electors, and on the fourth vote Luciani was elected.

Luciani was not expecting this nomination and he was in such a state of confusion that one of the cardinals at his side said to him: "Have courage. If the Lord imposes a burden, he also gives the necessary strength to carry it. Don't be afraid, there are many people around the world who are praying for you."

Cardinal Villot stayed at Luciani's side like a loyal and loving friend. One day as John Paul I, as he now was, accompanied him back to the door of the papal apartment, Villot turned to him and said, "Your Holiness, there is no necessity for you to be so attentive. Remember, you are the Pope, and I am just a cardinal." John Paul said to him, smiling kindly, "There are popes, and there are poor popes."

When they were preparing the papal apartments, John Paul was the guest of Cardinal Villot. After lunch the Pope was asked if he wanted to be on his own, for a siesta, and he declined, saying that he did not like being left alone.

The amount of work imposed upon John Paul I was formidable. He said to a cardinal one day, "Most people need a typewriter [literally, *writing* machine in Italian]; I could do with a *reading* machine."

Cardinal Villot told me that Luciani's feet used to swell up tremendously at night.

On September 23, the date of Luciani's last excursion from the Vatican, as he was asked to get up to reply to the acclamations of the crowd, he said, "I would prefer one hour's adoration of the Blessed Sacrament."

. . . Who would have imagined a death so sudden! Cardinal Villot was very affected by the loss of his new boss. Villot told me eventually the details of what happened on the morning of September 29. Not seeing him arrive in the chapel, the secretary went to his door. A light filtered through. He became worried and found him with his glasses still perched on his nose, the sheets of paper he was reading scattered around him. His bedside lamp was still on. He seemed to be sleeping peacefully with a soft smile on his lips.

His personal doctor, who had looked after him for many years, declared, "It was only in dying that he was ill." When some Italian newspapers demanded an autopsy, the doctor replied that this wouldn't be necessary seeing that the causes of death were more than evident: the Pope had suffered a serious heart attack.

Cardinal Sebastiano Baggio, present camerlengo of the Church, has since declared: "Was he crushed by the sheer weight of his pontificate? Did he die of a broken heart? Perhaps his body, fragile in aspect, had not been in any state to resist the impulsions of his soul which had said *yes* with a boundless generosity. Death must have crept up on him as if in anticipation of the prize that lay ahead of him."

Here were some fascinating new details, especially Luciani accompanying Villot to the door of the apartment against all precedent and protocol. And again, here was mention of the swollen feet. But Villot had evidently given his friend Bergère a sanitized version of the morning of September 29, complete with filtered light and peaceful smile, and Bergère had swallowed it whole.

28

Sister Irma, the nun who had "interviewed" Sister Vincenza, lived and worked in Rome, I eventually discovered. After much effort I persuaded her to come round for a chat, and she turned up one morning in time for coffee.

She was a dumpy little person with a face of startling innocence. She was dressed in the modern style, in a gray suit and short veil, and she was carrying a huge shopping bag. She told me that she had joined the convent at fifteen and had been a nun for some fifty years.

I asked her if Sister Vincenza had confided in her about the death of John Paul I.

"Yes," she said promptly. "You see, my sister was Vincenza's mother superior. I belong to another order, and I went on holiday up to Lamon in the Veneto where she lived after she left Rome. I think she felt she could confide in me somehow because I wasn't in the same community."

"Can you tell me the details as she related them to you?"

"She told me that the evening the Pope died he went into the kitchen to say good-night to all the sisters. Then he said to Father Magee, 'Look, stay with them a bit longer, because they're always on their own.' Apparently Father Magee stayed up talking with them till about eleven, reading through the lives of the popes. Then they went to bed."

"And the next day?"

"Around five-twenty Sister Vincenza left some coffee outside his room. After five or ten minutes she went to check and found that he hadn't taken it. So she thought he was resting a little longer. She went away again and came back later. She opened the door and saw the light was on, so she thought he must be dressing or still resting. So she went to the chapel. After seven or eight minutes he had not come out and neither of the secretaries was up either, so she decided she must do something she'd never done before. She went and knocked on the door. Getting no answer she went on in and saw him in bed, wearing his glasses, papers in his hand, his head bowed slightly forward. She told me she went toward him and said, 'But, your Holiness, you shouldn't play this joke on me!' Then she realized that something was terribly wrong and she got frightened and rushed back to the sisters. After that they went and got the secretary, Father Magee."

"So it was Sister Vincenza, definitely, who found his body?"

"She found him dead, but she said the priests decided to announce that the secretary found him because they were worried about the stories that went round about Madre Pasquelina and Pope Pius XII."

"And how about Don Diego Lorenzi? Did Sister Vincenza ever say anything about him?"

"Yes, she said that Don Diego wasn't made for the job. He used to complain to the Pope, saying, 'I wasn't made to be shut up like this in a cage!' "

"Did she feel that the Pope was unhappy in the Vatican?"

"She said he suffered in Rome because he was timid. He was shy. Although when he really believed that a thing had to be done, there wasn't a saint who could stop him. But yes, he suffered in the Vatican."

"What happened to Sister Vincenza after the Pope died? I've read somewhere that she was banished, sent as far away from Rome as possible."

"The papal apartment was locked up and she had no reason to

go back. She was from the Veneto, and she returned to a convent up in the region where she came from. It was all quite normal. She had a bad heart even before she went to Rome and so she went into retirement. She worked as sacristan and went out occasionally to visit the sick. That's all. When I first asked her to talk with me about the Pope, I was visiting her convent for a two-week vacation. She told me that she hadn't even told her fellow sisters what she had told me."

As Sister Irma made her way down to the street with her enormous shopping bag, I felt satisfied that the "missing hour"—created by the alleged 4:30 discovery of the body—had been a mistake. There had been two sources for this: David Yallop's interview with Sister Vincenza and an ANSA report on October 5, 1978, from "rumors" within the Vatican. I still wanted to attempt at least to find ANSA's source for that 4:30 claim.

Signor Mandillo of ANSA, having helped me with Mario di Francesco, was in no mood to help me any further. So I tried his number two, a Signor Besmelovich, who agreed to meet me at the Sala Stampa that same morning.

He was a huge man with Slavonic features and hair cut *en brosse*. He looked at me dubiously. "That would be a matter of divulging sources. I don't think it's possible; we are very secretive about these matters, but I'll see what I can do. Just give me a little time."

As we were walking to the door he said, "By the way, I am working on my own theory of John Paul's death. I am convinced it was a case of psychological murder."

"What do you mean, Signor Besmelovich?"

"Aha! That is my own secret. . . ."

29

My meeting with Dr. Buzzonetti was to be held at six o'clock in the Vatican Health Service, a modern building in the Vatican business sector. I gave my name at the door and went to the second floor. A young man met me at the lift and escorted me through a series of corridors to the papal doctor's office.

There were two besuited men in the room. A short round man with thinning white hair came forward. "I am Buzzonetti," he said. He wore glasses and his eyes seemed lidless, giving him a smooth, smiling look. His nose was pinched sharp at the tip. He wore a gray suit and pale-blue shirt with a striped club tie.

He introduced me to the other man who was dressed in tweeds; his blond hair was coiffed into an elaborate bouffant style. I gathered that his companion was there for legal purposes, as a witness.

The room was virtually bare, and the terrazzo flooring gave it an impression of coldness. Buzzonetti sat behind his desk, which was set in a corner of the room like a personal fortress. Above his head was a portrait of Pope John Paul II and a modern crucifix.

Dr. Buzzonetti regarded me coolly. I noticed that he had a tape recorder on the desk. I placed mine next to his.

"Shall we proceed?" he said.

We switched on our tape recorders simultaneously, which caused his companion to titter. It relieved the tense atmosphere a little.

"When did you last see the Pope?" I asked. "I mean, when the Pope was still alive."

"I can be very precise about that," he replied promptly. "Neither myself, nor Professor Mario Fontana—who was head of the Vatican Health Service then, and who died in 1979—were ever called to give our professional services to Pope John Paul I. I saw him at the end of the conclave. I was there as the deputy to Fontana. Then I think I saw him at a distance in the crowd at some function. Then I saw him dead. That's all."

The doctor spoke rapidly, his head cocked, the lenses of his spectacles flashing in the light of the neon strips above him.

"Were you aware of the Pope's state of health, even in terms of a rumor?" I asked. "It was said after he died that he was in very poor health."

"I wasn't aware of it," he said without a pause. "But even if I had been, I wouldn't tell *you* because professional secrecy comes into play. I've got to be abundantly clear about this. All the clinical aspects of this business of John Paul I are covered by two secrets: the first is the professional secret, which no one can release me from; then there's the secret of my office as vice-director of the Health Service of this State of the Vatican. But anyway, I don't know anything."

I paused to take stock of the situation. The Vatican, through its public-relations departments, was currently arguing that the Pope had been in poor health. And yet the only professional individual in the place responsible for making such judgments knew nothing. My attitude toward Dr. Buzzonetti was growing more hostile by the minute.

"All the accounts say that the Pope was taking various medicines. Can you say what they were?"

"I really don't know," he said bluntly. "I know nothing about his medicines."

I felt a spasm of anger. This was deliberate stonewalling. This man had signed the Pope's death certificate, and he knew nothing of his medication?

"Can you at least tell me at what time you were called to the Vatican after the Pope was found dead?"

Dr. Buzzonetti looked down at some prepared notes in front of him. "This I wrote down at the time," he said. "At five forty-two A.M. I was called at home on the morning of September twenty-ninth. I was, obviously, asleep in bed and the telephone woke me up. It was Father John Magee, and he said: 'The Pope is dead.' I made some comment of surprise or shock and he repeated, 'The Pope is dead.' Then he put the phone down. I got dressed quickly, took the car, which was parked under the house. I live in front of the Castel Sant' Angelo, so I'm quite close to the Vatican. Around six o'clock I entered the papal apartment. I got there so quickly that later on that day Cardinal Villot asked me, 'Do you live in the Vatican?' I hadn't understood why, but they were surprised how quickly I got there."

"Were you or another doctor available during the night?" I intervened. "I mean, if the Pope had suffered a heart attack, would you or another doctor have been able to come immediately?" I was trying to establish whether there was any responsibility on the part of Buzzonetti and his Vatican Health Service for the day-to-day health of the Pope.

"Of course, there was always cover in the Vatican," he said. "For many years there has always been a doctor on call, or a nurse, who give uninterrupted cover day and night, holidays and ordinary days. I was called at this time, I suppose, because it was clear that the Pope was dead and so didn't need an emergency doctor. I don't know. This is just my interpretation of things."

"After you entered the papal apartment," I said, "what happened then? Can you give me an account of the exact sequence of events through the rest of the morning as far as the Pope's body was concerned?"

Buzzonetti took a sheet from the file in front of him in a swift, professional manner. "I recorded in note form everything I did and observed at the time, so I can say with more precision than others what happened that morning. These are my notes here. I tell you all this without violating the professional code of secrecy, because others saw these things together with me."

He joined his hands together, elbows resting on either side of his notes. "When I entered the apartment, the Holy Father was in his bed. He was propped up, leaning forward slightly; his expression was composed and calm. He was wearing his glasses properly on his nose—that is, they hadn't slipped off. His head was turned slightly to the right. In his hands he was holding some printed or typewritten sheets, like a pamphlet or booklet. The lamp above the headboard was on. I don't know whether there were two or three cushions. With the blankets in the correct position. There was no gesture of agitation or untidiness." He was speaking with authority, in an almost snappy fashion.

"After seven o'clock Monsignor Noè, the master of ceremonies, assisted by me, and helped by a religious of the Order of Saint John of God from the Vatican Pharmacy, and the secretaries, prepared and vested the body in the papal garments. Obviously it wasn't something done in a few minutes.

"After this, I left. My part was finished. But I know that the body of the Pope was eventually moved to the Sala Clementina, where, if I am not mistaken, other preparations were in course. I know that things had to be hurried up because Sandro Pertini, the president of Italy, was waiting to go in to pay his respects to the body. So, practically speaking, the body was exposed in the Sala Clementina from around noon till around seven in the evening of that day.

"Then the body was removed from the Clementina to the Sala dei Forconi, which is nearby. It's known as the Hall of the Preachers. Here it was undressed again and the body was treated for hygienic preservation without the removal of organs, intestines or blood. The reason was to ensure as far as possible the feasibility of exposing the body to the faithful for some days, taking the climate and so on into consideration."

"Who was responsible for the preservation process?" I asked. "Who was there?"

"It was done by a team directed by Professor Gerin, Cesare Gerin, who at that time was director of the Istituto di Medicina Legale at the State University of Rome. He is an authoritative scientist of worldwide fame. He was assisted by his closest collaborators, amongst whom was Professor Fucci. Then there was Professor Mariggi and Professor Maragin. There was also a technical assistant in the person of one of the Signoracci brothers who also work at the istituto and who are very competent in this sort of operation. The treatment began at about seven in the evening of September twenty-ninth and finished at about three-thirty on the morning of September thirtieth. Then the body was vested again after a few hours, and exposed once again."

"There's an ANSA report," I said, "claiming that the Signoracci brothers were called to the Vatican at about five in the morning."

"That's silly," he said testily. "It's got to be an error in translation. It doesn't make sense."

I produced the ANSA agency-dispatch from my briefcase. "Here it is." I passed it across the desk to him. "On the twenty-ninth it says, they were telephoned at dawn, then a Vatican car called for them at about five in the morning and they came in here to start their work."

"It's not true!" snapped Buzzonetti, his eyes blazing. "These are lies. What date? The twenty-ninth? It's absurd, invented. Completely false, absolutely false. I can also say, and here I'm not breaking the seal, because there were other people there. When the shock of the first minutes had passed, Cardinal Villot said he would have to get in touch again with Professor Gerin's team because he would know who to choose to perform the process that was to have taken place in the evening. They were the same team who did the process on the body of Paul VI. They were chosen by Professor Fontana as director of the Vatican Health Service at the time and personal doctor to Paul VI. What I mean to say is that they were chosen after six, probably after seven in the morning. The Signoracci couldn't have been here at five."

I was now thinking of the contention in Yallop's report that the Signoraccis had put a time on the hour of death closer to 4:00 A.M. than 10:00 P.M. or 11:00 P.M. on the previous evening. I was remembering the standard principle that rigor mortis takes about twelve hours to establish itself in normal temperatures. I was also thinking of Don Diego's claim that the back was still warm.

"Had rigor mortis set in to the Pope's body; were there any parts of the body still warm when you found him?"

"I can't tell you that because I'm bound by professional secrecy," he said abruptly.

"I ask," I went on, "because there's a dispute over the time of death. I understand you thought it was about eleven P.M. The Signoracci brothers are quoted as saying they were positive that the Pope died at a different time."

"I repeat," he said insistently, "it's a professional secret and it applies to this area of discussion too. Anyway, the determination of the time of the death of the Pope was not done by me alone. I was the number two in the Health Service at the time. Professor Fontana was there. He is dead now, but he was a great student of pathology and was a top-class pathologist and doctor. He had more experience than me, much more in this kind of work. I can also say that the doctors from the Istituto Legale came later and saw the body, many hours after death. They too were used to estimate dates and times of death with great precision and competence, certainly greater than mine, but they never discussed it."

"Can you confirm that the Signoracci brothers were in no situation to make statements about the time of death?"

He shut his eyes, as if with forced patience. "What is certain is that the Signoracci brothers would not have seen the body close up until after seven o'clock in the evening."

It was time, I decided, to bring up the question of the cause of death, and I knew that this was likely to be the most controversial question of all.

"I understand you diagnosed myocardial infarction," I said. "Was this an exact verdict, or necessarily rather vague?"

Buzzonetti looked at me stunned for a few moments, as if speechless at my impertinence.

He glanced for a moment at his companion and cocked his head. Finally he said in a cool voice, "The diagnosis wasn't mine alone. There were two of us. I arrived first. Professor Fontana came at about eight o'clock. I gave him my opinion straightaway. He was entirely in agreement with the first bulletin, which was given not by me but by the secretary of state. Actually, I have now remembered that the preparation and undressing of the body began after eight o'clock. I remember now . . . Fontana then gave an order . . . I'd forgotten this, that the body should not be treated until at least nineteen or twenty hours had passed, in accordance with Italian law which insists that fifteen hours' observation pass before a body can be touched."

He was running ahead on a new theme, but I had noticed both his failure to answer the question, and his attempt to shuffle the responsibility onto Fontana, who was now dead. His correction about the time of the undressing and dressing of the body was also interesting. Earlier he had talked of seven o'clock; his change of mind, making it an hour later, was clearly to allow for the supposition that Fontana could have examined the body. The comment seemed to draw attention to the extraordinarily speedy process of diagnosis by Buzzonetti alone.

"But what of the diagnosis . . . " I began to say, to nudge him back on course.

"As for the method of diagnosis," he said rapidly, "one does it employing the following elements . . . this is important: analysis, historical details, clinical history, remote and proximate. Secondly, with objective data. Thirdly, with circumstantial evidence: the bed, the position of the body, the aspect of the underwear, all the elements that give suggestions, ideas as to what happened. Then there are statistical considerations. Based on all these criteria, sudden death by heart attack was diagnosed."

I found myself thinking that "clinical history, remote and proximate" would surely have included knowledge of his embolism in 1975, and information about his medicines.

"There is another point, which no one has pointed out: the diagnosis of sudden death. The adjective SUDDEN is not a journalistic description"—he managed a little smile at the word *journalistic*—"it is an exquisitely clinical diagnosis, and implies three fundamental concepts, as can be seen in all the textbooks: it is a natural death—sudden death is always natural; it is never not 'proper,' by definition; it's a death which is instantaneous or immediate, or premature, something like that. Thus, very little time is involved: in this case, instantaneous. And it is *unexpected*. These are the elements of a sudden death. All you have to do is look in any medical textbook."

The important-sounding terminology flowed on: "A confident diagnosis can only be made by pathological examination. It should be said that in many cases of sudden death, neither can the autopsy give a mathematical, anatomical proof of the cause of death in an absolute sense. So even the pathologist must form a hypothesis of this kind, putting various elements of the mosaic together in order to arrive at a concrete conclusion. Certainly in the hypothesis of a death which is not sudden, but violent, then there's another mechanism which would imply recourse to judicial processes, a problem which wasn't considered by anyone at that time. . . ."

It occurred to me that he was playing for time, hoping that I could be dissuaded from the question that he knew was hanging on my lips. I leaped in.

"Dr. Buzzonetti, I understand that it's now being suggested that the cause of death might have been a pulmonary embolism, due to the fact that he'd had an embolism in the eye three years earlier."

"Anyone can come up with hypotheses of this or that, or embolisms," he said grandly, and dismissively. "There's Professor Dino, a Catholic, who has been saying it, although he had never seen the Pope. . . ."

At this point, to my astonishment, Buzzonetti turned to his colleague and muttered under his breath, "This is the third degree, eh?"

His expression was idiomatic, but I caught it nevertheless. We sat in silence for a few moments.

"I'm sorry if you feel I'm being impertinent," I said at last, "but isn't it best that we settle these questions for once and for all? I don't really want to come back again after this."

He looked surprised, crestfallen. He raised a hand. "I'm sorry," he said. "I've got nothing against you personally. In fact I like you, but you understand I am bound by very strict codes of conduct."

I felt that the exchange had lightened the atmosphere a little. "Did you call Dr. Da Ros, the Pope's previous doctor, in the Veneto, at any time whatsoever? After the death?" I asked.

"He came either that evening or afternoon to Rome, I don't remember all that well. I met him, I think, in the Sala Clementina or outside. He embraced me, he said that he agreed with the diagnosis. We exchanged a few words, a greeting. He was upset, crying, you know. . . . It was a very short meeting. He said that in his view it was a heart attack, but we didn't initiate a medical discussion."

So much, I was thinking, for the remote and proximate data. Apparently no discussion about John Paul's medication, about the swollen ankles, the pain in the chest the previous day, the thrombosis or embolism in 1975 . . .

"Don Diego Lorenzi now claims that the Pope had a pain in his chest on the day before he died," I said. "I found it puzzling. Why would the priest not tell the doctor of this pain? On the other hand, why did you not ask him if there had been any strange symptoms on the eve of the death?"

"I don't know why Don Diego didn't report the pain," he said, thrusting his head back. "They certainly never called me. As for my obligations in the matter, I've said that the diagnosis was made with recourse to the remote and proximate data. Thus the proximate data would include news of the hours or days before. What they were I am not going to say, but I accept that a doctor should ask. Any doctor would."

"Did you feel at the time that an autopsy would have been a good option?" I asked.

"I honestly don't think so . . . I don't think so," he said emphatically.

"Have you ever spoken with any other journalist or investigator about these matters?" I asked.

"No, never. You're the first person I've spoken to about these things apart from the little bits of news which were given out to all the journalists and are of no consequence. And I'm only speaking to you because I was asked to do so as a special favor by the secretary of state in the interests of the Holy See and in my service to the Holy Father, whom we serve as humble doctors. We're educated into this spirit of service to the Church, otherwise I would never have spoken to you or to anyone else."

The grandiloquent statement reduced me to silence. All the same, I felt that he knew a great deal more than he was telling me.

"Do you think that the Pope was very overworked, or depressed, during his Papacy? Was he under great pressure?" I asked him.

"I know absolutely nothing of this," said Buzzonetti airily. "I kissed his hand the day he was elected Pope, while the conclave was still in force. He was greeting all the Vatican assistants. I kissed his hand, that's all. I saw him maybe once or twice from a distance, and then I went on holiday after the election. I hadn't had any vacation because of the death of Paul VI, I only returned a few days before he died. So I don't know anything, and I can't say anything."

"Can you tell me anything that would absolutely repudiate the theory that Pope John Paul I died by poisoning?"

"Yes . . . common sense!" He gave a sudden high-pitched laugh and flashed a look at his colleague.

As we were coming to a close I decided to change tack to a more personal line of questioning. "What were your duties as Pope's doctor," I asked, "and how are you chosen for a job of this kind?"

"I wasn't the Pope's doctor and neither was Professor Fontana," he said flatly. "I was vice-director and Professor Fontana was the director. I was called, I think, because they knew I lived nearby. That's what I think. I knew Father Magee because he was Paul VI's secretary, so we knew each other during the latter years of the reign of Paul VI. And we lived through the saga of the death of Paul VI and all the rest of it, and so we fraternized a bit with each other. So probably when the Pope was found he thought of me, knowing I was nearby, because Professor Fontana lived farther away, in the Trieste quarter beyond the Policlinico, and anyway he was too old to get up so early in the morning. . . . So they got me up instead. These are the facts, and life is made up of these sorts of facts and not just the things they write in newspapers and books."

This last sentence was spoken with evident distaste for the world of publishing, but I was pondering the clear message in the earlier part of his statement: the Vatican doctors were absolving themselves of any responsibility for the health of John Paul I. And yet how, I wondered, could they have taken responsibility for the diagnosis? Certainly under English law the death of any patient who had not been seen by his doctor within a period of six weeks must be referred to the local coroner.

I felt that we had come to an impasse, but I was far from satisfied with my encounter.

I rose and started to put the recorder into my case.

"Are you satisfied?" he asked.

I did not respond.

As I shook his hand he said, "I hope you don't get me into trouble!"

30

My meeting with Dr. Buzzonetti had left me with considerable antipathy toward the Vatican Health Service. I found it astonishing that neither Fontana nor Buzzonetti had organized a conference with Da Ros, the physician in the Veneto, and that they had not acquainted themselves with the basics of John Paul I's medical history. Buzzonetti seemed to me to be evasive and I was convinced that he was using the principle of patient privacy as a blind for something that was worrying him. I had not succeeded in solving the cause of John Paul I's death to my satisfaction.

In the meantime I returned to the problem of Bishop Magee, John Paul I's Irish secretary. I had decided to enlist the support of Archbishop Foley, and I once again made the journey to the office of the Commission for Social Communications in the Vatican.

As I announced myself to the valet in the lobby of the commission in Piazza San Carlo, the archbishop appeared in person from behind me. He was wearing a black flat cap which gave his round face an astonished, comic appearance.

"Let's go into my office," he said.

I took it as a gesture of special privilege; meetings with people from the outside world were invariably conducted in the anonymity of the official interview parlors. He showed me into a spacious, sunny room filled with heavy, dark-stained baroque furniture with brocade cushions. There were stacks of newspapers and magazines on occasional tables; a statuette on a plinth was situated in the center of the room: it depicted Francis de Sales—patron saint of journalism. He took off his cap, motioned me to sit on an upright sofa and drew up a severe-looking armchair opposite me. He joined his hands, fingertip to fingertip, and gazed at me benevolently. He had a folder on his lap.

"You know," he said, "you are sitting on the furniture that originally belonged to Pius XII; all these furnishings came from his private apartment."

Then he said, "How's it coming along?"

"I have a problem, Monsignor, and if I can't solve it I don't know how to proceed. Bishop John Magee is a crucial witness, but he's refused to see me. Is there any way you can twist his arm a little?"

The archbishop opened the file before him; he had a puzzled expression. "We wrote him a letter before Christmas asking for his cooperation," he said, "and he was here only a few days ago. I spoke with him, in fact. I wonder why he's holding out on you. . . . There's a priest who works here in the commission who may be able to help."

He went over to his desk, picked up a telephone and put a call through. "Father," he said, "would you come in here a moment?

"Bishop Magee," he said, returning to his chair, "is a member of the Kiltegan Fathers, the Order of Saint Patrick for the Foreign Missions. One of his confreres in that society works for me—Father Michael Glynn. Let's ask his advice about the best way to approach this problem."

There was a knock and a white-haired priest put his head around the door before entering. It was the *bagarozzo* I had seen in the corridor of the commission on my first visit. The archbishop beckoned him and he walked with hesitant steps across the room to sit gingerly on the edge of a chair that matched the archbishop's. His face was pale and heavily lined, he wore gold-rimmed spectacles through which he stole occasional glances at me, then at the archbishop, then into the far corner of the room. He looked tired and depressed.

"We have a problem, Father. Mr. Cornwell here is writing a book about the death of John Paul I, and we'd like him to meet with Bishop Magee. We wrote to the bishop before Christmas, but His Lordship has declined a meeting, it seems. I'm wondering the best way to go about this."

The priest rubbed his cheeks and chin and looked up at the ceiling. He breathed in deeply and sighed. "I've no idea at all, I'm sure," he muttered in a quiet Irish brogue. "I couldn't see the point in any meetings. Sure, it's all died down now, this murder theory. What's the point in going and stirring it all up again?"

The archbishop stared at Father Glynn and stretched his lips into a strange rictus, as though he were about to blow a raspberry.

Father Glynn sighed again, and continued, in a barely audible mumble, "Sure, I know the mind of the bishop pretty well, and he's decided not to talk to anyone any further on the matter. He wouldn't be keen, I can tell you that."

The archbishop looked at me. "I wonder if *I* should call Bishop Magee. What do *you* think, Mr. Cornwell?"

I was furious with both of them. I wanted to say to the archbishop, "For God's sake! *You're* the boss, *you* call him!"

I turned to Father Glynn. "You know, Father, it would look strange if we left the bishop out."

Father Glynn folded his arms and looked away, as if preferring to ignore my remark.

The archbishop seemed to fall into a reverie for a while. "I know what we should do," he said at length. He turned to Father Glynn. "Why don't you call the bishop first? Then, if you can't persuade him to meet Mr. Cornwell, I can then consider the matter further and come to a decision."

"Whatever you like," said the priest. "You want me to do it now, or what?"

I was uttering silent execrations.

"Just as you like, Father," said the archbishop in a mild manner. "That would be very kind, although he may well not be at home right now."

The priest had risen to leave the room when I said to him, "Father Glynn, if Bishop Magee is reluctant to see me, perhaps he would at least allow me to explain the outstanding problems connected with my investigation."

He paused to listen while I said this, but without looking me directly in the face. Then he proceeded to the door.

When the priest had gone, I said to the archbishop, "How official are the broadcasts on the Vatican's Radiogiornale? If they put out a story saying what the Pope was reading when he died, would that have been tantamount to an official statement?"

"The Vatican Press Office is the only guide to official statements, and if they hadn't published that story, then the radio found their own material. They use the wire stories independently; they have them over there and tear them off."

The archbishop delved into the file on his lap again and brought out a two-page document. "You should have this statement which we made available to the Episcopal conference in June 1984. It refers to the relationship between official Vatican sources and Vatican Radio."

He handed me the document (see Appendix, p. 347). Skimming through I immediately came upon a passage with the heading:

"The pages" and the Imitation of Christ

. . . The theory that the Pope held in his hand the *Imitation of Christ* did not originate from any official Vatican source. No official document ever mentioned it. A report which circulated among journalists, with no ill-will intended, was picked up even by Vatican Radio (which does not have an official character) and was soon afterwards corrected, when the real facts were verified.

"Who wrote this?" I asked.
"It was produced by us, here in the office," he said.
The last item in the document read:

The sister or the private secretary?

While it makes no real difference whether the Pope was found dead by a sister, or, as the Vatican communiqué said, by the

private secretary of the Pontiff, in fact, the secretary instantly
ran to the bedside of Pope John Paul I when he was summoned
by the sister who suspected that something might be wrong.
The secretary touched the Pope to awaken him and discovered
that he was dead. The secretary then called Cardinal Villot.

I considered the subtle wording: it still managed to avoid saying
that the nun had found the body, and still managed to claim that
it was the secretary who found John Paul I dead; a textbook example
of Scholastic equivocation.

As I put the document in my briefcase, there was a knock and
Father Glynn's anxious face came round the door.

"I've talked to Bishop Magee," he said, and he was now looking
directly at me. "He apologizes that he put you off that other time
there; he has only just received the letter from His Excellency.
Anyway, he'll see you just as soon as you can get to Ireland. Give
his secretary Father Sheehan a ring. Good luck to you now." And
he was gone.

Archbishop Foley beamed with satisfaction. As I rose to depart,
he said, "How about a blessing?"

Later that afternoon I waited for an hour at the porter's lodge for
Mario di Francesco, the former ANSA man who was going to tell
me the background to his story about the papal morticians. I waited
in vain; he failed to show up.

I returned to my room, called Father Sheehan and prepared to
fly to Ireland.

31

J drove in a taxi west along the banks of the River Lea some fifteen miles beyond Cork city. A bridge separated the mainland from Great Island and we climbed the bluff from which the slate-gray neo-Gothic Cathedral of Cobh dominated the sky like a decaying wedding cake, huge and redundant on its lonely, windswept vantage point.

Beyond the cathedral a dramatic vista opened up—the waters of Cobh harbor and a scattering of humped-back islands in the shimmering light of midmorning. Below was the huddle of unkempt houses and shops of the town.

The bishop's house was a rambling Georgian mansion situated in a mildewed garden of evergreens with views of the cathedral and the sea. As I got out of the car I caught my breath in the chill Atlantic blast.

I was shown into a parlor by a housemaid. She rubbed her rawboned hands together and said, "Sure, it's a mighty cold day." She turned on an electric convector-heater to take the edge off the freezing damp. There were some high-backed ecclesiastic chairs and, over the mantelpiece, an oleograph of the Virgin Mary. On the table was a copy of *Doneraile Schools' Magazine 1987*. I peered at the bookshelves: *Questions and Answers,* by Canon E. J. Mahoney, *Moral and Pastoral Theology,* by H. Davis, SJ, *The History of Catholic Emancipation,* by W. J. Amherst.

The door opened with a flourish and three clergymen peered in at me. The bishop was in the center of the trio, wearing a simple black soutane with a gold cross gleaming at his breast. The two flanking priests, one old and one young, were both bespectacled, ruddy and smiling; they were craning their necks forward to get a good look at me. The bishop had a squarish face with prominent, glaucous gray eyes. His mouth was wide, his lips slightly down-turned. One pale hand hovered above his pectoral cross.

"Let us go to the library," he said, with soft, careful enunciation.

We walked in a sort of procession down the corridor. The bishop entered a spacious, book-lined room and, as I followed him, the door shut behind me. His two acolytes had vanished.

There was a bay window with high views over the islands, the polished oak bookshelves gleamed in the light of a coal-and-peat fire in the grate. We sat in armchairs on either side of the fire. The bishop crossed his legs and brought his hands together, fingertips touching.

"Now, what I am going to tell you," he commenced, "I have never told to any human being before, because I told the Holy Father that I would remain silent. If I am breaking silence now it is because it is the express wish of the Holy Father that I should do so. Nothing less would have induced me to speak."

His delivery was well-modulated, elaborate, as if savoring the consonants of his educated Irish brogue.

"But first let me explain to you how I came to be secretary to a second pope. After the election of Papa Luciani," he began, "I went back into the papal apartments to help clear out Paul VI's extensive library on the Tuesday morning two days after the Pope himself had moved in. As I started work I didn't know where Papa Luciani was, but I knew that apartment, every inch of it, because I had lived there for four years as Paul VI's secretary. After half an hour, at ten-thirty, a door opened at the end of the corridor and I guessed who it would be. I happened to be carrying a box of books in my hands. I saw the Pope coming toward me and I felt like a thief in the night being caught. I put down the box and went toward

him, and he moved toward me rather timidly, his zucchetto a little
to one side on his head. He came with hands extended, saying, 'I
know you. You're Father Magee. I've met you. What are you doing?'
I explained how I was taking out the books, and he said, 'Would
you do me a favor? I have a terrible headache. Would you ever go
to the kitchen and fetch me a cup of coffee?' And with that he
turned back to the large *salone* where he was working. I got the
valet to get the coffee, and I went on about my work. Paul VI had
never so much as asked me to fetch a glass of water."

Bishop Magee closed his eyes demurely. John Paul I, he was
giving me to understand, had made a faux pas. It was emphatically
not within the scope of a secretary to go fetching coffee, even for
a pope. Bishop Magee, I guessed, was a man acutely conscious of
fine degrees of protocol.

"Then next morning, on the Wednesday," he went on, "I was
back in the same study clearing books just as before. Again, at
exactly the same time, the door opened and he came up to me,
saying, 'Ah! You again. You are going to be scandalized. I need
another cup of coffee.' I was about to go to execute this second
errand when he took me by the arm and steered me into a side room
and said, 'Now, what do you intend doing now that Paul VI is dead?'

"I began to tell him that I was going to present myself to the
Secretariat of State and ask Cardinal Giuseppe Caprio what I should
do, when he stopped me and said, 'Look, I know nothing about the
Secretariat of State, but you know it all. Wouldn't you like to come
and help me? It would be very useful for me to have you to help
me.' I said, 'Holy Father, anything you want.' Then he was no
longer timid. He became very definite, and he said, 'Right! You go
to the Secretariat of State and *tell* them that I have today nominated
you my secretary.' He became very full of himself. Then he said,
'But before you go, get me that coffee.'

"Now in all those thirty-three days of his Papacy, I did not go out
of the papal apartment once. I became extraordinarily close to John
Paul I because very early, at the very beginning, he asked me to
share with him in everything. I shared his whole life throughout the
day, from the time he rose until the time he went to bed.

"He was usually in bed by quarter to nine or nine o'clock, because he would rise very early in the morning to pray. He would rise at four-thirty and be in the chapel by five-thirty, when I would join him. Paul VI had a different routine. He used to go to bed at two o'clock. I used to work with him on Secretariat papers from nine o'clock to midnight, and I would go to bed. Then the other secretary, Monsignor Macchi, would continue working with him until two o'clock in the morning. He was reading, going through reports, writing; he was such a worker it was incredible. There were times, even so, when Paul VI rose before five o'clock. He would tell me that he had very little need of sleep.

"Now, when Papa Luciani rose at four-thirty, he would go to the bathroom, and while he bathed and shaved he would play a tape recorder, doing a Linguaphone course in English.

"I would arrive in the chapel at five-thirty and we would begin with readings of the Divine Office and morning prayer; then he would follow that up with a reading from the *Imitation of Christ*, which he kept in his prie-dieu in the chapel, and he would select a little passage and comment on it and meditate on it. So we would be praying in the chapel just together. The other secretary, Don Diego Lorenzi, was never there; he got up later and joined us to concelebrate Mass at seven o'clock. After Mass we would have breakfast together. That was the regular procedure every morning.

"The morning would be taken up with paperwork and private audiences, then we would have lunch at twelve-thirty. After that he would take a short sleep and go up to the rooftop garden. We never went out to the Vatican Gardens as such except on a few occasions at the beginning, because it meant he would be followed by the security people, and he didn't feel free. And Cardinal Villot would come into the gardens to meet him, and oftentimes he would start talking about various problems. So he stopped going out so as to avoid Villot.

"He would walk around and around the roof garden for about two hours, because he thought the exercise helped his ankles. One day he showed them to me. They were terribly swollen and his own doctor in the Veneto, Dr. Da Ros, had advised him to walk a lot. Sometimes he would take some files that Villot had brought so that he could study them.

"I myself would take him up to the garden, and I would say, 'I'll be back here in two hours.' He only wanted me to accompany him as far as the garden and then to leave him alone.

"Don Diego Lorenzi was very often out at that time. He often went to visit members of his community in the Vatican—the Don Orione brothers ran the telephone and the telegraphic system in the Vatican—and he would go and spend time with them relaxing in the afternoon and evening because he was lost in the Vatican and he didn't know people. So I was on duty virtually nonstop. I tell you this because Don Diego did not fully comprehend that there must be a secretary on duty at all times. His frequent absences meant that I must remain in the apartment. I tried to apprise him of this, to no avail."

The bishop was immersed in his story, gazing into the fire, as if listening to the sound of his own melodic voice. There was something fastidious, overscrupulous, spinsterish, about his delivery. He was curiously self-controlled in his diction, and yet occasionally he seemed to catch his breath, as with emotion, and I fancied I noticed tears welling in his great, protruding, glassy eyes.

"Now, just to show you how preoccupied Papa Luciani was," he went on in hushed and confidential tones, "I will share with you something that has never been told before. One day I was in the secretaries' room and I got a phone call from one of the Vatican police down in the Cortile di Sisto Quinto, where the entrance to the Vatican Bank is. He said, 'Father, there's something strange happening. There are sheets of paper falling from the sky, and they're not in Italian. I've been collecting them all up.'

"I told the man to hold on to them and that I would be down. And I thought immediately that something had happened to the Pope, who was up on the roof. There was a lot of wind that day. So I shot up in the elevator, out onto the roof garden, which was a walk around a series of arches. I could see the Pope's head protruding through an arch and peering down to the basement below, where this policeman was. There were scores of sheets spread all over the three descending rooftops and in the gutters. As I approached I heard him moaning, *'O Dio mio! Dio mio! Cos'ho fatto.'*

"I went alongside and said, 'Holy Father, what is the matter?' He was distraught and crying, 'Oh, look what I've done! It's a confidential document and Cardinal Villot will be coming to see me

about it. What shall I do? Can't you do something?' He said, 'I
wanted to sneeze, and I fetched into my pocket for my handkerchief
and a gust of wind came and blew the papers away. . . .' You see,
he was a very simple, beautiful man. I said, 'The first thing is to
take the papers that are left. Give them to me. I will hold on to
them. And come with me now, back down.' I brought him to his
bedroom, and I said, 'Holy Father, I recommend that you lie down
on your bed.' And he did exactly as I told him to do. I now went
off and I called the *pompieri*, the Vatican fire brigade, and told
them the problem. They came flying up within two minutes with
ropes and ladders. At extraordinary risk to their lives they clambered
all over the roofs and they retrieved every paper. And so it was that
I was able to reconstitute the document again. Every sheet was
found and put in its correct order and I then presented myself again
to the Holy Father. As I entered the bedroom there he was lying
curled up on his bed, his hands covering his head and holding
between his fingers his rosary beads, praying and praying and praying. When he saw me, he cried out, 'Oh, you are wonderful! How
could I do without you!' I share this with you to illustrate the fact
that he was a man who worried about small, little things."

He let this sink in for a few moments. I was noticing that he
rarely looked at me directly. He frequently looked down demurely
into his lap or at his soft-looking hands, and looked up to gaze into
the dancing flames of the fire.

The story had astounded me, particularly the image of the frightened little Pope lying in a fetal position having been sent to bed
by Magee.

"Every day through those thirty-three days," he went on, "he
walked on that roof for two hours. He would come back down again
and we would work together. We would sit together at his desk and
I would pass him document after document, letter after letter, everything that came up from the Secretariat of State, and he allowed
me to guide him through this great burden. I organized things so
that after supper in the evening he did not have to think about work.
He would read and then go to bed."

He paused for some moments, looking into the fire, breathing
deeply, as if considering some deeper confidence. Then he began:
"One morning the Holy Father said to me, 'Now, John, would you

do me a favor? I want you to celebrate Mass and I want you to allow me to be your *chierichetto*.' Which means little altar server—the little boy who serves the Mass. So I celebrated Mass at the altar, him kneeling there below me. He followed the Mass in a little missal, and did the action as any little altar boy, offering the wine and water, washing my hands, and knelt down at the end of the Mass to receive my blessing."

His voice fell to a hushed, reverential whisper. "I felt most embarrassed. Later he said, 'Thank you. You'll do it again another time for me. I'll tell you when I want it.' I did it for him in all three times. Now I've never published that. I tell you just to show you the relationship I had with him. The last time I did it was on the Tuesday morning in the week before he died. And on that morning at the end of Mass he said to me, 'Thank you very much. You know when I serve your Mass I know I am serving the person of Christ.' Now, for a pope to say that to an ordinary simple priest was . . . *tremendous*."

The bishop was overcome with emotion. He sat for some time swallowing hard, blinking away tears.

How many popes, I wondered, had behaved like this in recent history? And what did it mean? There seemed to me to be a link between the Pope humbling himself as an acolyte to his secretary and the incident of the fallen documents. It was as if John Paul had sought abasement, humiliation.

At last he continued. "The day he died was a cold day—Thursday, September twenty-eighth. There was a very cold, strong wind, the first cold wind of the autumn. After lunch he took his siesta, and I warned him against going up on the roof garden. He said, 'I won't go up because in fact I'm not feeling too good. I just don't feel myself.' I said to him that I would like to call Dr. Buzzonetti, and he said, 'Oh no, no, no. No need to call the doctor. I'll walk in the house.'

"It is important that you know that Dr. Buzzonetti had been chosen as Papa Luciani's personal doctor, not Professor Fontana—who had been considered too old. Buzzonetti had met his Veneto doctor, Da Ros, on the previous Sunday, and it was agreed that his case notes would be sent to the Vatican. Dr. Buzzonetti, I have to say, regrets that this was never done.

"So on that Thursday he began to walk in the *salone* next to the secretaries' room. I could hear him walking round and round and round. Even though he had shown me his ankles I knew that it was a blood-circulation problem: if he kept walking he would be all right. During this time I got a phone call from Cardinal Villot, who wasn't scheduled to come. You must remember that Villot, like anybody else, could only come in if invited. And the door had to be opened by me from the inside. Anybody who talks about Swiss Guards being inside knows nothing about the papal apartment. The only people who are inside are the priest secretaries, the valets, the kitchen staff and the sisters.

"Now, here I would wish to make a little diversion to tell you about the valets who worked for Papa Luciani. When Paul VI died, his valet left the apartment and he was replaced by two Vatican workers who had come from the Veneto region: Paolo and Guido Gusso. It was customary for the Pope to have people around him from his home region.

"These two men behaved in my view most inappropriately. They took over the papal household in an unprecedented way. From the day that I returned to serve the Pope, I was amazed to find that these two men were introducing photographers and various people into the private apartment without any reference to me or to the Pope. They would come in and photograph the Pope's private study, photograph the bedroom. They were everywhere and running everything; they were in the chapel, serving at table . . . They completely took over. The Pope did not feel free. It was a total break with previous popes. Under Paul VI it would have been unthinkable. The valets should be discreet, and nobody was ever allowed in at any time to disturb the Pope's privacy. The Pope and I talked about it and he said, 'I am now in their hands, what do I do?'

"In consequence I arranged that another, more discreet man from the Veneto should be hired, and I planned to dismiss the Gusso brothers. The day before this was done, toward the end of supper, the Pope said to me in the hearing of Don Diego, 'Tomorrow morning our friend is coming at ten o'clock. I want to meet him so that he can get to know the apartment.' Now Don Diego picked it up wrongly, because he thought that the Pope was going to replace *him* with Monsignor Senigaglia, his former secretary, something that had been in the wind. Diego was looking furious. As we left the dining room, the Pope said to me, 'I take it that you will deal with those Gusso brothers and make sure they don't return here.'

"The Pope went into his room and Diego and I went into the secretariat. As soon as we were out of the earshot of the Pope, Diego said to me abruptly, 'What's all this? Who's coming tomorrow? What are you doing behind my back?' I now informed Don Diego of the Holy Father's wishes and told him that he wanted the Gussos out, although I realized that Don Diego was very close to them, and indeed it was through him that they had originally come into the apartment.

"So I said, 'We'd better call Paolo, who is on duty, and tell him right away.' Paolo was called from the kitchen, and we ushered him into a sitting room. I went ahead of Don Diego, and just before he was about to follow me, he said abruptly, 'Talk to him yourself.' He disappeared. So I knew that he was having problems. But the Pope asked me to do it and I had no fear. I told Paolo Gusso that he and his brother must now return to their former jobs in the Vatican, and I asked him for the keys to the private elevator. Paolo received that very badly. He took those keys out of his pocket and held them up. As I went to retrieve them he dropped them on the floor at my feet, turned on his heel and walked out. I felt it very much, but didn't say anything. When I returned to the secretaries' office Don Diego had gone. I never saw him again that day; he went off with his *confratelli*. I have told you this because the activities of these brothers are very pertinent to the rest of the story and things that happened after the Pope's death. I should also tell you that the other brother retained separate keys into the apartment and it took some days and much persistence from me to have them returned."

There was a pause in his story as the housemaid appeared with a tray of coffee and four large slices of iced fruitcake. I declined the cake, and so did the bishop, although his large eyes dwelt on the plate a moment or two. She stayed to put coal on the fire, and I noticed that he was a little pained at the noise she was making with the scuttle.

He sipped at his coffee, then placed it delicately on a low table at his side. He waited for the woman to leave the room before recommencing his story.

The tale of the Gussos had affected me considerably. The Pope's household had evidently been in considerable disarray. Reading between the lines I guessed that the relationships between Magee and Lorenzi, Magee and the Gussos, had been deplorable. And in the midst of the domestic upset was a pope already crushed by the burdens of office.

Magee continued. "So that afternoon on the eve of his death he was walking in the *salone* and there was a telephone call from Cardinal Villot, who wanted to come that evening. I went in to the Pope. He was making a circuit of the room, saying his rosary, and I informed him.

" 'Oh! Cardinal Villot again!' he said. 'But I've no document to read.' You see, he thought that Villot was always chasing him for things he should have read, and he was really perturbed. So it was arranged that Villot should come at six-thirty. And he continued his walking. After a little I heard him from where I was in the secretaries' room making a sort of harsh coughing noise. I rushed into the *salone* and I found him standing near the table. He said, 'I have a pain! Send Sister Vincenza to me. She knows what to do.' I asked him, wouldn't it be better if I called the doctor. But he was insistent that I shouldn't call him. I pressed him on this very strongly. I said, 'Holy Father, it might be something serious.' But he was adamant. I should remark that Don Diego was not there at all during all this. The Pope went to his room and I went to the kitchen and to Sister Vincenza, and she said, 'Oh yes, this has happened before.' She took some medicine and went off to see the Pope. For her this was quite normal, although it wouldn't have been for any other nun. She had been infirmarian in Venice and evidently had this rapport with him. All this was at about five-thirty. An hour later Cardinal Villot came and I accompanied him to the Holy Father, who was now in his private study.

"The cardinal stayed until twenty-five minutes to eight, and by this time Diego had returned from wherever he was, about halfway through their meeting, and I remember him saying, 'Villot again!'

"Cardinal Villot was the kind of man who was strong in his approach to the Pope, and dominant. It was not possible for either of us on the other side of the door to know what was the subject matter that was being discussed between them. However, when the cardinal came out, I then accompanied him to the door and the Holy Father went to the toilet. When he returned we were ready to go to supper. In the meantime I had told Don Diego about the pain, and he, too, wanted to call the doctor. I said to the Pope, 'How are you?'

" 'Sto bene! Sto bene! Eccomi!' he cried, pummeling his chest. 'Andiamo! Those tablets of Sister Vincenza are miraculous. Let's go to supper!'

"I want you to know that my relationship with Paul VI was very much father and son. My relationship with Papa Luciani was more brother–brother.

"During supper he ate well and he was in good form. I used to ask him certain questions, because he was always anxious lest he forget certain things he had to do. I asked him, 'Holy Father, have you chosen the person to give the Vatican retreat next Lent?'

"He said, 'Yes, I have.' Then he immediately said, 'The type of retreat I would like at this moment would be for a good death.'

"He was constantly talking of death, constantly reminding us that his Pontificate was to be of short duration. Constantly saying that he was to go so that he would be replaced by 'the Foreigner.' All of this was a great enigma to us then. I said to him, 'Oh, Holy Father, not again! Coming again to that morbid subject! You're only beginning your Pontificate.' Now Don Diego, who was at the end of the table, said, 'That reminds me of a prayer we Italians have all learned, which we say when we go to bed at night. It was composed by Saint Alfonso Liguori and it goes something like this: *O Lord, grant me the grace to accept the death which you will send me, and wherever it will come from.*'

"The Pope immediately intervened and said, 'That's not correct. It was not written by Saint Alfonso, and it goes like this: *Lord, grant me the grace to accept THE DEATH BY WHICH I SHALL BE STRUCK*

DOWN.' The Italian would be—*dammi la grazia di accettare la morte nel modo in cui mi colpira.*

"I said, 'My God! What kind of a subject are we talking about?' That was almost exactly to the second at about a quarter-past eight.

"I must here make another small diversion in my story. I have told you that I never left the apartment in the whole thirty-three days, but in fact I did go out on that very day, when he was walking around and around the *salone,* on the eve of his death. I told him I was going out because I needed to have my books fetched from the house of the missionary society where I had lived during the conclave. Between two-thirty and four-thirty I had the opportunity because there was a van going from the Vatican. All my boxes were brought back and placed in my bedroom on the floor above the principal rooms of the private apartment. This will be relevant later in my story.

"Now, when supper was ended the Pope turned to Don Diego and said, 'Would you put a call through to Cardinal Colombo in Milan. I want to speak to him.'

"Don Diego went and I was left alone with Papa Luciani at the dining table. He turned to me and said, 'We have a problem that Cardinal Villot brought up this evening as to whom we should appoint as the new patriarch of Venice.' That was the subject of the meeting of Cardinal Villot and the Pope. He wanted to consult Cardinal Colombo of Milan. Then he said, 'Let's go!'

"I asked him how he was feeling and he told me that he felt fine. We got up and he said grace, then he went, as always, into the kitchen after the meal to greet the sisters. And he said, as ever, '*Buona notte! A domani, se Dio vuole!*'—Good night! Until tomorrow, if God is willing! That was his common expression. As we came out into the corridor, Don Diego called from the far end, 'Cardinal Colombo on the line.'

"The Pope then took off down the corridor at such a speed I was worried he would slip and fall on the marble floor. I couldn't believe the speed he went down there. He went straight in and took the call, which lasted about fifteen to twenty minutes.

"After this I went with the Pope to say compline. And as I said good night to him in his study, he bent down and took one of those homilies that I mentioned to you, which were in a box near his bedroom door. This was at about nine-twenty P.M.

"I followed the Pope into his bedroom because I wanted to bring to his attention the presence of the two alarm buttons on either side of his bed which had been fixed up only that morning. You may consider that to be a remarkable coincidence. But it is the truth. These alarms had been there in the day of John XXIII, but had been out of use because Paul VI opted to sleep in a little truckle bed near the bathroom. And he had divided the bedroom in two with a curtain.

"Now these bells, if the buttons were pressed, would wake God Almighty! They worked perfectly well, because we had tested them that morning while he was having a private audience on the floor below. When I said good night to him that evening, I said, 'Holy Father, if you should ever need us in the night, there are these two buttons.' And he said, 'All right. Now, *buona notte. A domani, se Dio vuole.*' And he had in his hand one of those homilies we spoke of.

"The night the Pope died, Don Diego was out, and he came in very late, long after I had gone to bed. Before I went to bed I went to see the sisters in the kitchen. I haven't ever said this to any living soul except the Holy Father, but you must now get all the facts. They asked me how the Pope was, and I said I was worried about the pain he'd had. Sister Vincenza said, 'No, no, don't worry!'

"I was most concerned as to whether he would push those buttons if he was in difficulty and we talked about that. Then I said a most extraordinary thing in the light of the subsequent events." The bishop put his hand on his heart and blinked. His eyes were brimming.

"Now. Believe it or not, this is the gospel truth! I said to Sister Vincenza, 'It would be terrible to lose a pope now after losing Paul VI. How many days is it now? Thirty-three?'

"Believe it or not, as sure as I'm sitting here now, there was in the apartment a copy of the *Annuario Pontificio*. It gives you a list of all the popes and the periods of their papacies. And I said to the sisters, 'I wonder how many popes lived less than thirty-three days.' And we sat down there in the kitchen and we went right through the list of the popes that very night. I can't remember how many there were. There weren't many.

"At ten o'clock I left the sisters. I had been preoccupied about the bell. You see, I had been used to Pope Paul, who had frequently used the bell at night if he didn't feel well. He rang the bell at Castel Gandolfo the night before he died. He had been practically dead and I spent the whole night with him.

"I went upstairs to my room. With all that had gone on I had forgotten about my books. There were all those boxes on the floor. In the first one I came across, there were two magazines that had been published on the death of Paul. I had now the opportunity, and the desire, to look at these things. I sat down on the floor and read them. I could see my own photograph in a number of them; in particular there was a beautiful photograph of the funeral. I was looking at that, flicking through, and I never noticed the time going; then I saw it was eleven-five. So I got ready for bed, because I had to be up at five in the morning.

"So it was that I went to bed not knowing that, according to the report on the next day, he was already dead."

32

The cathedral bells rang the quarters to the tune of a popular Catholic hymn entitled "Jesus, My Lord, My God, My All." With each quarter a bar of the melody was added until the whole tune was complete.

At one o'clock, as the belfry rang a resounding and complicated peal, the door of the library was thrown open and the housemaid entered with a tray for lunch. A circular table was laid up in the bay window and we sat down to oxtail soup, Irish stew, and semolina and apple pudding.

"Oh, Eileen," the bishop said with a sigh. Then turning to me, "Ah, the things the good woman provides. . . ."

The bishop produced a bottle of claret half-full and stoppered. "I never drink," he said, "unless I have a guest taking a drop." The bottle hovered above my glass.

"I'd like that very much," I said.

"Indeed," he murmured, "indeed. . . ."

The bishop held up the chilly wine to the light, the glass opaque with condensation.

I was somewhat preoccupied, looking out over the great panorama of the islands and the sea. I was thinking about Don Diego and the undercurrent of animosity that clearly existed between him and Magee. It had shocked me that the bishop had confirmed Father Farusi's contention that Don Diego had been out on the night of the Pope's death. Why had Don Diego not told me this? I wondered. Why had he made such an elaborate apologia about telling the truth, when all the time he was conscious of a major omission? Had there been other economies of the truth? I wondered.

With the soup in the bowl in front of him, the bishop now launched once more into his story.

"I am going to share with you something that I have never told publicly before. The whole question of how he was found. There has been a lot of controversy over that. I will tell you all the facts, because it was stated in the official bulletin from the Vatican that *I* found the Pope. I slept well that night, without any preoccupation whatsoever. I was awakened by my alarm at five A.M., but unfortunately I fell off to sleep again, to be awakened at five twenty-five by the sisters who came to my room—the sister superior and another. They were very agitated. They said, 'The Pope has not appeared.' Every morning they would leave him coffee at about five-twenty. That would have been left in the sacristy or just outside the door of his bedroom, I'm not sure which. As far as I remember they told me that Sister Vincenza had gone in and found the Pope in bed. They told me: 'She thinks he's dead.' I got up, threw on my soutane over my pajamas and rushed downstairs. The door was closed, everything was in darkness. Normally every morning when I went down, the lights were on and the Pope was in the chapel. I knocked at the door in the corridor. No word. I opened the first door, for it is a double-door system, then the second, knocking and calling as I went. I called the Pope from the curtain that divided the room. The main light in the room was not on, but there was a reading light over the bedhead still on.

"I pulled back the curtain, which was evidently what Sister Vincenza had done, and there he was, propped up with pillows, and his papers were still erect in his hands, his face turned to the right, with his spectacles on. And he looked, as it stated in the bulletin, like one intent on reading.

"I called him again. And I was convinced that he was asleep. I went over, touched his hands and found him absolutely cold and stiff. The sisters were behind me, all four of them, including Sister Vincenza. Don Diego was still in bed.

"I fell on my knees. I buried my head in the quilt. It was very soft. I shouted into it, my voice muffled, 'Oh God! No! Why? Why? Why?' And it suddenly came across to me what to do. I was the only one in the world, apart from the sisters, who knew that the Pope was dead. I remained for a moment, then I stood up and looked at him. He was smiling, that smile I had become so used to. I really loved that man. I turned round and the sisters were distraught. I said, 'Yes, sisters, he's dead. Now one of you go and call Don Diego. The others remain here and pray.'

"I now knew what I had to do. I had to call the camerlengo— that is, he who executes the obsequies of the dead Pope, and this was Villot himself. He it was who served as camerlengo for Paul VI.

"Now. The timing of all this. I would say I found the Pope dead at five thirty-two. Certainly at five thirty-seven I was sitting at my desk in the office just two doors away. I phoned the private apartment of Cardinal Villot. I knew that he also had heart problems and I was wondering how I would break the news to him. In the meantime I could hear the sisters praying out loud by the bedside. I could also hear the voice of Don Diego.

"The phone was a long time ringing and eventually Villot's secretary answered. Then, as I was waiting to be put through, all the worries came upon me and my feeling of guilt that I hadn't called the doctor the day before. Eventually, when the cardinal answered, I found him extraordinarily affable for that hour of the morning, so much so that he took my breath away and it was quite a time before I could come to the point. 'The Holy Father is DEAD.'

" 'No, no, no, no . . . he *couldn't* be dead. I was with him last night.'

"I said to him, 'Listen, he's stone-cold DEAD.'

" 'I'm coming,' he said, 'but I can't believe you.'

"As soon as I put down the phone I rang Buzzonetti, who lives in Piazza Adriana. He was so tired that he didn't even seem to grasp what had been said. He told me later that he got into his car and halfway to the Vatican he nearly turned back because he thought

that he had been dreaming. The next thing was that I knew I had
to face Don Diego. Personally, I liked Don Diego. He was a very
nice man and we had become very close in those days. I shared
with him many things and he knew all about my own life. I went
back into the bedroom and Don Diego was at the bottom of the bed
leading the Rosary. I moved on and went out and down in the lift
to the Cortile below and, just as I went out there, next to the door
of Archbishop Marcinkus, Dr. Buzzonetti arrived.

"We came up together in the lift, and as we arrived in the
apartment the door on the tertia loggia rang and it was Cardinal
Villot. As he came in he was very agitated. He said to me, 'You're
mad!' We went straight in the bedroom. It was at this time that I
actually witnessed what the Pope was holding in his hands. It was
indeed the homily, as I have told you. Now that is the gospel truth,
for I saw it with my own eyes.

"Don Diego stayed with Dr. Buzzonetti. Cardinal Villot said to
me, 'We must go to prepare a statement.' And we went into my
office and I gave him a piece of paper and he wrote out the bulletin.
Now in fact he was putting in my name, but it wasn't published
immediately. Then later it was asked—why not?—and it was put
in. I asked Cardinal Villot, 'Please do not put my name in.'

"He said, 'The question will be asked, "Who found him?" I can't
put that the sister found him dead. In any case, de facto, you came
down, went in and found him *dead?* No?'

"I looked at the bishop quizzically. De facto—the Roman Catholic Church had lost none of its penchant for Scholastic hairsplitting. I could see the old cardinal scheming over the various
implications of the word 'found.' "

The bishop returned my look. I was convinced that he knew what
was running through my mind.

"I said to him," the bishop continued, "that it was the sisters
who came up and told me, and that they had already found him.
But there it was . . . in effect. . . ." His voice trailed away with a
trace of embarrassment.

"Now. Don Diego, with all due respects, he held the view and
spread the word amongst his community, and he told some journalists, that I was nowhere to be seen. He said that the sisters

called him first. I've explained how this happened. He didn't have
to pass by the secretariat and so he would have been unaware of
my activities that morning.

"We then called Vatican Radio for their first news bulletin, which
goes out at seven or seven-thirty. It was later in the day that I found
that somebody from the radio had put in the idea that he was reading
the *Imitation of Christ*. This was to have extraordinary repercussions
because holy women and holy nuns all over the world were calling
in to ask us what page was open. I suppose it was an understandable
thing for anybody to say, because Thomas à Kempis was one of his
favorite writers. And I suppose it was to avoid anyone saying he
was reading a pornographic magazine . . . or, you never know what
they'll say, a cowboy story. . . . Put something into his hands,
something reasonable! In any case, the *Imitation of Christ* was in
the chapel, not by his bedside."

I interrupted. "Monsignor," I said, "I've got a problem about this
Imitation of Christ story. It's just a small thing, but it's been dogging
every account of the death right from the beginning. Don Diego
tells me that there was not a copy in the whole apartment and that
he had to go out to borrow one several days before the Pope died.
And yet you maintain there was one in the household chapel."

The bishop had a pained expression. He looked baffled for a
moment.

"I never knew about that, now," he said. "It's possible, at the
beginning, before the books arrived . . . It might have been missing . . ."

"Don Diego is adamant that there was no copy during the week
that the Pope died," I said.

"The Pope certainly had one in his prie-dieu in the chapel,"
insisted the bishop. Then he said, with some feeling, "Don Diego
was never there, so how should he know? He never asked *me* about
the book, because I would have told him where it was."

He sat for a while thinking. And during this pause I was also
considering the discrepancy between the secretaries' stories over
the writing of the bulletin. Ten years had passed, and it would have
been remarkable if both men's accounts had coincided exactly. And
yet, they were both so clear about details: Don Diego insisting that
Buzzonetti held the pen, and had even scored out Sister Vincenza's

name; Bishop Magee insisting that it was Villot alone, and that there had been an exchange of quibbles.

As if reading my thoughts, he said, "You know, I never got together with Don Diego really to reconcile our accounts."

"There was just one thing Don Diego wanted me to corroborate with you," I replied. "It was about the pain on the evening of his death. He said that some months later he telephoned you . . ."

The bishop broke in: "Did he ever bring up the subject of the Gusso brothers?"

"No," I said, somewhat taken aback at the vehemence of his interruption.

He was breathing deeply now with emotion, swallowing hard.

"The only one I've ever talked to about this was the present Holy Father," he said in reverential tones. "After the Pope had died I was required to move out of the Vatican and into the Maria Bambina Institute next to Saint Peter's Square. On the day after the funeral I developed a terrible pain in my heart, and I met Dr. Buzzonetti. He said I was suffering from stress and I must lie down. The next thing was that a telephone call came through to me in my bedroom and it was a man from a news agency, and he said, 'There is a story going around that the Pope was assassinated and that you are put at the center of the plot. Would you like to comment on that?' I slammed the phone down on him.

"Later, I was crossing the courtyard of the convent and I saw a crowd of people, including schoolgirls, at the gateway. As I passed them they all stared at me because the person they were listening to was pointing directly at me. And this person was none other than Paolo Gusso, the man who dropped the keys at my feet.

"I thought no more of it until the mother general of the order, who lived there, came up to my room and said, 'I'm very upset. One of my sisters was standing with a group at the entrance this morning, and they were all listening to a gentleman from the Vatican who was giving an account of John Paul's death, and you happened to pass by, and he turned and pointed his finger and said: "ECCO L'ASSASSINO!" There goes the murderer!' I told the nun not to worry, but I was torn to pieces inside.

"Now I am convinced that he must have been one of the sources of what has been said in this regard. You see, he never spoke to me all that time after I had put him out of the apartment. He ignored me, although I met him many times. He cut me dead, and I felt it, too. But he continued to be a very close friend of Don Diego's.

"Straight after this another nun turned up and said that there were journalists outside waiting to interview me. Then she showed me a newspaper in which there was a headline saying, DOUBTS ABOUT THE NATURAL DEATH OF JOHN PAUL, and my name and my photograph were in the middle of it. Through the window I could see the journalists and the TV cameras all collecting at the gate. I was completely torn apart.

"I managed to find a back entrance to the convent; I crossed Saint Peter's Square and went up to the Secretariat of State to see Cardinal Caprio, and he listened to my story. I was emotionally distraught and weeping. I told him that I was publicly accused and pointed out as the assassin, and I told him about Paolo Gusso.

"I said, 'How can I live here with all this speculation going on?' He said that my best plan was to get out of Italy altogether. He told me that he thought the rumors would continue until the next conclave began. I got the distinct impression that he was telling me I was an embarrassment to the Vatican. They wanted me out of the way.

"Buzzonetti took a different line. He said, 'Father Magee has been defamed in front of witnesses. We should let the law take care of it.' But I wasn't getting Caprio's support at all. He couldn't have cared less about my personal predicament. He just wanted me away from Rome. So I came out of the office and I was at my wit's end. I had lost two popes within two months, all that strain. I had no home, no job. I couldn't stay in Rome, and yet I didn't know how to begin to get away. It seemed that I hadn't a friend or ally in the whole of the Vatican." Tears were welling in the bishop's eyes, and he sat forward, his arms folded in front of him, rocking slightly as he recollected the episode.

"Then," he went on, "I remembered what people had often said. That the only man you could turn to in any kind of trouble in that entire place was Archbishop Marcinkus. In any kind of difficulty he was the one man with a human heart, who would help you. I went over to his office, and as I went in there he called out, 'John!' and he came over, hugged me in his arms and I burst out crying.

'Tell me, what can I do for you,' he said. 'You've had a hell of a time.'

"I said, 'Believe it or not, I'm now accused of having killed him.' I told him about the press and that I needed to get away, that I wanted to get to England to stay with my sister Kathleen, who lives outside Liverpool—she's a nurse.

"He said to me, 'Just you sit down there and take it easy.' Within twenty minutes he had an air ticket. He sent somebody over to collect my things. He summoned a car, and I was off to the airport. Nobody knew, and I got on a flight to London, and from London to Manchester. I was absolutely exhausted. My sister put me to bed and knocked me out with some tablets.

"The next morning she brought in the papers—and there it said, in the *Liverpool Echo,* that I had 'fled' from Italy the day before, and that all ports were on the lookout for me. It even said that Interpol was looking for me. I stayed there in hiding for ten days— the whole thing was so traumatic—until the next conclave began.

"I returned to Rome after midnight on a Saturday night. On the Tuesday morning I was watching the new Pope's first Mass on television with all the sisters. Afterward I went up to my room and the phone rang. It was Cardinal Caprio. He said, 'The Pope wants to see you. The Pope has asked for *you.*' Apparently as the Pope left the conclave and went to break the seals of the papal apartment to enter for the first time . . . They told me afterward, at the door he turned to Cardinal Caprio and said, 'I want the Irishman. Send for the Irishman.'

"So I went back to the Vatican. I still had the keys to the papal apartment. I went up in the lift and could let myself in. I went through to the secretaries' room . . . and that's where I found him, Pope John Paul II. He was sitting at *my* desk. His zucchetto was just thrown to one side, his cassock was all unbuttoned down his chest, no collar, and he was sitting sideways on the desk, writing, not as Pope Paul VI did, upright and elegant, but slouched, his hand on his head, like a man more used to physical action than to scholarship. I knocked, and as he turned it was the physical posture of a man of the world—it was unpopish. This was a very human, down-to-earth man. He jumped up and came over. He wouldn't let me kiss his ring. He caught hold of me, put his arms around me. 'Welcome home,' he said. 'Now you stay with me.' He didn't ask me whether I wanted to or not. He just said, 'Now you stay with me!'

"That night at supper he explained to me that he wanted me to help them to get started and to train his Polish secretary Father Stanislav. He said, 'I won't keep you always here. Eventually I'll put you out.' "

The bishop was looking at his watch and his eye had roved to the desk where there was a pile of correspondence. "Let me take you to the airport," he said. "I'd like to do that for you."

As the bishop drove at breakneck speed to the airport, I asked him: "Do you recollect John Paul I ever talking about Vatican finance? Was he preoccupied with such matters?"

He thought for a few moments. "You know, his one big financial headache was the problem of his Italian state pension. You see, he had been entitled to this like every other Italian citizen when he was patriarch of Venice, and he used to give it to a little community of nuns. Anyway, he kept bringing this up at meal times: 'Do you think they'll go on paying my pension?' he would say. In the end I said to him, 'Holy Father, you're a head of state of a foreign country; you won't get an Italian pension.' I must say, I also felt like telling him he had all the money in the world if he was worried about the little convent there."

"Do you reckon he appreciated the problems of the IOR, the Vatican Bank, or Vatican finances in general?"

"Not at all!" said Bishop Magee. "Not at all."

"He sounds a nervous man . . ." I said.

"He was, he was," said the bishop. "I'll never forget the day we were expecting Dr. Da Ros in from Venice. I'd left word at the Porta Sant'Anna that this man was coming through the gate in the afternoon, and I described him as a big fellow with a beard and glasses. Well, it just shows you how coincidences happen. It so happened that a madman turned up at the gate answering exactly to Dr. Da Ros's appearance. He had come along and said, 'I've come to see the Pope!' He was swept straight through, past one set of guards after another, and finally admitted to the lift which comes straight up into the papal apartment.

"As it happened, I was just accompanying the Pope to the roof garden and we were waiting outside the lift door, and we noticed that the lift was on its way up. As the door opened this fellow came bursting out, fell at the Pope's feet and started kissing his toes. The Pope screamed out! 'Get him off! Get him out of here!' "

The bishop laughed softly to himself at the memory.

Before I left him at the airport, I asked him, "Do you have one memory of John Paul that stands out?"

Almost without hesitation he said, "You know, he repeated over and over again, 'Why did they choose *me*? Why on earth did they choose *me*?' He said it every mealtime, repeatedly, every single day of his Papacy. He spoke repeatedly of the 'Foreigner' who was going to follow him. 'I am going soon,' he would say, 'and the Foreigner is coming.' One day I asked him who this Foreigner was, and he replied, 'He it was who sat opposite me during the conclave.' Now, after I had left the papal apartment as secretary to John Paul II, I was appointed master of ceremonies in the Vatican, and I had access to the plan of that conclave for the first time. The cardinal who sat opposite Papa Luciani was Cardinal Wojtyla!"

The bishop was silent for a while. Then he said, "I am convinced that John Paul I had a great insight into the fact of his imminent death."

Back in London I called Marjorie Weeke. Was there some way, I asked, for the Vatican to check whether either of the Gusso brothers had made accusations against John Magee?

She said that she would see what she could do.

33

On the way back to Rome I broke my journey at Zurich to meet Hans Roggen, former sergeant of the Swiss Guard, now a security official in a bank.

Roggen had been the source of the single most damning piece of circumstantial evidence against Marcinkus in David Yallop's *In God's Name*. The text reads:

> In the courtyard near the Vatican Bank Sergeant Roggan [*sic*] met Bishop Paul Marcinkus. It was 6:45 a.m. What the President of the Vatican Bank . . . not a renowned early riser, was doing in the Vatican so early remains a mystery . . . Roggan blurted out the news. 'The Pope is dead.' Marcinkus just stared . . .

Marcinkus, as Yallop points out, did not even lodge at the Vatican; his home at that time was at Villa Stritch—at least twenty minutes' distance from the Vatican by car.

In a later passage Yallop claims that in a personal interview with Roggen the sergeant admitted that he had been trying to get to sleep with little success while on duty the night the Pope died. "This is the officer in charge of Palace security on the night of Luciani's sudden death," comments Yallop, "tossing and turning in his bed as he tries to *sleep*."

What I found odd about Roggen's evidence was that while it might have appeared courageously honest in the case of Marcinkus, it was foolhardy in respect of his own conduct. Sergeant Roggen had condemned both Marcinkus and *himself* out of his own mouth. At all events his evidence had added essential ingredients to the dramatic atmosphere of conspiracy that pervades Yallop's description of the Vatican on the morning of the Pope's death. I was deeply intrigued at the prospect of meeting Roggen at last.

He came to my room in the Hotel Simplon off the Bahnhofstrasse at nine o'clock in the evening. He had come in out of the snow, the collar of his navy loden coat up, his round, fresh face ruddy with the cold. He was broad-shouldered, athletic and had a grip of iron. He looked pleasant and open-faced, but nervous. As he was taking off his coat he said in a heavy Swiss accent, "I've got some very important things to tell you."

He settled himself in the chair by the dressing table and I offered him a beer from the room's drinks' cabinet.

"What were the circumstances of the interview with you that appears in Yallop's book?" I asked him.

"I never met him," he said. "I spoke only with a man called Philip Willan, his researcher."

"I've talked to Marcinkus," I said. "He maintains that when he met you on the morning of the Pope's death he was getting out of his car after driving in from the Villa Stritch. Now, in Yallop's evidence there's no mention of a car, which would have explained a great many things. . . . Marcinkus is depicted as wandering guiltily and without explanation. Did you tell Willan that Marcinkus was still in his car?"

"I don't remember. But the truth is that Marcinkus had come into the Vatican by car, as he always did."

"So you can't be sure that you told Willan about the car?"

"No, I can't be sure," said Roggen despondently.

"Let's put it another way. Did Willan ask *you* what Marcinkus was doing? Or what the situation of the meeting was?"

"I don't remember."

"Did you tell Willan, as far as you can remember," I went on, "that this was Marcinkus's normal time of arrival?"

"I don't think I said anything about that. I know that Marcinkus is, in fact, an early riser. But I didn't tell Willan that."

"Do you remember the Signoracci brothers, the morticians, arriving in the Vatican that morning?" I asked.

"No. Definitely not."

"Were you awake all night? Did you have difficulties sleeping?"

"The night before, I went out with my mother visiting some priests and I had a good Italian dinner, and I had trouble falling asleep. We saw the Pope's light on at about ten-thirty P.M. to eleven P.M. It wasn't unusual. I used to live just below the Papal Palace in an attic on the top of the barracks and I could see up to the windows; the lights were always on until late. There was nothing unusual about that."

"There's mention in Yallop's book of emergency lights being on during the night. Did you tell Willan that?"

"I never told him that at all."

Roggen was sitting on the edge of his chair. I could see that he could scarcely contain himself; he was wringing his hands and screwing up his face. I realized that he wanted to unleash a storm of words. I said, "Those are the most important questions for me at the moment, Hans. But why don't you just tell me what's on your mind."

"My testimony has been made the basis of circumstantial evidence against Marcinkus!" His voice was high-pitched with emotion. "It's all rubbish. This is what happened: A man called Noel, who had been at the Beda College in Rome, called me and asked if I'd like to make an interview about the life, a biography, of John Paul I. I said we'd see what we can do. I didn't think anything wrong. Then this Mr. Willan came over and we talked.

"He said he was writing about Pope John Paul I. He was saying what a wonderful saintly man he was, and all that. Then he said, 'Oh, but everybody must have been heartbroken when they heard the news!' He wanted me to tell him how people reacted to the news. 'And how did *Marcinkus* react?' You see?

"Then I explained to him that I had been on special checking rota which means this: you go to bed as normal, because you are on day duty, you see; then, at an unspecified time each night, you get up and check on the guards who are on night duty. There are three of us do this during different segments of the night. It's a random check: the night guards never know when it's going to be. On that particular night I did my check at four in the morning. It's like a doctor on night call. What! Does he expect we never go to bed at all? Then he goes and puts in the book that I said I was asleep on duty!"

His voice was high and indignant. He stopped a moment, as if struggling to overcome his emotions.

"On the night the Pope died nothing happened. I checked all the night guards, and all the doors. Everything was normal. Then I went back to bed. There had already been other checks made earlier in the night by the other checking officers, as normal. My mother, who was staying with us, had to get up early to take a train back to Switzerland at about seven o'clock. I got up at five-thirty, quarter to six, I took Mother down to my car around six-thirty and drove her through the Sant'Anna Gate around six thirty-five. At the gate a guard stopped me and said that the Pope had died. I was flabbergasted. I drove my mother to the nearest taxi rank and went straight back to the Vatican: two minutes. I went to the barracks— I was just in jeans and sweater—I talked to somebody there. I went up to the tertia loggia, the main entrance to the Pope's apartment, around quarter to seven. Cardinal Villot was coming out of the door and his face was streaming with tears. He was completely broken down. He was *heartbroken*. Villot was a very dignified man, and on that morning it was obvious he was heartbroken. To depict him as a murderer is a wicked slander.

"Anyway, I made this all clear to Willan, and after a bit something about his questions seemed fishy. I stopped straightaway. Then he called me a day or two later and he asked for another interview, and he kept asking me questions about medicines and the Vatican Pharmacy. And I said to him, 'Please stop that. I know now what you are trying to do. And don't use what I told you when you came to see me.' "

"Let's go back to Marcinkus. You were telling me about how Willan broached the subject."

"He wanted to know how Marcinkus reacted when I told him

about the Pope's death. It was in the context of how different people reacted when they heard the news, not what they were doing on that morning. If he'd asked that I would have told him. But let me continue the story. After I'd seen Villot I went down to the Cortile di San Damaso. I was standing talking with a guard and saying how I never thought Papa Luciani looked healthy. Then Marcinkus drove in. He'd come from outside the Vatican as usual. I went over to his car and said, 'The Pope's dead. It's like a bad dream.' And Marcinkus said to me, 'You should never have bad dreams!' It was something like that. I genuinely think that when people received the news, they were still thinking of Paul VI, because he had died so recently. When they heard the words—'The Pope is dead!'— they were often baffled for a few moments, because the last thing they expected was that the Pope should die so soon. It was a shock for everybody.

"Look, I knew Marcinkus very well, I had good relations with him, he was a *good* fellow. . . ." Hans Roggen's voice grew perceptibly louder and broader. "I liked him very much. He was always very friendly to me and to the guards."

He stopped for a moment, his head bowed. He went on: "Willan asked me the question: 'How did Marcinkus look when you told him?' I told him honestly that Marcinkus looked surprised, you know—stunned. I said he didn't believe me, he was speechless . . . you know."

"So, let's just get this straight for the record. You can confirm that Marcinkus wasn't lurking suspiciously at what would have been an unusually early hour for him?"

"No! No!"

"So what was his usual pattern?"

"He was an early riser, always. I'll give you an example. I went on many of the trips abroad which were organized by Marcinkus. He was *always* the first to rise: four-thirty, five o'clock. He usually took a shower, said Mass, then started the day. He's a man who needs very little sleep. When we were abroad on trips he always spent much of the night outside the Pope's door, guarding him, checking that he was properly protected."

"What was his regular time for arriving in the Vatican during the days when he lived out at Villa Stritch?"

"Always regular—six-thirty, quarter to seven."

He stopped for a while to sip his beer. I got the impression that he was frustrated, with so much to say and yet not knowing how to say it.

"I'm so upset about all this," he went on. "Try to see my point of view. I became a Swiss Guard at the age of twenty in 1966, after doing my national service in Switzerland. We have had Swiss Guards in my family for more than two hundred years. We go right back to 1784 in our family. It's an honorable tradition, and I had a great loyalty and devotion to the Holy Father. This was my life, my career. Now how does this look? As if I betrayed innocent people. Why should I *do* such a thing? And I'm made to sound like the sort of guy who sleeps when he should be on duty. How does that seem, now?"

"Is it possible," I asked, "that Pope John Paul I could have raised the alarm that night and that it went unnoticed?"

"No! There was no alarm raised."

"Anybody coming and going to the apartment would have been seen?"

"There are guards on all the entrances to the apartment. Nobody came or went until Villot's arrival at six o'clock. The timing of Magee's call to Villot at six-forty A.M. is absolutely definite. We know this on excellent authority because the conversation between Magee and Villot on the phone was overheard on the Vatican switchboard."

"There are only two entrances to the papal apartments," I said: "The door on the tertia loggia and the service lift. If anybody had tried to gain entrance to that apartment, would it have been noted?"

"There's a third way, too: a staircase by the lift which is kept locked. But it's absurd to say that anybody could go in any of these ways without being seen. All entrances are covered day and night and you can only get in if the door is deliberately opened on the other side. Okay: if you had keys by some means or other you might gain entrance, but you would still be seen."

"It was said that you had a very restless night, as if you were filled with apprehension of some kind."

"That's rubbish! I said that I had this big meal and so my stomach was a bit uneasy. That's all."

"You'd had a lot to drink?"

"Absolutely not."

I helped Roggen on with his coat and accompanied him down to the street. I remembered the strange stories about John Paul I wandering like a child all over the Vatican City without proper security. There was even a story about him popping out of the main gate one morning and looking, smilingly as ever, into the streets of Rome.

"Was it true," I asked as we said our farewells, "that John Paul once went down to the Porta Sant'Anna and looked out into the street?"

"Believe me, the Swiss Guard would have known that. We're there day and night. It's nonsense."

I watched him walking off into the snow until he turned into the Bahnhofstrasse.

The one shred of "circumstantial evidence" against Marcinkus, I was convinced, now seemed very tenuous indeed.

Before leaving Zurich I called Marjorie Weeke.

"I've spoken to Guido Gusso," she said. "He's adamant he never spoke to anybody, and never accused Magee of anything. But what's more interesting is this: apparently Don Diego spent the evening in Guido Gusso's apartment on the night the Pope died and, according to Gusso himself, he stayed until about midnight."

34

J took a train from Zurich to Milan and made a second journey out to Piazza Tripoli to talk with Don Diego Lorenzi. I arrived at the Piccolo Cottolengo at seven o'clock in the evening and found Don Diego pacing up and down in the lobby. He looked restless and nervous.

He took me down into a basement in an empty part of the house, to the room where I was to spend the night. There was just sufficient space for the narrow single bed and a wardrobe. I deposited my bag on the bed and he immediately took me up for supper in an echoing, high-ceilinged room near the kitchens.

We were served with *penne all'arrabiata* and veal with spinach by nuns in white habits; we drank a bottle of red wine between us. When the dishes had been cleared I led with the one question that had brought me back to Milan:

"Don Diego," I said, "Bishop Magee was very definite about the fact that you went out the night the Pope died. I've also heard this from two other sources: Father Farusi, who was head of Radiogiornale on Vatican Radio, and one of the Gusso brothers, who said you were with *him* the evening the Pope died. Is this true?"

Don Diego looked up at the ceiling; he shut his eyes and took a deep breath. He was silent for almost half a minute.

"Listen," he said, "I went to see Guido Gusso on August twenty-seventh, the Sunday after Luciani was made Pope. And I don't think I set foot in his place ever again. It is true that during the period I was the Pope's secretary I paid a few visits to my confreres, who lived only a hundred yards from the private apartments; they are in charge of the post office. And the last time I had gone out was on Wednesday, which was the day *before* the day the Pope died. This Father Farusi I met a few days after the funeral of the Pope. . . ."

"Did you speak to Father Farusi about the *Imitation of Christ* story, either on September twenty-ninth or any other day?"

"No! I never spoke to him until after the funeral, and it was about something quite different. There was a story going around that the Pope had been upset on the evening he died about a television report that a young Italian had been killed in some kind of political vendetta. That's what we talked about, and I told Farusi it was untrue."

"Last time we met you were emphatic that you had to go outside the apartment to borrow a copy of the *Imitation*," I said. "Bishop Magee tells me that he used to read from the *Imitation* every morning with John Paul. That's been bothering me. How do you account for that discrepancy? How did the Pope let you go out of the building to find a copy when he knew all along that there was one in the chapel?"

"I didn't know that," he said in a small voice. His face was glum. His schoolboy youthfulness seemed to me less innocent this time around. And yet, what possible motive could he have to lie? I wondered whether Don Diego was simply a bit disorganized, or whether he was so depressed in the Vatican he would have used any pretext to go out of the papal apartment.

"I suppose it was a misunderstanding," he went on. "We were at the table eating our supper at eight o'clock on Monday night. As far as I remember I went looking for the book; I just presumed that the book hadn't come up from Venice and went to borrow another copy."

"How long were you gone?"

"Fifteen minutes."

"Not long."

We were silent for a while.

"At all events," I said, "Magee insists that on the evening of the Pope's death you disappeared from the apartment after supper. He is quite definite about this. And he's definite that you frequently went out, whereas he only left the apartment once during the Papacy—and it was on that same day, in the afternoon, when he went to fetch his books."

"I think John Magee went out twice," he said. "But look, I went out at about eleven o'clock in the morning to be fitted for a new cassock. That cassock was used by me on the day of the funeral. I was back by half-past twelve. I didn't go out in the evening. I was in."

"All right. Bishop Magee also says that the Pope had a sharp pain while walking in the *salone* in the afternoon, around five-thirty, and that you were out at the time. When you told me your version, you said that the Pope complained of a pain at a quarter to eight as he was coming into supper."

"I was definitely in the apartment," said Don Diego vehemently. "And the pain he experienced was definitely in the evening, after Villot had left. And I did *not* leave the apartment in the evening to go to the Gusso brothers, or anywhere else."

One of these two priests, Magee or Lorenzi, had been mistaken, or was not telling the truth. But which of the two had a motive to lie? I could see no reason for Magee to lie, and yet, if Don Diego had indeed gone out of the apartment, why would he lie about it ten years later, when there was no longer anything to lose?

He was looking at me quizzically. He said, "Who got John Magee into the private apartment, did he tell you that?"

"He told me in great detail," I said. "According to him the Pope himself appointed him, when he was collecting Paul VI's books. . . ."

"This is all nonsense. *I* was the one who asked for Magee to be returned as secretary. *I* arranged for it through the proper channels. The Pope does not make those decisions. It would be lacking in respect to the establishment. And Luciani was very conscious of the proper hierarchy and so on." Don Diego started to laugh. "I'm not blaming Bishop Magee." He laughed again. "I don't know . . ."

He went to a cabinet and brought out a bottle of brandy and two small glasses. "Here," he said, "let's have a nightcap."

As we sat sipping drinks, I said to him, "You know, the only way I can account for all the discrepancies in your stories is that perhaps you, all of you, feel a little bit guilty about the Pope's death, that perhaps you are hiding something even all these years later. Wouldn't it be best to make a clean breast of that now?"

Don Diego eyed me. At length he said, "I wasn't shocked by Luciani's death. I saw it as the will of God. God gave him to the world for a few weeks, then took him back to himself. God made him Pope for a short time to teach lessons of faith, hope and charity, the lesson of Jesus Christ throughout the ages." He was speaking in reverent, well-modulated, homiletic tones. He said at last, "I did not feel the death of Luciani as a personal loss. And I have nothing to hide, nothing to cover up, nothing to pretend."

I felt irritated, as if I were being subjected to special pleading. And yet I wondered, too, whether the fault lay in myself: was I perhaps blind to the perspective of a man of faith? Was it worldly cynicism that encouraged me to believe that this was just another diversion, a confabulation to avoid confronting uncomfortable facts?

Reluctant as I was to play the policeman I decided nevertheless to press him more closely.

"Would you mind, Father," I said, "just to clear the matter up in my own mind. . . . Could you tell me exactly where you were on the evening of the Pope's death, from the time you finished supper until the time you went to bed?"

"Of course I can tell you. I was in the secretaries' room writing letters, and preparing sermons for a trip I was to make back in the Veneto. I didn't go out. I didn't! In fact, it might be possible to check the letters I wrote, with the dates, and compare it with the typewriter I used on that day . . . to prove it."

I sensed a hint of desperation. It did nothing to inspire my confidence in him.

"Let's go back to the afternoon, when, according to Magee, you were absent. He told me the Pope was walking in circles in the big *salone*, and he, Magee, was working in the secretaries' room. Where were you?"

"In the secretaries' room."

"John Magee says you had gone out. Why would he have said that if you were sitting in the same room? It doesn't add up, does it, Father?"

He smiled and shrugged.

"Let me go back to my feelings about when the Pope died," he said. "The Good Lord had given him to us, and he has taken him away from us. We did not deserve him. I think he went straight to heaven without passing through purgatory. He used to say, as I told you, 'I pray to the Lord every day to take me away.' He did not want to stay in this world. I lost the Pope, but I did not lose the message he gave me and gave the world. And so there was no sense of loss. . . ." Don Diego poured himself another glass of brandy. His voice had become weary; he was beginning to drone.

"What happened to you after the Pope died?" I said. "Have you been disappointed with your career since then?"

"I went to a little house near Mestre. They moved me from there a year or so ago. People said I was banished to a 'hidden place.' I have taken a vow of obedience. I do what my superiors tell me to do. We *need* faith to deal with these facts. We need it."

He sat looking at me bleary-eyed for a while. "Did you ask about Villot's death?" he said. "He died quite suddenly."

I sensed that he was no longer inclined to talk about the details of John Paul's death. He fell silent again, gazing at me. Then he said, "I did not mean to cover up anything; we didn't know anything about the later rumors. We didn't suspect anything about it. We *could* have suspected . . ."

He was staring into his empty glass. "Look, I have to get up early in the morning. I have to go to bed."

He rose and walked very slowly to the door. He paused, waiting for me to join him. We walked down a corridor and he opened a door where a television could be heard blaring. Inside I could see a group of nuns sitting in a semicircle in front of the television set. Some of them were sewing.

"Thank you for the wonderful supper!" he called out to them. "Good night and God bless you."

The nuns looked up, beaming and nodding.

As we walked down to my basement lodging he said, "The poor

man was overburdened. They put too much on to him. It was all nonsense, asking the Pope to make all those decisions, all that paperwork. He had much more important work to do—pastoral work, prayer! He should have sent all those documents back and told them to get on with it themselves."

He bade me good night outside my room and I watched him as he walked slowly back up the stairs, switching off the lights as he went.

35

The mystery of the Signoracci brothers—Ernesto and Arnaldo—their dawn telephone call and the sinister ride in a Vatican car to the "morgue in the tiny city-state," had dogged me throughout my inquiries. However many other mysteries receded on scrutiny of the evidence, this one item had failed to budge. It was one of those dramatic elements, which, when thrown in with the other circumstantial oddities, served to cast an atmosphere of intrigue over the entire situation.

Navarro-Valls, the Vatican press officer, had originally misled me by suggesting that they were in the employ of Dr. Buzzonetti. Buzzonetti had denied any association with them, indicating that I should apply to Professor Gerin, their official employer. I had called upon Professor Gerin, to find that he was deep in retirement and that his mind was a complete blank about everything and anything to do with John Paul I. The only positive information I had received about the Signoraccis to date was Mario di Francesco's assertion that they were dead.

One afternoon I resolved the matter by picking up the telephone book in the *salone* at the English College and dialing a Signoracci listed in the Rome area.

A hoarse voice sounded in my ear. It was none other than Arnaldo Signoracci, embalmer of popes. Very much alive, although reluctantly available for comment. When I told him of my mission, he said at once that he would have to discuss the possibility of a meeting with his brother.

Several days passed and more phone calls, while the brothers, who lived some distance from each other, consulted. They were anxious about the venue, and there were protracted disputes about the timing. Ernesto, who was still in business, was unusually preoccupied with autopsies, inquests, embalmments . . . There were all manner of misunderstandings leading to further delays, and further confusions. Then finally we all managed to agree.

So it came about that on a morning of brilliant light and long shadows I went to my encounter with the Signoracci brothers outside a church not far from Saint Peter's.

They came ambling along an hour late, hands poking outward in their coat pockets as if they were each packing a pair of secreted guns.

Arnaldo was tall, about six feet two, with long and grizzled sideburns, wearing a car coat with a knitted woolen collar. Ernesto was bald and dressed in a black raincoat. Their long craggy faces looked bloodless, putty-colored, their jowls collapsing in concertina folds. The whites of their eyes were marbled with brown seams, like aged mastiffs.

They apologized for the delay, Ernesto explaining that he had been doing a "job" that morning and that they had then got lost. When Ernesto shook my hand I caught a daunting odor of formaldehyde.

We talked for a while about the best place to conduct our meeting and they decided without demur on the church. The place was deserted and chilly, the brothers' macabre tones echoed high to the clerestory. Arnaldo had a nervous blink and an occasional neck spasm; he was looking about the building suspiciously.

We found a place in a side aisle and they settled down, one on either side of me; they sat with hands still firmly in their pockets, as if to keep them out of mischief.

Ernesto, the bald fellow, took the lead: "We're used to churches. We were born on Tiber Island, and there are three churches there;

we were altar boys. We've been in this business for three generations. It began with our granddad in the old morgue on the island,
then they moved it to the Department of Legal Medicine in 1921.
I'm Ernesto, he's Arnaldo. Arnaldo there was born in 1912, he's
seventy-six tomorrow; I'm sixty-five next birthday. He's been in the
morgue for fifty-eight years. He was a twin but the other one died.
We're real Romans, brought up on a wolf-cub's diet, as they say.
Now our children are in the business, including the children of our
brother Renato. The trouble is, our memories are going; working
with the dead all the time, there's no reason to remember."

"I can understand that," I said, "but this is a pope; you should
be able to remember a bit about the Pope."

"You're right," said Ernesto.

"You're right, see," added Arnaldo, "but we've tried to sort things
out, and we've made a bit of a mess, because, look . . . it's a sin
to tell lies and mislead everybody.

"But we've fixed up three dead popes. . . . When they're dead
they're all the same to us. . . ."

"You enjoy your work?"

"Well, the technical stuff is very interesting, the autopsies, because the human body is fascinating . . ."

"Very fascinating," broke in Arnaldo, who was content to let the
younger Ernesto take the initiative, adding a hoarse rejoinder occasionally for good measure.

". . . But working in the morgue does something to your brain,"
continued Ernesto. "There are too many sudden deaths, hangings,
road accidents, stabbings, shootings . . . Then there's the living
ones who come in—screaming and shouting, a proper madhouse.
You'd think it was quiet as the grave, but it's always full of women
and gangsters, types like that, all screaming and shouting together—
you know the kind of thing—all day, all night."

"Well, I can imagine that's a bit of a strain, Ernesto," I murmured. In fact, I was thinking of the revered corpses of the popes
against the background of all this homicidal mayhem. I decided to
steer the conversation back to the matter at hand. "But do you
recollect being interviewed on the day that the Pope died by a Mario
di Francesco who was then with the ANSA news agency?"

"We're used to journalists, because we always get pestered at

the morgue by all the papers when something sensational happens, such as big accidents and suicides."

"Homicides—there are lots in Rome," added Arnaldo, nodding agreement.

"Lots of homicides . . . So, given that we're bound by the 'Secrecy Code,' we can't say anything at all. We can't even tell the truth, so these journalists invent stuff. . . . There's the guy lying on the slab in front of me with his skull caved in, and I read in the paper he died of a stab wound in the stomach, and I think to myself, 'Oh ho!' . . . But not a word passes my lips, see."

"This is important, Ernesto," I said in a solemn voice. "Let's see if we can remember one or two things about John Paul I. On the day that he died, ANSA news service said that you and Arnaldo received a phone call at dawn and that a Vatican car called for you at around five in the morning. Can you explain where that story came from, and whether there's any truth in it whatsoever? It was published at seven-thirty P.M. on that very day."

Arnaldo grimaced theatrically, looked at Ernesto and up into the vaulting of the church, as if for inspiration. "In the morning? At five?"

"Listen," said Ernesto, "we're a bit confused with the times and hours because we've been fixing up the corpses of the popes since John XXIII. I can remember John with the big fat tummy because it was the evening and the sculptor had to go in first to do the death mask before we could get to him; there's a way of remembering. Also, it was our first pope. The other one, Paul VI, was up at Castel Gandolfo, and I wasn't in Rome. But this one, I can't remember properly. I know we prepared our stuff in the morning, but what time we went to the Vatican I can't remember."

"You came to the Vatican in the morning?"

"During the morning, but not at dawn," said Ernesto emphatically.

"No, not at dawn," added Arnaldo, watching his brother closely for a cue.

"Monsignor Noè at the Vatican told us that Papa Luciani died at five o'clock in the morning," went on Ernesto, "so how could the car have called for us at five? Why don't you talk to Professor Gerin? He was in charge."

"You say Noè said the Pope died at five o'clock?" I asked incredulously. "Look, I'll come back to that. . . . I've tried to talk to Professor Gerin, but he's ill. He's incapable of telling me anything."

Ernesto looked knowingly at his brother: "Hey, you hear that? Gerin won't talk! Maybe he's got good reasons, eh?"

Arnaldo, head in a slight spasm, picked up the cue: "Aha! Maybe he's got good reasons, because, listen, he's a great man. . . ."

"It's not that he doesn't want to talk," I said. "He can't talk because he's not very well, he doesn't remember anything."

"Anyway, they would have called Gerin, not us. He's the boss."

"So Gerin was called?"

"Of course. He's the director of the Institute of Legal Medicine, the state morgue and all that."

I felt as if I were trying to pick up mercury with a fork. "Look, let's forget who was there and who wasn't there for a moment. Why don't I just let you tell the events of the day, as far as *you* remember them, starting at the beginning without any prompting. Okay? Right, let's go."

"Okay, but there was a doctor there, too, what's his name . . . Buzzonetti . . . he'll know what time we came."

"Buzzonetti. I've talked with him and he's given me his version of events. Now I want *your* version, you see."

"Fontana was already there too when we arrived."

"Yes, Fontana was there from about eight in the morning," I said with a sigh. "But look, I'd really like *your* version of the timetable. Fontana's dead."

"Well, we'd like to do that, but unfortunately we can't."

"What do you mean, you can't?"

"My memory . . ." Ernesto looked at me, eyes wide open, shaking his head.

"But you're absolutely certain there was no phone call at dawn?"

"Absolutely no call at dawn," said Ernesto. "No call at all. The only time I got a call was for Paul II, no, Paul VI, sorry it was for Paul VI. I got a call. I was on vacation . . ."

"So who called you for Papa Luciani? Gerin?"

"No, we were already on duty. Gerin was there at the institute and came in and told us to get our stuff and start preparations. We could say it was about twelve o'clock, or eleven o'clock. I just don't remember. We got the preparations done, then came to the Vatican and started work with Professor Gerin."

"Yes, we did," added Arnaldo, shaking his head vigorously.

"So that's the whole story. Got any other questions?"

I looked at Ernesto in amazement. He was fiddling with his coat buttons and had a bland expression of finality. I gasped with frustration. Ernesto looked at his brother and shrugged, then he screwed his forehead and shut his eyes for a while.

"Listen, it seems to me that there's a month's difference," he said at length. "I was on leave when Paul VI died, so I had to suspend my vacation. Then I think I took my vacation again a month later because I'd missed out."

"You were on leave when Paul VI died?" I asked.

"And also when Papa Luciani died."

"No . . . surely not. . . ." Arnaldo was looking at him askance, eyes narrowed.

"It's all confused," said Ernesto, looking at me plaintively, "I'm sorry."

"Well, just tell me what you remember."

"We prepared our stuff. There was Professor Gerin. I don't remember if they came to get us, or one of us took our own car."

"I think it was in a car they sent from the Vatican," Arnaldo said to his brother, "because . . ."

"No, I think that was the other time, but this time, I don't remember. . . ."

"Gerin's car . . ."

"I don't remember. I think I came in my own car. . . ."

"Well, can you remember what time you came into the Vatican?" I insisted.

Ernesto looked up at the ceiling. "The time? . . . I'd say . . . It could have been at seven in the morning . . . or . . . it could have been at ten in the morning . . . or . . . at three in the afternoon . . . I don't know. . . ."

"What? At seven?"

"No, later. . . . It could have been at eleven. . . ."

It occurred to me for a moment that the brothers were playing games. I blew a silent whistle. They looked at me a little pitifully.

"So it was Gerin who got the phone call?"

"Yes, yes . . ." said Arnaldo, nodding at his brother.

"Not us, we're just the assistants," went on Ernesto. "There are two departments—the morgue, where we are the technicians, and the pathology department. Gerin is the director of both sections."

"Sections!" said Arnaldo with a macabre chuckle. "He's the head and we're the thorax . . . if you want to be anatomical. . . ."

"Don't mind him, he's a bit of a comic," said Ernesto. "No, Gerin's the boss. He holds the chair."

"Is there a morgue in the Vatican?"

"No," said Arnaldo, "the Vatican has no morgue. Has the Vatican got a morgue, Ernesto?"

"Of course not," said Ernesto with authority.

"ANSA, the news service, says that you conducted work in the morgue of the Vatican."

"Absolutely not. We're talking about the Italian State Institute of Legal Medicine. By the way, if I'm not mistaken Dr. Mariggi was there. . . ."

"Marascino also," said Arnaldo.

"But Marascino died," countered Ernesto.

"Ah, yes, he's died," confirmed Arnaldo in a mournful voice.

"We're always together and so we don't really take much notice of anything, and that day was a long time ago."

"You see?" said Arnaldo. "I mean, we do lots of this sort of work, so we get confused."

"Why don't we talk to Dr. Mariggi, see what he knows?"

"He'll know."

"Look," I broke in, "let's just see what *you* know. So you came to the Vatican, and what did you do when you got there?"

"Who, us? Well, we began to prepare the liquids; there are liquids to be specially prepared."

"Liquids," said Arnaldo, blinking and nodding his head vigorously.

"We opened the femoral arteries," went on Ernesto, "and then began to inject this liquid."

"In the morning?"

"In the morning?" Arnaldo repeated to his brother.

"But the Vatican people say you did the preservation in the evening."

"It could have been, but first we could have prepared and then left. But just the preparations take nearly a whole day anyway."

"Tell me about the liquid."

"We inject an antiputrid liquid," said Ernesto enthusiastically, "that's what we call it."

"Where did you do this, in which room or place in the Vatican?"

"In a room . . . a little room, wasn't it?" he said to Arnaldo.

"I think so." Arnaldo looked hazy.

"Was it in the Vatican?" Ernesto asked his brother again.

Arnaldo looked blank, shrugged.

"Do you understand what the law is in Italy about embalmment? How long does one wait?"

"Yes, twenty-four hours. The same for an autopsy," said Ernesto.

"Now, was the Pope prematurely embalmed, in your view? Were you conscious of breaking Italian law by performing the embalmment before the due time? You see, I'm trying to get a fix on the timing of the embalmment as far as you're concerned."

"But we did the same with Pope John," said Ernesto. "We began the same day that *he* died. There's no problem, because the Vatican is a foreign country, even Professor Gerin couldn't object—the great professor of legal medicine, see? It's whatever the Vatican wants. They're not bound by the Italian magistrates who impose a limit of twenty-four hours, especially with sudden death."

"We don't like magistrates," intervened Arnaldo. "Even twenty-four hours increases decomposition." He screwed up his nose.

"Now, was Papa Luciani embalmed before he went on exposition?"

"Before exposition? Yes, without a doubt. Always beforehand, because with the vestments they wear, we couldn't have done it, because it would have soiled them. Without a doubt."

"If not, there would be gaseous decomposition and then it could explode. So you have to do everything before."

I looked at the brothers, horrified. I had an image of the Pope exploding in a shower of putrefying flesh and ghastly liquids in Saint Peter's Basilica. Could this possibly be true? I had a sudden image of Pope Alexander VI and his hissing, erupting black cadaver. Ernesto saw my reaction and came to the rescue.

"Listen, he doesn't mean the *body* would explode, but that the decomposition, the gas, would explode!"

"Oh yes," chuckled Arnaldo, "the decomposition."

"It's an unfortunate term," said Ernesto.

"Do you remove any of the organs?" I asked.

"No way."

"Blood?"

"This shouldn't be done either," said Ernesto. "It was laid down by Pope John [XXIII]. But we lost a bit with Papa Luciani because we had some difficulty getting the injection in. There was some coagulation there."

"There's something intriguing me. Why is decomposition a problem in the Vatican and not in the outside world?" I asked.

"It's only a problem because they go on view for four days, and the heat and all that. . . . You have to do it in good time."

"Buzzonetti, who is now director of the Vatican Health Service, tells me the body was not treated until after six in the evening and that you never even saw or came anywhere near the body till that time. Does that sound likely?"

"Maybe they exposed it before we got there and then undressed it again," said Ernesto. "I don't think so . . . but we don't know."

"When you arrived, was the body dressed in vestments?"

"Absolutely not. . . . A nightshirt or something, we didn't really notice much, it doesn't bother us."

"After you injected the body, what then?"

"Who? Us? Well, we checked the nose, the mouth, for seepage. Gerin always said we should stay around to watch for losses."

"We slept in the Vatican," added Arnaldo.

"That's right. We slept in there. There's a kind of hotel with nuns, for guests. We were on duty in shifts."

"Yes, us two, on shifts," confirmed Arnaldo.

"When no one was there we touched it up a bit and cleaned it up. We kept checking . . ."

". . . Because decomposition can advance rapidly . . ."

". . . Yes it can spread . . ."

". . . It begins in the soft parts of the face," said Arnaldo, "and we have to feel it and make sure. . . . We developed our own method. Just to see."

"We stayed three or four days. There was a nun who gave us breakfast in the morning."

"We had lunch there, too." Arnaldo's eyes were bright with recollection.

"Yes, lunch, I remember those great slices . . ."

". . . Really beautiful steaks," interrupted Arnaldo, smacking his lips.

"Doesn't this work spoil your appetite a bit?" I asked.

"On the contrary!" said Arnaldo. "When I think . . . I suppose there's no harm in saying it now, I don't suppose I'll get into trouble, as it was back in the war. I had a little gas ring and I used to cook in the operating room of the morgue, because I couldn't get out for lunch, we were so busy. One minute I'd be up to my elbows in intestines, and the next minute I'd be tossing the spaghetti. But it was all clean, everything disinfected. . . ."

"That was the war," said Ernesto, with a bleak smile.

"I was in the morgue on my own then," Arnaldo continued. "Even Dad didn't help. I got to know all the presidential council, all the Germans . . . They've all been through my hands. . . ."

"He frightened everyone in those days. . . . He went around like a body snatcher. . . ."

"I was so tired I used to forget to take off my apron. . . . I went around with blood on my apron. . . . Do you think I could smoke in here?" Arnaldo took out a cigarette for himself and offered me one as an afterthought, which I declined.

"You don't smoke?"

"Not at all?" inquired Ernesto.

"Don't start," advised Arnaldo, inhaling deeply on the cigarette, "it's bad for you. . . . I'm sorry, I'm suffering. I've seen everything. . . . My brains don't work, my memory doesn't work anymore. . . ."

I decided that it might be best if we continued our conversation outside, in the fresh air. We left the church and ambled a little until we found a spot in the sun. My head was dizzy with the gyrations of my two witnesses, and yet I was becoming more and more con-

fident that their dawn trip to the Vatican had been, at the very least,
a "mistranslation," as Buzzonetti had charitably put it. I wondered
what a hostile counsel would have made of their evidence in court,
and yet, it seemed to me that they were not totally unreliable. I
was convinced that they were extremely honest in what they could
not remember, and I was impressed by the fact that they had not,
at any point, confabulated a response for the sake of appearances.

When we were settled again, I asked Ernesto, "Did you see any
marks on the Pope's body?"

"Absolutely not."

"Could he have been poisoned?"

"Anything is possible . . ." said Arnaldo.

"Anything. . . . But listen, we didn't see any signs . . ."

"It would have been a disgrace," added Arnaldo, "if the Pope
had been poisoned."

"But had he been poisoned, you would have seen a sign?"

"It would depend on the nature of the poison. Sleeping pills
wouldn't give a sign. Only carbon monoxide would make the gut a
different color, because the liquid blood would be tinted. There are
other poisons which you can detect, but you need an autopsy, and
there's one where the corpse smells of sour almonds. But we weren't
asked for samples, and we didn't take any. There was no question
of suspicion."

"Has anyone at the Vatican ever asked you to be discreet and
not to say anything?"

"No," said Ernesto emphatically. "We've got nothing to do with
the Vatican. Professor Gerin is the boss, and he always told us to
be careful talking to journalists—but that's about anything."

"Have you had any sort of contact with the Vatican since the
death of the Pope?"

"Absolutely nothing."

"Were you paid by the Vatican?"

"Absolutely nothing," said Arnaldo, "only medals."

"That's right," added Ernesto, "Professor Gerin insisted that we
didn't want any money. They made us Knights of Gregory, with a
diploma and that sort of thing."

"Have you ever been paid by journalists?"

"Nothing," said Ernesto.

"Tell me something else," I said. "Did you perform a sort of secret autopsy on the body at some point? Make a kind of examination?"

"People have asked us that before," said Ernesto. "There wasn't any autopsy. People who think he was murdered always ask that question. Mind you, that gossip was all around Rome, and even our friends asked those sorts of questions. But we were certain he had died normally. We didn't see any reason for an autopsy. But people keep asking, 'Why didn't you do an autopsy?' They don't understand that it's not up to us anyway; it has to be requested by a magistrate."

"You're reported as saying that John Paul I died at four in the morning," I said. "Is that right, Ernesto? Did you or anybody else examine the body for time of death?"

"A journalist asked me about the temperature of the body. I told him that we take it at the institute, using a rectal thermometer. That's the way you do it. But this was the Pope. And no, there was no need to do this. We were only there for the preservation treatment. Nothing else."

"Listen, Ernesto, you've been quoted as saying that in view of the condition of the body, the Pope died at four in the morning. Did you ever say anything remotely to suggest this?"

"No! No! . . . What I said was that he was *found dead* at five in the morning. But that's what *I* was told, by Monsignor Noè."

"Earlier you told me that Monsignor Noè said that he had *died* at five. Now which is it?"

"I'm sorry, I get confused. I meant to say that Monsignor Noè or one of the priests at the Vatican told me he was *found dead* at about five in the morning . . . sitting up in bed, reading, with his glasses on. That's all I ever said."

"Ernesto," I said, "do you know why I'm asking these questions?"

He looked at me a little bleakly. "Yes, of course I understand. . . . There's been some deception, and we've been deceived a bit too."

"I want to be quite clear with you about this. It's been claimed on your verbal evidence that you were called to the Vatican before the body was found."

"No, no . . . I've always been absolutely certain, and I've said that it wasn't early in the morning. I know that."

"And we were never called," Arnaldo added.

Ernesto raised his hand, then placed it on his head. He was quiet for a few moments.

Ernesto turned to me. "You know . . . I'm certain I was on vacation again when Papa Luciani died. I went away again a second time because I'd missed my vacation returning for Paul VI, so I took it again later. The reason is that I definitely heard the news on the radio. Then *I* phoned the institute from outside. I think I remember now. I heard it on the radio . . . I called. I'm sorry, now it's all coming back. . . ."

"What makes you think you were on vacation?" I asked.

"I'm sorry, I'm confusing things a bit. I was definitely at Circeo on the coast when I heard on the radio that Papa Luciani had died."

"But you told me this earlier, and Arnaldo here thought you were mistaken."

"I think you called *me*, didn't you?" said Arnaldo.

"Listen," said Ernesto, "I can remember now. I was away, and you were already retired. You weren't going into the office then."

"When did you retire?" I asked Arnaldo.

"Nineteen seventy-seven," he said promptly. "With Paul VI and Papa Luciani I was recalled for the job of head technician."

"Okay," I said. "Now, Ernesto, how far is Circeo from Rome?"

"One and a half hours or so. I phoned in . . . and they said they needed me definitely, and Arnaldo."

"Now you, Arnaldo, where were you?"

"I was at home, and Ernesto rang to tell me that Gerin had asked for me."

"And then?"

"I think we prepared our stuff in the afternoon, and then began in the evening."

"Did you come by Vatican car?"

"No, it's coming back now. The Vatican brought in Gerin and his assistants and the stuff, but not me. I came by myself, I think."

"Where did Gerin come from?"

"From the institute in Piazza del Verano."

"Ernesto, where do you stay in Circeo?"

"I've got an apartment, it's got no phone. That's why I had to go out to call from the public pay phone."

"Now, are you sure you're not confusing this with Paul VI?"

"Definitely not, because on that occasion they rang somebody else in Circeo, who called me at the apartment. I don't know how they managed to do that, but they did. With Papa Luciani I went to the public phone. I can see myself doing it." Ernesto was triumphant with the discovery of the missing episode.

"Are you absolutely clear about this now?" I asked.

"Finally and absolutely," said Ernesto, beaming.

"Finally," parroted Arnaldo. "If only we had clear minds, like we had once upon a time. Gerin always trusted us, but we've worked too hard for too many years, at least twelve hours a day in that tomb of a morgue, full of screams, shouts, crying. . . . All the relatives coming down to see the stiffs. . . . Homicides, suicides, accidents, sudden deaths, all packed together. It was always full. So just think of these things we do all the time."

"Ernesto, would your wife remember about Circeo?"

"Not a chance. She's not interested in this stuff. She's not even a Catholic—she's a Jehovah's Witness."

We began to walk toward Saint Peter's. Arnaldo seemed to be basking in the satisfaction of a considerable achievement. He was looking about him enjoying the sunshine and the grandeur of Bernini's Colonnade.

He turned to me and said, "Have you got any pull with these people at the Vatican?"

"Why do you ask?" I looked at him expectantly.

"Do you think you could manage a pass to visit the Vatican Gardens? I'm a widower, you know, but I've got a lady friend, wonderful, Christian, well-bred, a Roman, and then there's her sister, and they'd like to visit."

"Next time I talk to Archbishop Marcinkus, I'll see what he can do," I said.

I was feeling benevolent, and especially toward the Signoracci brothers.

36

The day after my meeting with the Signoraccis, I went to the offices of *Il Messaggero* to meet Mario di Francesco, the author of the original ANSA report. He came down to the vestibule of the office, a tall man in his late thirties wearing a dark-gray suit and club tie. We sat on a low sofa in the reception area and talked.

"Did you write the report in ANSA about the Signoracci brothers being fetched by a Vatican car at five in the morning?" I asked.

"Yes, it was me," he said.

"Can you remember how you got your information?"

"Very simply. I got it from the brothers themselves. I can't remember which ones. There are five of them. One of them, at least, is dead. Have you managed to meet any of them?"

"Yes," I said, "I met the ones who embalmed the Pope's body. Incidentally, in your report you mentioned Ernesto and Renato . . . in fact, it was Ernesto and Arnaldo."

He looked at me mystified.

"No matter . . ." I said.

"On the day the Pope died," I went on, "did you speak to them on the phone, or meet them in the flesh?"

"On the phone."

"What time?"

"In the afternoon, I think. Certainly in the afternoon, because I always worked in the afternoon. Perhaps at five o'clock."

"Where were they at that time?"

"What do you mean?"

"Were they in the morgue, in the Vatican, at home?" I said.

He pondered the question for a while.

"Let's think," he said. "I think I called them in . . . I don't know if it was their office, or the mortuary. Probably in one of the offices of the mortuary."

"So they weren't in the Vatican at that time?"

"I don't understand the question."

"I'm just wondering what they were doing in their offices and not in the Vatican."

He looked at me warily. "Yes, but listen, the problem is that there were five of them at the time, five brothers, and all five of them were in the business. Possibly I spoke to one in the office who had not gone to do the job, but just heard about it from one of the other brothers. Understand how it went. . . . Look, I don't think I can help you any more. You see, I wrote something which surprised me a bit at the time. . . . I mean, it surprised everyone. . . . I didn't follow it up, but it wasn't my job to do that, just to get the basic information. I never bothered with it again. But I think about it a lot, and there are still questions remaining about it."

"Do you think you might have made a mistake?" I said. "Or do you think the brother you spoke to might have made a mistake?"

"Sure. That's very possible. He could have been mistaken about the time."

"Is there anything else you'd like to tell me?" I asked.

He looked at me apologetically and shrugged.

"I've been thinking about it a lot recently," he said. "No, I can't add anything. If there was any way I could help you to reconstruct things better. . . . Have you spoken with the brothers yourself?"

"Yes."

"What, the ones who actually did it?" He looked surprised.

"Yes."

"Ah, well. . . . You see, my information was always filtered through another of the brothers. So sure, they could have been mistaken. In fact, a brother could have told another brother, then that one tells another brother, and so on and so on. In the end the information is already at fourth hand. You see?"

As I came away from the offices of *Il Messaggero*, I found myself laughing. I was speculating at the quality of information one would acquire at fourth hand through the Signoracci family.

PART
III

Even the pathologist must form a hypothesis . . . putting various elements of the mosaic together in order to arrive at a concrete conclusion.

—DR. RENATO BUZZONETTI, papal doctor

37

After my meeting with Mario di Francesco I felt that the time had come to review those ten circumstantial oddities that had given rise to the mystery surrounding the death of John Paul I, and to see how many of the contradictions had been satisfactorily resolved by my research so far.

1. Who found the body. The two key surviving witnesses, Don Diego Lorenzi and Bishop Magee, had both admitted to me unequivocally that Sister Vincenza found the body. This was also supported by Sister Irma's account of her conversations with Sister Vincenza. The Vatican's official position was published in a memorandum issued in June 1984 to the Episcopal Conference by the office of the Commission for Social Communications (see Appendix, p. 347). Yet the document managed to engage in a superb example of "amphibology," as my moral theologian friend would have it: ". . . the secretary instantly ran to the bedside of Pope John Paul I when he was summoned by the sister who suspected that something might be wrong. The secretary touched the Pope to awaken him and discovered that he was dead." In the meantime Silvio Oddi, the retired cardinal referred to by "Monsignor Sottovoce" and Don

Diego, continued with the full fiction that Magee was the original discoverer of the body, and—despite Don Diego's assertions to the contrary—was claiming that he conducted an official investigation with all the principal witnesses, including Sister Vincenza. I called on Dr. Navaro-Valls to establish whether Cardinal Oddi had any official standing either as an investigator or as spokesman for the Vatican in the matter of John Paul I's death, and received an official and categorical denial.

The overwhelming evidence was that the nun had discovered the body first. But it was clear that the Vatican had lied, and had continued to lie in isolated pockets, about this essential question. Cardinal Oddi's motive seemed to be a reluctance to admit that the Vatican should confess its past errors, and even the Commission for Social Communications was still hedging. Whatever the case, it warranted extreme wariness of the Vatican's regard for truth.

2. When the body was found. Both secretaries, and Sister Irma—reporting conversations with Sister Vincenza—are adamant that the timing was about 5:30. There was an ANSA news report, however, asserting that Vincenza had found the body at 4:30. And in David Yallop's *In God's Name* there appeared a further assertion of an earlier discovery, at 4:45.

When I attempted to probe the original source of ANSA's story, which had been based on *"indiscrezione"* in the Vatican, I received no information from the ANSA Vatican journalistic team. The most sympathetic of them told me: "The source will never be known; it has to be kept secret."

I now tried to discover the source by enlisting the help of a close friend who is a Rome correspondent, giving him a month to report back and authorizing him to pay for the information if necessary. He finally wrote me the following memorandum (the names used are pseudonyms):

I failed to discover the source of the famous ANSA story. Antonio went off on an assignment; he handed me on to his colleague Giovanni, who rushed out of the Sala Stampa almost before I'd finished explaining; then I spoke to the ANSA man you'd already spoken to. He refused to tell me. So then I got another Italian friend to speak to him and he finally disclosed that the writer of the ANSA story was a certain Pietro. I wrote this Pietro a letter, suggesting he could simply disclose even who his sources were *not* (not a group, for instance). When two days later I rang up, he broke into a show of extreme irritability. It would take so much work, he said, and he was too busy; he had work for the next five months and could and would do nothing, and rang off.

Where could such *"indiscrezione"* have come from? Curial cardinals? Sister Vincenza herself? Lift attendants? My brief journey through the Vatican had taught me that the place was rife with rumor at every level, and that much of it was inspired by motives of mischief or self-interest. But what possible motive could there have been to spread such a rumor had it not been true?

Despairing of finding the source of the ANSA report, I now turned to David Yallop's evidence. Yallop claimed to have spoken with Sister Vincenza herself, but had declined during my interview with him to reveal anything more than what he had cited in the book for fear of compromising her sister nuns. Knowing that Yallop had used researchers and interpreters to handle Italian-speaking witnesses, I was keen to get as close to the original source as possible. I eventually contacted one of Yallop's researchers in Rome, Philip Willan—a journalist working with UPI, who had interviewed the Signoracci brothers and Hans Roggen.

Willan said this to me:

"I didn't interview Sister Vincenza on David Yallop's behalf. I traveled up to her convent and tried for three days to speak to her, and she adamantly refused. In the end I capitulated; I was rather relieved, to tell you the truth. Nevertheless, a reference to a personal conversation with the nun appeared, as you know, in Yallop's book. I spoke to Yallop about it and asked how he'd got it. He told me that she had eventually relented and that he had sent another of his researchers to interview her because I was away at the time on another assignment. I don't know who this other interpreter was. Yallop apparently kept his assistants incognito from each other for reasons of security."

My curiosity about the status of both the ANSA and the Yallop versions of the earlier discovery stemmed from an examination of internal textual evidence.

The text of the ANSA story read thus: "It was not . . . John Magee who found John Paul I dead at 5:30 on the morning of Friday, September 29. It was a nun one hour earlier . . ." The ANSA story then went on to describe how the nun had brought coffee at 4:30. "She went away and returned some minutes later," said the report, "to find that it had not been touched. She knocked on the door. She went away yet again. Then she came back once more a little later. She knocked once again; not obtaining any reply, and worried, she looked through the keyhole and saw that the light in the room was on. Opening the door a little she saw the Pope on his bed, his eyes open, his glasses on, in his hand four sheets of paper . . ."

The report first states that the nun *found the body* at 4:30, then it subsequently says that she only brought the coffee at 4:30. Yet it was only after returning on two separate occasions that she decided to investigate. How much time had elapsed between each of these visits? Fifteen, twenty minutes? We are not told. Is it conceivable that the nun would be in a state of panic within a minute or two? What is certain is that by the admission of the report itself the nun could not have both brought the coffee and found the body at 4:30.

But there is another problem. In order for Sister Vincenza to see the Pope in bed by "opening the door a little" she would need to peer through a second set of doors and a heavy curtain, as well as round a corner. Whoever launched the Sister Vincenza story knew nothing about the layout of the papal apartment and the papal bedroom.

Yallop's version of the discovery of the body supplied a possible answer, at least as to how the nun could have immediately seen the Pope on opening the door. He has the nun placing a flask of coffee not outside the bedroom door proper—which adjoins a corridor leading to the sisters' quarters—but in the "Pope's study." This door does indeed open within a few feet of the papal bed. Yet in order to reach the Pope's study, she would have had to pass the first bedroom door in the corridor (the logical place to leave the coffee), turn right and walk down the corridor leading to the *salone* as far as the secretaries' study and the chapel opposite, then pass back through the secretaries' study to enter the Pope's study. It seemed extremely unlikely to me that she would have done this, not only once but several times. None of the many other reports suggest that she left the coffee in this place: all other sources agree that the coffee was always left outside the bedroom door in the corridor, which is close to the Pope's bathroom. What is more, every account of subsequent entries into the bedroom refers to the door from the corridor, not the door from the Pope's study.

But something else bothered me about the Vincenza episode in Yallop. Instead of quoting her verbatim on the details of her discovery, his narrative is written entirely in reported speech. How much of it was based on his interview, how much on speculation or on other sources? Is it an amalgam, or a seamless piece of firsthand evidence? Then again, just how reliable was the information she was giving him?

When I talked with Yallop on January 6, 1988, he told me that Sister Vincenza had informed him that the Signoracci brothers had laid out the Pope's body in the papal bedroom on the morning of the death. I was now convinced that this could not have been possible, and it thus cast serious doubts, as far as I was concerned, on anything else Sister Vincenza apparently told him.

But there was something else again—the details of John Paul I's normal routine in the Vatican. By all accounts Pope John Paul I rose in the Vatican between 4:30 and 4:45. He spent half an hour or so over his ablutions and dressing, during which time he listened to an English-lesson tape. According to the recollections of Sister Vincenza in the Belluno newsletter, she normally prepared him coffee at about 5:30 every morning, which he took before going into the chapel to say his office and morning meditation in preparation for Mass at 7:00 A.M. I had satisfied myself that the evidence for this pattern was so overwhelming that the idea of a major variation just for the morning of September 29 was so unlikely as to be incredible.

As a result I could not buy either the 4:30, nor even the 4:45 discovery of the body by the nun. I believed, on the evidence I had collected so far, that she had come across the body at about 5:30, and I was convinced at this stage that it was not just the fact that he had failed to drink the coffee that alarmed her. Magee had not appeared, and the Pope was not astir and ready to go into the chapel. As Magee told me, the lights in the corridor leading to the chapel were still off as he himself had overslept that morning.

The conspiracy theory has it that the extra hour was employed in cleaning up the vestiges of the crime. It is equally true that without the "extra hour" the conspiracy theory looks a little less plausible.

3. The official cause of death.   I believed at this stage that in the absence of an autopsy I would never know for certain what killed the Pope. Buzzonetti's diagnosis seemed to have been made in great haste and without a proper knowledge of the patient's medication or medical history. In Britain and the United States a diagnosis by a physician who had not known the patient, or visited him in recent weeks before the death, would have been illegal.

I had attempted to contact the Pope's "family physician," Dr. Da Ros, and been repulsed. I had applied to Professor Rama in Mestre, the specialist who had treated him for his eye problem in 1975, but the professor would only "correspond" with me. I had sent through the Vatican a detailed list of questions in Italian on February 24, but despite several telephone calls I had as yet received no reply.

The idea of a pulmonary embolus was intriguing, but where was the evidence? And had not Navarro-Valls merely produced this theory because he thought it answered the problems of such a *sudden* death?

On reflection it seemed to me that there were still many questions to be answered about the manner of the Pope's death. But how and where should I get the answers?

4. The estimated time of death.   Buzzonetti had estimated the time of death to be about eleven P.M. on September 28. This has been contradicted by Yallop in his report of the Signoraccis' testimony. When I questioned the brothers myself on this point, I was more than satisfied that it had been a result of a confusion, in which the brothers had mistaken Monsignor Noè's statement about when the body was found for when the Pope had died.

What is certain is that the brothers had been in no position to estimate the time of death from an examination of the body.

In view of the reported onset of rigor mortis in the hands and arms, it appears that he must have died at least late in the evening of September 28.

When I attempted to interview Archbishop Vergilio Noè, master of ceremonies at the time of John Paul I's death, he agreed to see me, but when I arrived at his office, he said, with some feeling, "*Please* leave me out of it."

When I told him that it was essential for the sake of the historical record to put down the correct order of events on the morning after the Pope's death, he said, "I agree with whatever Dr. Buzzonetti told you. I went through all the details with him before he saw you."

5. *The timing and legality of the embalmment.*   If the Pope had been on Italian territory it is certain that the law would have been broken, since the preserving process had begun at seven in the evening on September 29, well within the twenty-four-hours' observation required in Italy.

I contacted the Vatican City lawyer, Vittorio Trocchi, to question him on this point. He said bluntly, "But Italy is Italy, and the Vatican is a foreign state with its own laws. We can do what we like."

In view of the fact that the Pope's body was due to go on show for four whole days, in what might possibly be extremely hot and humid weather, it seems reasonable to expect that the body would require prompt treatment to avoid unpleasant "explosions." I was fully satisfied that there was no evidence that the body had been hastily embalmed on the morning of September 29.

6. *What the Pope had in his hands at the moment of death.*   There were four versions of the "truth": the *Imitation of Christ*, sermons and discourses, a talk to the Jesuits, and a list of new Vatican appointments and sackings.

The significance of these contradictions centered on whether or not the Vatican had lied. I was convinced that the *Imitation* story had not been planted officially by the Vatican and that it was an invention by journalists in the Vatican Sala Stampa picked up by Vatican Radio, which has a measure of independent news gathering. The outstanding mystery was whether Don Diego Lorenzi had indeed told Father Farusi that John Paul had been reading the *Imitation*. If he had, it was baffling. And if he hadn't, was Father Farusi simply confused—or what?

Apart from this, I failed to see that the Pope's reading matter, even if it had been a dossier on Roberto Calvi, could prove anything about the way in which he had died. What was beginning to bother me more at this stage was the *insistence* that John Paul I was holding something in the first place. Why had it been made such an issue? I would be returning to this point at a future stage.

7. The true state of his health in the months leading up to his death.   I was convinced that I had not been given a clear picture of John Paul's health, and there had been no assistance on the part of the medical men to help me acquire it, despite the fact that the Vatican had used its good offices to obtain interviews for me. I was alarmed that Buzzonetti had failed to answer certain unobjectionable questions that would have set the historical record straight. Da Ros had refused absolutely to see me.

As with the diagnosis, I was wholly unsatisfied with the fruit of my research into the Pope's state of health in the weeks leading up to his death.

8. The whereabouts of personal belongings from the papal bedroom.   Stories that the Pope's spectacles and slippers had gone missing from the papal bedroom were pure rumor. According to Kay Withers of the *Chicago Tribune*, the Pope's sister-in-law had possession of these objects. There had also been talk of a missing will and an absent death certificate.

According to Don Diego, the Pope, in a note of several lines, had left everything to a seminary in the Veneto. When I asked Vittorio Trocchi of the whereabouts of this "will," he denied all knowledge of it, saying that it was with the family. He pointed out that a Vatican idea of a papal will was more a spiritual testament like that of Paul VI, published after his death. Naturally John Paul I had had no time to prepare such a document.

I could see how a conspiracy theorist would make much capital of the absence of a testament, but it seemed to me unlikely that the testament had been written in those brief thirty-three days and then destroyed by the Vatican. And where was the proof?

As for the death certificate, this was promptly produced by Vittorio Trocchi (see Appendix, p. 347).

9. Whether or not the Curia had ordered and performed a secret autopsy. Rumors that medical personnel had done an autopsy late at night in Saint Peter's Basilica during the period of lying in state were suggested by Italian newspapers at the time of the Pope's funeral. Professor Cesare Gerin, in charge of the process, does not speak; Buzzonetti and the Signoracci deny it. Can it ever be proved?

What is certain is that medical men working for many hours on a body that they are struggling to preserve would be in a position to make all manner of observations about the condition of the corpse. Were specific tests made? Were organs examined for particular reasons? I had seen no evidence that they were.

10. Whether or not the morticians were summoned before the body was officially found. The Signoracci brothers had convinced me that no dawn call and five-o'clock ride to the Vatican had taken place. Mario di Francesco had further demonstrated the flimsy basis of his ANSA story.

The only other source for the dawn call was Yallop's three interviews with the Signoraccis which had been conducted by Philip Willan of the Rome UPI. I called Willan at his offices and he confirmed that Ernesto Signoracci had told him also that he was actually away on vacation on the morning the Pope died. When I expressed surprise that this had not appeared in print, he commented that the Signoraccis had said a great many contradictory things.

Finally, as the dawn story had made mention of a Vatican car, I made a cross-check, for what it was worth. As Marcinkus himself was overall head of the Vatican car pool, I asked his secretary Vittoria Marigonda to produce for me that same day a copy of the logbook relating to September 29, 1978. She had it sent for, and it arrived in the space of twenty minutes. It indicated clearly that a car was sent for Gerin and his team, not at five in the morning, but 5:15 in the afternoon. It also confirms that Professor Fontana was fetched in the morning.

Naturally, a conspiracy theorist would argue that the logbook

could have been fixed, but it would have been remiss of me not to
go through the motions.

Reviewing my progress so far, I was still unhappy with the general
feel of my inquiry. I was astonished at the lack of candor among
the witnesses, the number of varying stories, a sense that *saving
face* was more important than telling the truth. I found the attitude
in the Vatican toward John Paul I disturbing. They had not liked
him. They felt that a mistake had been made.

It was clear to me that the remaining areas of true contention
related to medical matters: the actual cause of death, and the actual
state of the Pope's health before death. Given the Vatican's avowed
support of my investigation, the lack of solid information on this
score was attracting attention to itself.

It had also struck me that there was something peculiar about
the witnesses' preoccupation with who found the body and the posture of the body in death. It was no longer a question of which
version I should believe, but whether I should believe in *any* of the
versions given. I had been intrigued by Dr. Roe's suspicions about
the posture of the body—that it was unusual to die in the midst of
an activity without response to the trauma. I was beginning to wonder
whether I should not be alert to the possibility of some new expla-
nations.

But what should be my next move?

I had virtually despaired of gaining any new medical information
from the Vatican or from Da Ros and Rama.

Then I had an extraordinary breakthrough from a quite unexpected source.

38

From the very outset of my investigation I had attempted to make contact with members of the Luciani family. I was particularly interested in meeting one of the dead Pope's nieces, Lina Petri, who was said to be a qualified doctor resident in Rome. Eventually we spoke on the telephone and she came to the English College for tea.

She was an unassuming, fair-haired northerner in her mid-thirties. She wore a white T-shirt, homely lavender cardigan, khaki slacks and desert boots. In a city which takes *la bella figura* in women of her age as a religious precept, she seemed utterly indifferent to fashion.

I made tea for her in the staff kitchen and we sat in the *salone*.

"I studied medicine here in Rome at the Policlinico Gemelli," she began. "I'm also married to a doctor. He specializes in radiological diagnosis." She talked in a forthright, energetic manner, with swift gestures of the open hand. I detected a note of suppressed emotion revealing itself in occasional catches of the voice.

"My uncle was very fond of me, because I was the only daughter of his sister," she went on. "He was very close to her. We were a close family and we saw a lot of him. When he was in Venice I used to stay with him four or five times a year, and when I came to study medicine in Rome, I used to see him every two months when he came down to the Episcopal Conference. He was thought to be a bit naive, you know, the 'smiling' Pope, but actually he was strong. He was shy, but he knew what he wanted and how to get it. He was humble, but he was quite determined. Don't forget he was a patriarch and a cardinal.

"When I was sixteen years old, in the fifth year at the *ginnasio*, I stayed with him on my own, without the rest of the family, during the Christmas holidays in Venice; he had two little guest rooms in the house. I spent a lot of time with him, especially at lunch and at supper. He would tell me where to go in Venice, he paid a lot of attention to me, just like a father or mother.

"He gave me money to buy new clothes. He even did this when I was here in Rome. He said to me, 'Here, take this money and go and buy yourself a new dress.' I was just a student; it meant a lot to me. He knew that the family on my mother's side was poor, and he had it on his conscience that my mother didn't get an education because she had to start work at the age of eleven to help pay for him to go to the seminary. Whenever he gave me money he used to say, 'Listen, Lina, this isn't the Church's money; this is my own money given to me personally as a conference fee. I can use it how I wish, and *you* are the very first of my poor.' He was always scrupulous like that. And he always told me that he would be deep in debt to my mother for the whole of his life.

"He and my mother were really close. When it was announced on TV that he was Pope, she collapsed on the ground, not with joy or happiness, but with sheer pity for him, because of the huge burden he would have to bear. Nobody thought for one moment that he would be made Pope. We have a photo of him that we all keep and cherish. He's holding her face in his hands after he had become Pope. They were on their own at the beginning of the audience with the family, and she said to him, 'Just think, Albino, if only Mama were here!'

"On the day of the audience I realized that there would be a big change in my relationship with him. Don Diego Lorenzi, who had grown in power too, really put me off. He said, 'You're not in Venice now, you know, you can't just come and go in here as you please. He's the Pope and you can't disturb him just when you feel like it.' I'm already a pretty shy person inside, and it really upset me; from that day onward I didn't even consider trying to contact him. In any case, I was frightened by all the Vatican pomp and ceremony. I didn't even know how to make a phone call into the Vatican.

"The last time I saw him alive was at a ceremony at the Lateran Basilica on September twenty-third. I went there with some friends and they lifted me up high on their shoulders so that I could get a glimpse of him. I think he saw me in the midst of the crowd because he passed in front of us just in time. All the people were cheering like mad. Later I heard from Sister Vincenza that it was on that day that he said I should be invited to the papal apartment for his birthday on October sixteenth. But as we all know . . . he didn't make it.

"I don't give much weight to anything the Vatican says. I've always seen the Vatican as an obstacle. He was simply my uncle, but there was all the fuss and bother about whether or not I could see him. Even in death the obstacle continued, and when my mother came to Rome to see his body, she had to stand in line. We didn't create a fuss about it. It was all part of the structure around him. But we needed a lot of patience; we suffered. When a person dies, the family normally looks after the body until it is buried. But it wasn't like that for us, nor afterward. Even now when I want to visit his tomb I often have to wait in line for half an hour and listen to all those people passing by and saying stupid things about him being murdered. And on special days, like All Souls', I can't visit because it's closed so that the Pope can go. There's that distance even after death.

"On the morning that he died my brother called me here in Rome at around seven-twenty. I was determined to see him. I went straight to the Vatican and stood at the Porta Sant'Anna. I told them at the gate I was the Pope's niece and they wouldn't believe me; after a lot of messing around—they wanted me to prove it—they phoned somewhere and eventually someone came and escorted me up to the doors of the papal apartment. Even then I wasn't let in; I was kept waiting outside, with more messing around. Then Father Magee came along and luckily he recognized me. He took me right into the apartment, and into the Pope's bedroom, and there was my uncle.

"I was left alone in there. The room was completely bare except for a crucifix and a photograph of my grandparents. The covers on the bed had been removed. I was standing there looking into his face. His head was turned toward the door and looked as if he had been smiling at someone the moment he died. His face showed no sign of suffering. His hands were joined together, but they were deformed and in a rigid position. They were . . . well, sort of bunched up.

"Somebody came in after ten minutes and gave me a chair to sit on. I stayed there for about twenty minutes, just looking at him. It then occurred to me that there was something very strange. He was wearing the clothes that we see the Pope in every day, the white robe, and the sleeves were all torn. Why should they be torn like that? I wondered.

"Then they came along and asked me to leave so they could prepare the body to take it to the Sala Clementina where it was to be placed on view. I wondered at the time why, if he had died in bed, he wasn't wearing his pajamas. I was convinced somehow in my own mind that he had died working at his desk.

"I went into the kitchen to see Sister Vincenza—I'd known her in Venice. She told me that they had been thinking of inviting me in before he died. She said she simply couldn't believe it because he had been so well, much better in Rome than in Venice. He'd said to her, 'Isn't it true, Sister Vincenza, we're much better off here?' I believe he said this to encourage her because she'd had a heart attack the year before, so she wasn't too well either. She was upset. She said he'd felt really well the evening before. Don Diego now reckons my uncle had a severe pain the evening before he died. Somehow it doesn't add up.

"Then another strange thing happened, and if you were a person with bad intentions you could extract all sorts of suspicious things out of it. Sister Vincenza was crying and pouring out her heart about all these things. I was listening to her patiently—we're not the sort of people who cry in public and make scenes, my family—but I was crying inside and I was suffering. Then in rushes Don Diego.

I don't know whether I should tell you this, it's not in his favor, but he made a bit of a scene. He said, 'Listen, Sister Vincenza, what has happened has happened! There's no need to mull over all the details.'

"To me, it was the wrong moment to talk like that. Here was the poor old nun suffering and weeping. Why start hectoring her? And what were these 'details' she shouldn't talk about?

"It wasn't until the following evening, when Sister Vincenza was with me and my mother, that she said something that perhaps explained what Don Diego had been talking about: that the circumstances were different from the official bulletin. She said, 'Don't worry. The truth is that I found him myself that morning when I took him his coffee. He had passed away peacefully in the night without pain or suffering, and I was the first to find him in death.'

"This was the background I think to what Don Diego was saying to her: that people must never know that she had found the body. Personally I don't see what's wrong with a nun taking him coffee. Anyway, she found him and not Father Magee, although they go on saying that it was him. Unfortunately this is one of the facts that adds to the hypothesis that there was some sort of intrigue. Incidentally, I should tell you that all that stuff about his personal items, his slippers and glasses, being spirited away by Cardinal Villot is nonsense. My aunt got his spectacles and slippers." She grinned mischievously. "She actually *wears* them."

I went to the kitchen to make more tea. I was deeply moved by what Lina Petri had told me; I sensed in her a strong element of the character of Luciani, such as I had gleaned from many accounts of him. She came from a down-to-earth working-class family, and her loyalty to her people and her origins was unassailable. Lina's testimony seemed crucial to me. She was highly intelligent, forthright and independent; I was convinced that she was incapable of connivance of any kind.

As a qualified doctor and close family member I believed that she, almost more than anybody else, except for his personal physician, Da Ros, could shed light on Papa Luciani's true state of health in the months leading up to his death. I was also intrigued to learn what she felt about Buzzonetti's diagnosis.

When I returned to the *salone* I asked her if she would mind answering some explicit questions about her uncle's health.

"Were you aware," I asked her, "of your uncle's state of health in the last years of his life?"

"Very much so. He didn't have outstanding health, but he was far from being an invalid. There were all the familiar ailments of an older person: he had a bit of arthritis, an operation for gallstones, an operation for hemorrhoids. He had some respiratory problems that went back to his youth. There had been a suspicion of TB and he spent time in a sanatorium, but it was straightforward pneumonia. All this was fairly normal. In fact, he'd led a reasonably vigorous life. He liked walking in the mountains, although toward the end of his life he was *in* them rather than climbing or walking up them. He even cycled a bit, especially during the petrol shortage in the early 1970s.

"But something drastic happened in 1975. I was already in Rome at the Gemelli by then. He went on a trip to Brazil to see Italian migrant workers from the Veneto. On his return he had an eye problem, a loss of vision. He went into hospital in Mestre under Professor Rama, who diagnosed an embolus or thrombosis in the retinal artery. This is really significant because it means the blood doesn't circulate properly; certain substances are formed in the arteries and veins which coagulate into clots and close the arteries. If something like this happens, it means that there are serious circulation and coagulation problems. It indicates that what happened in the eye could occur in the leg, the intestine or the pulmonary artery. If there is a precedent it is serious, and one must be very careful, because a person can no longer be considered in full health."

"Was he aware that it might occur again?" I asked.

"Certainly. He discussed it when we visited him that Christmas. He said in so many words that if it recurred he could be seriously ill. He also said that he would be a slave to his medicines— anticoagulants and so forth—for the rest of his life. Incidentally, all this rubbish about his taking Effortil, which is sometimes prescribed for circulation problems, can be ignored. There was some crackpot idea that perhaps he had overdosed on Effortil. Every doctor knows it is completely harmless and pretty useless. You can drink it like lemonade if you want to. The important medicines are the anticoagulants, which can be exceedingly dangerous."

"But if he was taking his medicines, would he be out of danger?"

"That's the problem. On becoming Pope, with all the hectic new way of life, he was probably neglecting to take essential medication."

"Don Diego talks of his having a severe pain on the eve of his death," I said. "Is this significant?"

Lina gave me a faintly knowing look, shrugged and extended her hands. "It's odd that it took Diego nine or ten years to come up with this. Such a pain would have been more consistent with a heart attack, but then a heart attack is rarely so sudden and painless as his death obviously was. The manner of his death is more consistent with embolism and, as I've said, he had a history of it. One is not aware of death with pulmonary embolism; it's a question of a fraction of a second."

"What exactly happens?" I asked. I was perplexed, skeptical even. Dr. Roe had insisted that he had never known a patient to be unresponsive to the trauma of death by pulmonary embolism.

"If the large artery that carried blood to the lungs is blocked," she continued, "one dies immediately, with no warning. Another thing is that he had swollen legs; everyone knew this during his Pontificate. He couldn't wear shoes at all, neither the new ones nor his old ones. His legs were very swollen. This is a sign of venous stasis, that the blood isn't circulating in the veins, and it's probable that clots have formed in the arteries. Incidentally, according to my professor of pathological anatomy at the Gemelli, he heard that when they were preserving the body, they had great difficulty injecting the fluids. This could be further indication of massive blockage in the pulmonary artery."

As Lina was saying this, I was thinking of my conversation with Don Diego in Milan, which had largely convinced me that Papa Luciani had been "killed" by overwork and unhappiness.

"Could stress," I asked, "have played a part in his death?"

"It's not like that. Stress can exacerbate an illness, but it's not necessarily a direct cause. It's much more likely that through stress he neglected to take his anticoagulants, which may have proved fatal."

"But how was it that the Vatican failed to spot the possibility of an embolus?"

"As far as I know, Buzzonetti had never been his doctor, and had never seen him. It seems that he didn't have a doctor at all in the Vatican, although he really needed a great deal of attention and care. In Venice he had one, of course, but not in Rome. He was a pope without a doctor to all intents and purposes. It was only a month, but that was a crucial month."

I had two thoughts running through my mind at this juncture. Her statement squared with what Buzzonetti had said, but not with what Magee had told me. Magee had maintained quite explicitly that Buzzonetti had accepted responsibility for Luciani's health in the week previous to his death. My second thought was that it had been the custom of popes in this century to surround themselves with doctors to the point of apparent hypochondria: Pius XII, in fact, had rivaled Churchill and Tito for his obsession with medical attention.

When she rose to go I accompanied her down the main staircase to the front door. We talked about the possibility of acquiring more information, and I asked her if she would call her uncle's doctor in Venice to find out more about his medicines and treatment.

She said that she would try to call Dr. Da Ros as soon as possible.

As I watched her walking down the Via di Monserrato and into the darkness, I felt that I had seen the story of Papa Luciani's death from a completely new angle. I was now convinced more than ever that Buzzonetti's diagnosis of myocardial infarction was incorrect. At the same time I felt that for the first time I had a clear picture of John Paul's state of health prior to his arrival in Rome.

But her evidence had raised some major problems about the operation of anticoagulants, which would require expert comment. In the meantime I still had no reply to my written questions sent via the Vatican to Professor Rama in Mestre.

39

s I considered my conversation with Lina Petri during the next twenty-four hours, something dawned on me. Mention of anticoagulants raised the likelihood that John Paul I had been taking the most common form of anticoagulant—Warfarin, which is also used as rat poison. Was it possible, I wondered, that the Pope might have died because of some misuse of the drug? Then I remembered reading of a rumor that had circulated in the weeks following his death: that he had died of an *overdose* of his medicines. That rumor had largely been discounted because it was widely thought that his medicines were merely mild tonics and multivitamins.

I would now need to explore that thoroughly, but excited by the possibilities of the new factor, I immediately contacted a doctor friend in England, a police surgeon with extensive experience in the field of forensic medicine.

"The patient in question was taking anticoagulants," I told him. "He died suddenly, so suddenly that he had no time to press a button at his side. At the same time, he died peacefully; there was no sign of a struggle—he still sat up, holding the papers he had been reading in his hands. The two diagnoses on the table are pulmonary embolism and myocardial infarction. But could such a death fit with misuse of an anticoagulant drug?"

"Well, frankly, it sounds more likely to me than the other two. Most anticoagulants are extremely dangerous, because in the action of preventing clotting they can work the other way: you can bleed to death. Bleeding to death is one of the quietest ways of dying I've come across: you can just slip away. Was he on aspirin?"

"He'd had severe headaches in the previous weeks. He was certainly a fiendish coffee drinker, all day long as far as I can tell." I was thinking of his early-morning coffee, of Sister Vincenza taking his coffee midmorning, of Magee being asked to bring coffee to the *salone*.

"With anticoagulants that could be decisive. In fact, aspirin— which can cause stomach bleeding—with coffee and anticoagulants could be the worst possible combination, particularly if the patient was under severe stress. If ulceration occurred, he could have bled to death. Why don't you ask his doctor what sort of anticoagulant he was taking and whether he was on anything else? Anticoagulants are the most sensitive to drug interaction of any medication available."

When I explained the situation in full, and the lack of information available, he was aghast.

"You *must* find out if he was on anticoagulants. They can't keep that from you unless they're trying to make a bloody fool of you!"

40

Delving through my files I eventually came across the reference I was looking for—an interview with one Father Giovanni Gennari in the now-defunct newspaper *Il Globo* in May 1982. According to Father Gennari, who claimed a close friendship with the dead Pope, John Paul I had been killed by worry and severe stress, which caused him to take an overdose of medicine on the night he died.

It was not difficult to trace the whereabouts of Father Gennari. He was no longer Father but plain Mister; he had left the priesthood to get married in 1984 and was now religious-affairs correspondent on *Paese Sera*, a left-wing daily in Rome. He agreed to see me that same day in the offices of the paper on Via Tritone.

I found a plump and happy-looking man with swept-back hair and an impressive Roman nose. There was still a hint of clericalism in his soft-spoken voice.

He took me into a deserted room to tell me his story.

"I used to teach in one of the seminaries here, the Lateranense," he began, "and I used to meet Luciani regularly when he came to the bishops' conferences. I lived under the same roof as him during the last session of the council and for the first synod. We ate together every day and we walked almost every afternoon in the garden, often alone.

"The problem with John Paul I after he became Pope was a terrible loneliness. I was stunned by what I heard from a close priest friend of mine called Don Germano Pattaro. Father Pattaro died four years ago. He was a theologian in a seminary up in the Veneto, and therefore well-known to John Paul. A few days before his death, John Paul sent for this priest and asked him to come to the Vatican. Pattaro was completely mystified; when he got there he said that Luciani, the Pope, was totally disoriented, struggling to cope with being Pope, and absolutely alone. He wanted to consult Pattaro about the theology of the priestly orders of separated churches. Papa Luciani was going to meet the Patriarch Nikodim, the one who dropped dead at Luciani's feet after taking a coffee. Anyway, the Pope told Pattaro that he didn't know who to turn to because he didn't know how anything worked, and whom he could trust. He was utterly lost. They prayed together and talked; Luciani seemed reluctant to let him go. The Pope eventually cheered up a little, but Pattaro said that as he left he could see this terrible sense of loneliness descending once more. The curious thing is that they had never been bosom friends exactly. It seemed to Pattaro that John Paul was just clutching at anybody he had known in his life up in the Veneto.

"Now the rest is based on excellent sources inside the Vatican. I know for a fact that certain things happened the evening Papa Luciani died. He had it in mind to change things at the top of the Curia and make certain new appointments. He wanted to substitute Cardinal Villot with Cardinal Benelli. Casaroli would have gone to Milan, taking Cardinal Colombo's place. This sort of thing. Papa Luciani talked with Villot about these plans on the last evening of his life and received a very straight reply. Villot told him that it would be a tremendous change from Paul VI's policies, and it would indicate the triumph of the Curia over the council. He said it would be the end of the openness that had been the hallmark of the Catholic Church for the previous twenty years.

"The Pope was shocked to receive such a forceful and opposing point of view. Anyway, he then called Cardinal Colombo, who gave him the same answer, which only made him more worried and anxious. That's how his day ended. He went to bed taking with him various papers pertaining to those appointments, but he could not sleep. So he called Dr. Da Ros, who prescribed a tranquilizer; it was of a vasodilatory kind. It was necessary to open up the Vatican Pharmacy to get it. Going back to bed he mistakenly took an overdose and this caused a collapse and a heart attack. He was found the next morning leaning on one side curled up a little. He was stiff to the point that in order to lay him out for his exposition and burial it was necessary to break his knee.

"Now I heard this on good authority from the inside, and I believe it to be true. The problems started when those people who had quarreled with him the night before now found themselves having to control the news. All the lies, the half-truths, the rumors, the obscurities, started up because of blind fear and shock.

"They made the poor man Pope and he found himself on his own. He could not carry the burden of it. He tried to make a go of it, but he didn't have the psychological resources."

As I walked back to the English College I was wondering whether there would be any end to the gyrations. My conversation with Gennari underlined the importance of getting Dr. Da Ros and persuading him to talk at last. In the meantime I would approach the Vatican Pharmacy for confirmation of the story about the late-night prescription.

41

The Vatican Pharmacy is situated in a utilitarian-style modern building in the so-called business sector of Vatican City, to the right of the road that leads in from the Sant'Anna Gate. Its director, Brother Fabian, an Australian, was a square little man with limp hair and spectacles. He wore a chemist's white coat over his black cassock. When I expressed surprise at the size of his domain and the large numbers of clients queuing for service, he told me that the pharmacy had a clientele numbering more than eight thousand: the Vatican employees and their families. "You see, we can sell all sorts of stuff you can't get in Italy," he said.

He took me in an elevator to the top floor of the building, which housed the John of God community that ran the operation. We sat in a parlor where an ugly glass statue of the Virgin shared a sideboard with a white plaster polar bear.

"It was such a short time John Paul was in here it's difficult to remember anything about him," said Fabian. "I know he was on Digoxin for heart trouble." He winked at me. "That's a kind of digitalis. Whether he had anything on the night he died I've no idea, but I can find out."

He made a phone call summoning his colleague Brother Augusto to come up and to bring with him the papal medicine book. I was astounded at the promise of candor that seemed in store.

Brother Augusto was a frail little man with a wide mouth and liquid eyes. He was carrying a red book, which he handed to Brother Fabian.

"You were on duty the famous night, Brother," he said. "Was anything asked for from the papal apartment?"

"No," said Brother Augusto, "I would have remembered that. But in any case it should be in the book."

Fabian was already rifling through the pages. "We keep a record just for the popes in this book. I could get my head chopped off for showing you this, but they tell me you've been okayed."

He had stopped at a page. "Well, that's funny. It goes straight from Paul VI to John Paul II. John Paul I evidently had nothing from here whatsoever. That's strange. . . . And now I see that it was Paul that was on Digoxin, not John Paul I. What a stupid mistake to make—I could have sworn it was John Paul. Well, it just goes to show!"

"May I see the page?" I said, leaning over his shoulder.

"Well, I'm not supposed to," said Fabian, distinctly uneasy.

I could see that the book had numbered pages. The record of medicines was in pen. I could see a list ending on one page, and "John Paul II" underlined on the next, with a new list starting beneath it. It did not look as if pages had been torn out.

As we sat staring at the page, Brother Augusto said to me: "I was in that conclave which elected John Paul I, as infirmarian. There were just two of us—Brothers of John of God."

"Can you remember how John Paul reacted when he was elected?" I asked him.

The brother's face broke into a broad smile. "He was an angel fallen from the sky. . . ." He thought for a moment. "But he was very timid. After he had accepted, he kept making supplicating gestures as if to heaven, raising his eyes upward. He kept looking upward with swift movements of the head, smiling nervously and weeping. He was lovely."

Brother Fabian was now watching Brother Augusto as he imitated John Paul's election behavior. He was smiling benignly at him. Then he snapped the drug book shut.

"Well, that's it!" said Brother Fabian. "I guess it's back to work. Sorry I couldn't have been more help."

Before taking me back down to the ground floor, Fabian showed me the community chapel. As we stood at the door admiring the stations of the cross, I was wondering whether Giovanni Gennari's story was just another example of rampant Vatican rumor, or whether the Brothers of John of God were leading me up the garden path. I found it difficult to believe the latter, and yet, it occurred to me that Signor Gennari's tale might have had at least an element of truth in it.

42

The following day I called Lina Petri to see if she had had any luck with Dr. Da Ros. "I'm sorry," she said, "he refuses to talk to me. He was extremely abrupt."

"The anticoagulants. Did your uncle tell you in so many words that he was taking them?"

"I'm not a hundred percent sure whether *he* told me, or whether it was my mother. But I had a clear impression that he was taking them."

"Is there any possibility that you might have been mistaken?"

"He told me that his medicines were a matter of life and death. This is fixed in my mind because we had a conversation about a friend of mine who had died of leukemia. My uncle said that he himself was on a knife edge of life and death, which was why he was a slave to his medication. That doesn't sound like any old mild placebo."

As I came off the phone I found myself stunned for a moment by Da Ros's lack of cooperation, even with Lina Petri—both a niece of the Pope's and a doctor.

I felt it was time to ring Francis Roe, the cardiovascular specialist, for another consultation.

"Pope John Paul I died suddenly," I said. "Given that he had a retinal thrombosis or embolus diagnosed three years previously, given that he had recent swelling of the legs and ankles so that he couldn't even get into new shoes bought for him at the beginning of his Pontificate—neither his normal shoes nor bedroom slippers: what might a specialist deduce about the possible cause of death?"

"It certainly suggests that for one reason or another his blood was abnormally coagulable," he said. "The other main cause of swollen ankles would be congestive heart failure. But this is usually accompanied by breathlessness and consequent difficulty with mobility. Not only would his legs be full of fluid but also his lungs."

"There was no report of difficulty with breathing," I said, "and, in fact, he was able to rush down the corridor of the papal apartment the evening he died without difficulty."

"In that case you can almost rule out congestive heart failure, and we're left really with a probable thrombosis of the inferior vena cava."

"What would happen," I asked, "if he overdosed on an anticoagulant, or took it with another drug or substance that caused an increase in the anticoagulant effect?"

"It depends on the type of anticoagulant. Excess of Warfarin is how we kill rats, by internal hemorrhages," he said. "But the evidence for increased effect of Warfarin would depend on where the bleeding took place. There are two main areas. The first is into the head, a cerebral hemorrhage, and, depending on the size of the blood vessel involved, this would cause severe headaches as the intracranial pressure increased, possibly blindness, paralysis . . . but it's unlikely that it would be something huge and dramatic, happening within seconds.

"The other is in the gastrointestinal tract: anywhere from the mouth to the anus. As a rule this will generally take place over a period of hours, and if it's in the stomach, the patient will invariably vomit up large amounts of blood; lower down in the intestine he'll have diarrhea with blood, and there is a really evil odor. Anybody in the sickroom would have remarked on it."

This appeared to demolish my police-surgeon's theory, I reflected.

"And what would be the effect," I asked, "of a patient suddenly stopping or interrupting a course of anticoagulants?"

"Ah! That could be catastrophic! You get a *rebound* phenomenon. If you stop taking the anticoagulants abruptly, the effect gradually reduces over a period of three to five days. And the effect doesn't stop when the coagulability of the blood returns to normal, it *rebounds*—and for a period of time the blood is even more coagulable than was normal in that patient. So the patient is acutely at risk from the very thing that the Warfarin was supposed to prevent. If he had been on Warfarin throughout his period in Venice and then ceased taking the proper dosage in Rome, he would be a candidate for a thrombosis after three to five days of stopping the drug. If you were to make those assumptions, it would very neatly explain the death of John Paul I, given all the known facts."

Dr. Roe's theory, I noted, accorded almost exactly with that of Lina Petri.

"What would you prescribe given the history of such a patient?" I asked.

"The immediate treatment would be Heparin, which is one of the most *powerful* rapidly acting anticoagulants. The patient would require careful observation in bed—preferably in the hospital—for ten days or so. Walking massages the veins with the expansion and contraction of the muscles. Exercise helps bring blood back up into circulation, but, of course, if there's a clot there it's going to help liberate it."

"On the eve of his death," I said, "John Paul was walking vigorously around the *salone*, taking his two-hour exercise for his swollen legs and, according to Secretary Magee, he made a harsh coughing sound and complained of a sudden pain in the chest."

"That's extremely interesting. What may have happened: with the walking he dislodged a piece of thrombus, it traveled up into his lungs, gave him his sudden pain—which is fairly characteristic—but it wasn't big enough to kill him. Quite often with small pulmonary emboli you get a much more transient kind of pain than with a heart attack—with a myocardial infarction. The detail is certainly supportive of a massive pulmonary embolus later in the evening."

43

fter it was all over Don Diego Lorenzi said to John
Magee, "Don't you think that we had not done enough
of certain things to save his life?" Magee replied, "Oh, forget
all about it!"

"I was not very pleased with this answer," said Don Diego.

To answer Don Diego's question in some detail, the last hours
of John Paul I require close examination.

On the morning of September 28, John Paul I begins his private
audiences at 9:30. He meets the African Cardinal Bernadin Gantin
and the secretaries of two Catholic action groups, Cor Unum and
Justitia et Pax. They discuss Third World problems. He acknowledges material needs, but emphasizes the importance of evangelism.
He tells Gantin: "It is Jesus Christ alone we must present to the world.
Outside of this, we have no reason to exist, we will never be heard."

At the end Gantin watches with amazement as the Pope jumps
up to rearrange the chairs for a group photograph.

The morning passes with visits from papal nuncios from Brazil
and Holland, a chat with the editor of *Il Gazzettino* from Venice;
an *ad limina* visit for nine bishops from the Philippines. Again the

Pope stresses the need to preach the "fullness of life in the kingdom of heaven."

He breaks for lunch with his secretaries at 12:30. He has appeared cheerful, energetic throughout the morning.

On this last afternoon of his life, after a brief rest, the Pope tells Magee, "I'm not feeling too good. I just don't feel myself. . . ."

"Let me call Buzzonetti," says Magee.

"Oh no, no, no. . . . No need to call the doctor. I'll walk in the house."

According to Magee, "Dr. Buzzonetti had been chosen as Papa Luciani's doctor. . . . Buzzonetti had met his Veneto doctor, Da Ros, on the previous Sunday, and it was agreed that his case notes would be sent to the Vatican." So far as Magee is concerned, the responsible doctor is Buzzonetti. Why does Magee not, at least, consult the doctor and allow him to decide for himself whether the Pope should be persuaded to be examined?

Despite the fact that the Pope has complained of feeling ill, Magee by his own admission goes out for two hours, between 2:30 and 4:30, to collect some books, leaving the Pope alone. The Pope is walking in circles in the *salone*. Don Diego Lorenzi is absent from the scene, according to Magee.

The Pope is still walking when Magee returns to the secretariat. One hour later Magee hears him choking with a "harsh coughing" sound. Magee rushes in.

"I have a pain!" says the Pope.

"Wouldn't it be better if I called the doctor?" says Magee for a second time. "Holy Father, it might be serious."

But the Pope declines. He retires to his study and, according to Magee, Sister Vincenza brings him some unspecified medicine.

The Pope has almost certainly suffered a minor pulmonary embolism. He is gravely ill and in need of immediate specialist treatment.

At 6:30 Villot appears for a conference. Magee fails to inform the secretary of state that the Pope has twice complained of feeling ill that afternoon. Villot enters the Pope's study and they talk for one hour and ten minutes. Various Vatican sources will later claim that the interview is acrimonious, charged with emotion. According to Magee the subject is merely the appointment of a new patriarch for Venice. Both Don Diego and Magee are in the secretariat when

Villot emerges. Magee sees Villot to the front door of the apartment. According to Don Diego the Pope complains of a "dreadful" pain. The Pope has now complained of feeling ill three times since two o'clock.

"At about quarter to eight, or ten to eight, he came to the door of his study and he said that he had had a dreadful pain, but that it had passed."

Don Diego says to him, "We should call a doctor."

Again the Pope refuses. Don Diego fails to consult Buzzonetti or Da Ros in Venice.

The Pope, Magee and Don Diego go in to supper. The Pope raises the subject of death: "The type of retreat I would like at this moment would be for a good death." In the subsequent discussion both the Pope and Don Diego recite a popular prayer for resignation in death: "O Lord, grant me the grace to accept the death by which I shall be struck down." According to Magee, this is "exactly to the second" at a quarter past eight. The Pope seems to have an intuition that his death is imminent.

After supper Don Diego is instructed to call Cardinal Colombo of Milan on the phone. The Pope and Magee, according to Sister Irma's conversations with Sister Vincenza, go to the kitchen together. They say good night to the nuns and the Pope asks Magee to remain with them: "They are always on their own."

When the call comes through from Colombo, the Pope rushes down the corridor at immense speed. This is the last vigorous act of his life, the act that triggers a major embolus.

Accounts of the subsequent movements of the members of the household are contradictory.

According to Magee: he accompanies the Pope to compline, they return to the papal study, he witnesses the Pope retrieving a sermon from a shelf, he enters the bedroom with him and points out the alarm buttons. Only then does he go to the kitchen. Don Diego has already left the apartment.

According to Don Diego: he, too, accompanies the Pope to his bedroom and warns him of the alarm buttons. He then returns to the secretariat to type sermons and letters. In another version, he writes the letters in his own room. He retires at 11:45.

According to Sister Vincenza's account, as told to Sister Irma:

Magee does not see the Pope to bed; he remains in the kitchen for a long time. He is studying the lengths of the reigns of every one of the 263 popes in history. Magee tells the nuns he is worried about the Pope's health and speculates whether he might not die that very night. He whiles away the evening rifling through the *Annuario Pontificio*, reminiscing about the deaths of former popes. Magee, the romancer, is a fount of curious stories; he has an Irishman's gift for narrative, a sense of history.

The Pope is dying in his room.

Did Don Diego go out on the evening of the Pope's death? I returned to Milan to cross-examine him on this point, and he was adamant that he had stayed in—he had *not* gone out. For some weeks I puzzled over who was most likely to be telling the truth. They could not both be right.

Then it occurred to me that perhaps neither of them was telling the whole truth, and that perhaps the story of Don Diego's absence might have been a curious alibi, and not necessarily his own.

Throughout the confused story of the Pope's death I frequently found myself wondering why the witnesses were preoccupied with certain marginal factors, drawing attention to aspects that would otherwise be unremarkable. The most suspicious phenomenon, perhaps, was the description of the Pope propped up in bed reading. Dr. Roe remarked, "I've seen many deaths of this sort, but I've never known anybody die unresponsive to what was happening to them." Pondering Dr. Lina Petri's conviction that the Pope had not died in bed, I called Don Diego again to ask him point-blank whether in fact the Pope had been found on the floor of his bedroom or bathroom and only subsequently removed to the bed. He adamantly denied the suggestion, and repeatedly remarked, "It is not possible to pick up a dead body by oneself!" And yet I had never at any point suggested that it was the work of a single person.

It was this telephone conversation, together with Dr. Roe's and Dr. Petri's statements, that prompted me to construct a hypothesis that would resolve the outstanding discrepancies.

John Magee is in the kitchen, mulling over the possibility that the Pope might die that very night, reflecting on the Pope's frightening attacks of that afternoon and evening. He and the sisters stay up late talking, drinking tea. They go right back through the lists of the popes to Saint Peter, counting the days of the shortest papacies. "What if John Paul were to die after thirty-three days!" says Magee. At last, at eleven o'clock according to Sister Vincenza, he wishes them good night.

John Magee is the man who nursed Paul VI until his death, who thought of himself and John Paul I as having a brother–brother relationship, who even sent the new Pope to bed when he became distressed. Is it conceivable, in view of the manner in which he has spent the evening, that he now passes by the Pope's bedroom without stopping?

Surely his concern, his compassion, prompts him to pause; he listens, notices the bedroom light still on. He opens the door just a crack, peers in. The surefooted Magee has spent four years padding around these apartments. It is Magee's domain; he belongs here.

What does he find? The Pope is lying dead on the floor, in a fetal position far from the alarm buttons. Perhaps, as Lina Petri will suggest, close to his desk. He is still dressed, his hands bunched in agony at his chest, his head pressing into the floor to the right. The death is anything but "sudden."

Magee is distraught. He awaits Don Diego's return. They go together to the bedroom. There is panic, remorse. Popes do not die like this—on the floor, in agony and uncared for. All popes in recent history have died in their beds in dignity, fortified by the rites of the Church. Many questions are going to be asked about the state of the Pope's health on the preceding day. How will they explain why they had not fetched a doctor, despite so many warnings? How will they explain their absences throughout the afternoon? Don Diego's disappearance in the evening? Their failure to inform the Secretariat of State or the Vatican Health Service? In the heightened atmosphere of the Vatican they are terrified of the consequences. And what of the vast community of the universal Catholic Church beyond? Will they not be condemned for allowing the Pope to die in such an ignominious manner? Will they not be condemned for failing to do "enough of certain things to save his life"? And yet he is dead and nothing will bring him back. *Surely the best solution for all concerned is to construct both a dignified and a "sudden" death, a death that has come, as the Scripture says, "like a thief in the night."* A death which Dr. Buzzonetti will later describe as "instantaneous or immediate, or premature, or something like that . . . unexpected."

They pick up the body between them. Don Diego notes that the Pope's back and legs are still warm. They take off his cassock; he is wearing his day shirt and underclothes beneath. There is some difficulty and they tear the linen summer garment at the sleeves. They put the body, still in a fetal position, half-dressed, on the bed (this, after all, according to Don Diego, is how he was found). It does not look right. They prop him up with cushions and pillows so that his chin is slumped to his chest, but sideways askew, to the right. They place his glasses straight on his nose, put sheets of paper in his hands. It is essential that he appears to have died without warning, during a normal activity. No mention will be made of the Pope's pains and attacks that afternoon and evening.

But when should the alarm be raised? Now? In the dead of night? How to explain their presence in the room? How to maintain the semblance of a "sudden" and totally "unexpected" death? Better that everything proceeds as normal. He will be "found" in the morning when he fails to appear in the chapel for morning prayers.

They sit up much of the night talking, sharing many things in whispers, attempting to pray, weeping, coming and going from the room, ensuring that the corpse and the reading material remain in place. At half-past four they retire in order to create the appearance of a normal routine.

But they are unaware of the old nun's discreet routine of actually entering John Paul's bedroom with the coffee, possibly at 5:20 or even earlier. Sister Vincenza walks in on the dead Pope, without any of the coy formalities reported on the following day. His posture with the papers and spectacles in place looks like a strange "still life."

Magee is called by the frantic nuns before he can put in his routine appearance in the chapel. He will announce that he didn't hear his alarm, reinforcing the impression that he has slept soundly through the night. Then it is the turn of Don Diego.

Both secretaries will claim that they did not meet or consult on being called. And yet, separately, like clockwork, Magee calls Buzzonetti and Villot, while Don Diego calls Da Ros and the Pope's niece.

Dr. Buzzonetti arrives and sees the corpse's extraordinary pose. Is he fooled by the ludicrous spectacle of a dead man propped up with cushions, the papers stiffly upright in his hands? Does he voice his skepticism? Whatever the case, after a private discussion with the secretaries and Villot, the doctor writes an instant diagnosis, a catchall verdict: myocardial infarction. He reaches a verdict without sight of the patient's notes, without a second opinion and, according to Don Diego, without questioning the secretaries about John Paul's recent symptoms. There will be no autopsy.

Villot writes in the bulletin that Magee found the body. On this occasion, at least—perhaps—he has written the truth.

The body is laid out. The first privileged mourners come and go.

One of the earliest visitors is the Pope's niece. She is a medical student at the Gemelli Hospital in Rome. By this time the body has been reclothed in the torn cassock. The room is stripped bare. She, too, has been told the story of the body being found in bed. She does not believe it. Ten years later she will still say, "I was convinced somehow in my own mind that he had died working at his desk. . . ."

In the aftermath the secretaries are plied with questions. What seemed to be trifling details are now magnified to monstrous proportions. What was the Pope reading? What expression did he have on his face? Who, exactly, found the body? Rumors proliferate.

Father Magee breaks down at the Maria Bambina Institute in weeping fits, and with severe pains in the heart. He believes that people are pointing at him, accusing him of murder. At last, with Marcinkus's help, he departs for England; he claims that a newspaper says that Interpol is on his tail, that every port is on the lookout. His sister has to knock him out with sedatives.

The garrulous Don Diego cannot keep his story straight. After the funeral he is packed off to a hidden place in the north of Italy where he will have no further opportunity to meet with Magee. He will keep silent about the Pope's chest pains until October 1987 when, under pressure, he lets it slip while confronting David Yallop in a prime-time television show. Magee follows suit in February 1988 in his interview with me at Cobh. They break silence in the belief that they are counteracting a conspiracy theory based on the assumption that the Pope was in perfect health.

But why does Magee want people to know that Don Diego was absent from the apartment that night until after he himself had gone to bed? Is it not an excellent alibi for both of them? For how indeed could one man have coped with the weight of the body? Don Diego's absence on the night of the Pope's death is corroborated by three separate sources. So why should he deny it? As Father Farusi commented, "Look . . . Mister, you have to understand the Vatican. Everybody is making a big attempt to let it be known that they were doing their jobs properly." Did *bella figura* in this instance get the better of an alibi?

Don Diego, "the Pope's widow," talks frequently and at length about the death—Ancient Mariner–like. And with good reason does he tearfully relate that he never thought to give John Paul conditional absolution. In an unguarded moment he admits to me that the body was still warm when he lifted it. By the morning, when the body is cold and stiff, it would have been too late, as he well knew, for absolution. He nowadays comforts himself with the repeated assertion that his pope "went straight to heaven."

Villot, it is widely reported, is in a state of enraged anguish on the morning of the death. If he is an accomplice in such a cover-up, it is surely a measure of his own guilty feelings. It is said that he died believing that he had "destroyed" John Paul I.

I telephoned Bishop Magee and asked him whether there was any truth whatsoever in my hypothesis. Like Don Diego he denied the suggestion promptly.

"No," he said emphatically, "we definitely did not find him on the floor. We found him in the morning, dead in his bed."

And yet, I would much rather have believed that in his concern for the Pope's health Magee *had* paused on that night, that he had listened, seen the light still on, perhaps opened the door a crack and found the Pope dying, or already dead.

As it is, we can only believe that Magee's respect for papal dignity and authority overcame his natural compassion; for with anxieties about John Paul's very life still fresh in his mind, he nevertheless insists that he walked straight past the bedroom door, returned to his own quarters and retired for the night.

44

Cardinal Léon-Joseph Suenens tells the story of two encounters with the newly elected Pope John Paul I. As Suenens went up at the end of the conclave to thank him for accepting his election, John Paul said, "I would have done better to say no." After the final night spent in conclave, Suenens walked into the Sistine Chapel for the last time with him. "How did you sleep, Holy Father?" he asked. "I spent the entire night," said John Paul, "with nothing but doubts."

There is ample evidence that John Paul believed from the very outset that his election had been a mistake and that his Papacy was doomed. He longed to die, he prayed and begged God to die, and he was convinced that it would not be long before his wish was granted.

John Paul I had managed to rise in the Church while avoiding the grind of bureaucracy and financial responsibility. He had been sheltered from political conflict and had no time for theological dispute. His path to a bishopric had been in the enclosed world of a seminary where he taught general subjects. His special expertise had been catechetics—the communication of Christian doctrine in clear and simple formulas.

He replaced his secretary in Venice because he could not abide conversations about the state of the world and Church politics. He was suspicious of theology, which he thought could lead to heresy: ". . . too much theology, too little pastors of souls . . ." As his secretary Lorenzi said, "Luciani wasn't interested in big issues."

He loved the simple freedoms of his routine life: the ability to walk out and mix among the people, the freedom to take his siesta, to take vacations walking in the mountains, to spend time with his own family. As his secretary Magee remarked, "He was a man who worried about small, little things."

His constant sustenance was the *Imitation of Christ,* a work of spirituality that emphasizes asceticism and personal piety. Aimed at the spiritual formation of monks and nuns in enclosed communities, it is uncompromising in its rejection of the "vanities" of this world.

When he took over the patriarchate of Venice he had clearly arrived at an extraordinary summit for his intellectual and administrative gifts, and he had achieved it without apparent ambition or desire for promotion. He had been chosen by general acclamation: a token of that periodic nostalgic longing in the Church for the simple, pietistic answers to the world's problems and evils.

But how much of a challenge was Venice in reality? The ancient patriarchate, rich in history and pageantry, is probably less onerous an adminstrative chore than a large inner-city parish. As Don Diego relates, his secretarial predecessor had run the diocese single-handed. "You are going to be bored," said the patriarch when he took on Don Diego, and bored indeed he was.

Luciani was patriarch, he was a cardinal of the Church, but he managed to continue a pastoral style of life untrammeled by worldly or administrative anxieties. His only discomforts were the minor embarrassments of pomp and protocol that went with the job.

All this came to an abrupt end in August 1978 when he was elected Pope. Without seeking it, lobbying for it or even vaguely suspecting it, Luciani at the age of sixty-five was placed in one of the world's most demanding executive hot seats, with three thousand Vatican employees at home, three thousand bishops abroad and the spiritual leadership of nearly a billion souls. The burden of papal office combines a huge weight of moral responsibility as well as the legacy of history—the oldest surviving autocratic institution on earth. The bureaucratic, political and financial ramifications of the modern Papacy are incalculable.

It was, perhaps, with a sense of nostalgic longing that the conclave had decided on a *pastoral* choice: a *holy* man, a *simple* man, somebody who would short-circuit the wheeler-dealing of the Curia. Everything would be safe, they had decided, in the hands of a man of true prayer and saintliness. When they flew back to their various countries, the large majority of foreign cardinals were congratulating themselves on a job well done. They had got what they wanted: they had found "God's Candidate"; they had been guided by the Holy Spirit. But what did this mean, practically and immediately for Luciani?

It is apparent, from the vantage of hindsight, that Albino Luciani was singularly ill-equipped by experience and by nature for the role of pontiff. It is equally clear that he was seriously ill. And, as the Jesuit Father Farusi remarked, "The burden on a pope is enormous, but to shoulder all that and not be in good health is an added psychological weight . . ." John Paul I's phenomenal task was further exaggerated by illness.

Don Diego miscalculated both the nature of the papal task and the art of the possible in the Vatican. In this he can hardly be blamed; he had had no experience nor preparation for such a role. "Papa Luciani," said Don Diego, "was a man of prayer; they should have left him to be quiet and he would have been effective."

Magee, on the other hand, seemed mesmerized by the situation of strange power in which he found himself. "We had a brother–brother relationship." "The Hermit of the Papal Apartment," as many called him, was entranced by the Pope's vulnerability and spirit of assentation. He was, as one official described him to me, a "romancer," a daydreamer. John Paul I was sorely in need of men of sound sense and emotional stability.

Without compromising his personal approach, and despite his handicaps, John Paul nevertheless attempted to accommodate himself to the enormous burden: he rejected the pomp of the coronation, he asked to be called Pastor rather than Pontiff, he brought out his old sermons and polished them. He gave his winning smile before the cameras and did his best to behave in Rome as he had done throughout his priestly life.

But the public exterior was masking a private agony. For much of the day he was trapped, a prisoner in the "gilded" cage with his daily nightmare: the two suitcases of papers that came from the Secretariat of State, and on "every sheet of paper a problem."

Villot's miscalculation of the Pope's administrative capacities, his poor state of health, was disastrous and surely culpable. Villot was at him day and night; John Paul tried to walk in the Vatican Gardens, he was dogged by security men and Villot would hurry out to meet him and ply him with yet more problems. Night and day Villot appeared, pressing him for answers and solutions, nagging and goading. We shall probably never know the full extent of the administrative pressures he imposed on the new Pope; all we know for certain is that far from allowing him an easy introduction, Villot—the fidgety man who liked an empty desk for himself— attempted to get rid of Paul VI's backlog in the first few weeks. Normally "frightened of his own shadow," Villot was nevertheless, in the euphemistic words of Magee, "strong in his approach to the Pope, and dominant . . ."

My attempts to interview the man who had been Cardinal Villot's secretary at the time of John Paul I's Pontificate led to a series of ludicrous evasions. The monsignor in question refused to talk despite repeated instructions to do so from above. It is unlikely that the story of Villot's impact on John Paul I will ever be known in detail. We know that Don Pattaro found the Pope completely "disoriented" in the last week of his life. And after John Paul's death Villot would tell people that he believed that he had "destroyed" the Pope with pressure of work.

A more detailed description exists of the state of affairs in the papal household. The picture is one of disarray and distress. Don Diego and Magee were emotional, at loggerheads. Don Diego— known as the *ragazzino* to the Vatican gossipmongers—was "lost in the Vatican," restless, impatient, running off at every opportunity. The papal valets were, according to Magee, depriving the Pope of privacy and peace of mind—introducing strangers and photographers even into his bedroom. Sister Vincenza was homesick and ill.

There was no escape from stress and tension for John Paul I, even in the inner sanctum of his private apartment. John Paul was suffering from blinding headaches, loneliness and claustrophobia. The only relief he got was in pacing around a concrete roof garden like a caged animal. By the second week of his papacy, his legs were swelling up to elephantine proportions.

It was at this point that Magee records the extraordinary behavior of the Pope at morning Mass, requesting that he should be the secretary's *chierichetto*—an Italian term for a little altar server, the lowliest liturgical role in the Church. It was an act of abasement performed three times by John Paul I and gives a clue as to his state of mind. It suggests a deep need for a symbolic act of humility, humiliation—as if to assuage feelings of unworthiness and incompetence. John Paul I was convinced that the conclave had made a mistake. He was *not* the choice of the Holy Spirit. He was a usurper, a "poor" Pope, doomed.

At every mealtime, says Magee, he would say, "Why did they choose *me*? Why on *earth* did they choose *me*?" "He was constantly talking of death," says Magee, "constantly reminding us that his Pontificate was to be of short duration. Constantly saying that he was to go so that he would be replaced by the 'Foreigner.' "

According to Don Diego, ". . . he was fed up with this world and he wanted only to die. '. . . I ask the good Lord to come along and take me away . . .' I think that this prayer of his—'God, please take me away!'—was said thousands of times that month of his Papacy." Then, Don Diego again: "He did not want to stay in the world." On the evening that he died he recited, as if with extraordinary prescience, the prayer—"Grant me the grace to accept the death by which I shall be struck down"—and expressed a desire to make a retreat for a holy death.

Day after day, says Sister Vincenza, he insisted that he had usurped the papal chair he sat in. "Look, Sister, I should not be sitting here in this seat. The Foreign Pope is coming to take my place. I have *begged* Our Lord."

He had *begged* God to let him die. He was convinced in his own mind that his prayer would be answered.

There is extensive evidence of a connection between the loss of will to live and sudden death. Among the best documented categories are: people who have experienced recent loss, people who believe they have violated a sacred taboo, people in situations that are utterly uncontrollable, and, above all, those who "will" their own deaths through some idée fixe. Research has centered on the effect of states of mind on autonomic activity and the immune system; there is strong evidence that in stress the blood of primates can increase in coagulability to the point of death.

It would not be difficult to construct a plausible hypothesis that accounts for John Paul's death along these lines. Did he, as his niece believes, neglect to take lifesaving medicines? What is the dividing line between "giving up," suicide by deliberate neglect, and "resignation," or "abandonment" in a religious sense—where a person believes that it is God's will that he should die and eagerly embraces that prospect?

There is no evidence that John Paul abandoned himself to despair, but he was *ready* to die, and there was not only a sense of ripeness but a strong desire. It took only his refusal to see a doctor and the heedlessness of others to ensure the end he so devoutly wished for.

In the modern Italian culture of violence there is a sinister new word in currency: "to suicide," used in both the active and passive senses of the verb. Calvi was said to have been "suicided"; so was his secretary when she "conveniently" took a jump from a high window of the Banco Ambrosiano building the day after her boss's death. The term implies an attempt to make a homicide look like a suicide. The analogy in the case of John Paul I is not a fanciful one. By remaining silent about the Pope's symptoms on the day he died, those close to him in the Vatican effectively made a death, which involved symptoms clearly visible while he was still alive, appear like a "sudden" death. The analogy can be taken further. John Paul I wanted to die, the conditions conveniently prevailed, the spectators did not rush forward to prevent him.

John Paul almost certainly died of a pulmonary embolus due to a condition of abnormal coagulability of the blood. He required rest and monitored medication. If these had been prescribed he would almost certainly have survived. The warnings of a mortal illness were clear for all to see; the signs were ignored. Little or nothing was done to succor or to save him.

. . .

A little more than a hundred yards from the Pope's apartment stands
the Vatican Health Service, with doctors and nurses on duty around
the clock and a twenty-four-hour pharmacy, operating freely of
Italian drug restrictions and large enough to serve eight thousand
patients. The Vatican's health facilities are first-class. Its chief in
John Paul I's time was Professor Mario Fontana, a leading Roman
specialist in pathology who had been the personal physician of Paul
VI. All the facilities and personnel were theoretically at the disposal
of John Paul I during his brief reign, and yet John Paul died without
once having been seen by a Vatican doctor. According to Magee,
the changeover from Da Ros to Buzzonetti had been made during
the previous weekend, but the medical notes had not arrived at the
Vatican. As far as Buzzonetti is concerned the Vatican was not,
and had never been, responsible for the Pope's health. It is an
extraordinary irony that for nine hours through the night of September 29–30 six top specialists slaved over the Pope's corpse to
preserve its appearance for protracted funeral pomps, and yet not
one doctor can own to have been responsible for his health during
the last few days of his life when he was seriously ill and might
well have been saved by timely treatment.

The neglect of the physical well-being of the new Pontiff revealed
in this state of affairs is symptomatic of the Vatican's regard for the
man they called the "smiling Pope."

During the weeks that I spent in the Vatican talking with scores
of officials, I gathered that John Paul I's difficulties, both in health
and in coping, had been common knowledge throughout the almost
five weeks of his reign. Don Diego Lorenzi told me "the Vatican
does not exist . . . People do not know what they mean when they
say the Vatican." And yet there is no mistaking the extraordinary
speed with which any item of information, rumor or gossip will
travel through the corridors and offices of the city-state. The Vatican
does exist as a corporate entity, an extraordinarily self-conscious
community. I heard the Vatican described by its inmates as a
"goldfish bowl," "a village of washerwomen," "a palace of eunuchs."
The whole place, I was told, "floats on a flood of brilliant bitchery."
At the same time nobody is responsible; there is a pervasive sense
of pusillanimity, a reluctance to speak out and take responsibility,

a meanness of spirit. The old Jesuit Farusi warned me: "Look, mister, you have to understand the Vatican. Everybody is making a big attempt to let it be known that they were doing their jobs properly." Passing the buck is a favorite Vatican pastime, and when all else fails, blame everything on the Italians, the Americans, the reactionaries, the liberals . . .

It was common knowledge that John Paul I was overwhelmed by his task; as one official put it, "Everyone in the know said he was at his wit's end." It was common knowledge that he was seriously ill. I spoke with a Vatican official who told me, "I shook his hand at an audience a few days before he died, and I knew that I was holding the hand of a dead man." The description of his swollen legs was all over the Vatican. As his niece, Dr. Lina Petri, commented, "He had swollen legs; everyone knew this during his Pontificate. He couldn't wear shoes at all, neither the new ones nor his old ones."

Why was nothing done? Throughout scores of interviews I was told: "But you can't tell the Pope what to do. It is always for him to decide what he wants." The unique instance I recorded of an official attempting to help the Pope in his administrative difficulties was, ironically, Archbishop Marcinkus, who advised him to tell Villot to send in résumés of agendas.

How was it that this community of people, the majority of them dedicated to a life of religion at the center of Christendom, could fail to extend a helping hand to a man who was so clearly suffering?

I have found no evidence that the Vatican nowadays harbors isolated coteries, or even individual instances, of assassins, crooks and gangsters. I found occasional evidence, on the other hand, of men of holiness and prayer. Their pervasive faults and foibles are pitched in the "venial" category of imperfection. Their crimes are not "murder," "major theft," "fraud"; they are "equivocation," "economy of the truth," "mental reservation," "petty ambition," "pusillanimity," "denigration," "cynicism," a signal lack of "kindness" and common "charity." John Magee knew what this meant when he was at breaking point after John Paul's death. He commented: "I hadn't a friend or ally in the whole of the Vatican." Vittoria Marigonda knew what this meant when she described how monsignori and priests would open the door and stare at her without a word. Marcinkus, hardly a man of delicate sensibilities, summed it up thus: "What *is* this! I thought this was a place of love? . . . I don't want to work like a Hoover, pick up dirt—pass it on. I guess it sounds as if I'm trying to excuse *myself*, but that's basic fact. In this place, of all places . . . You can get caught up in this exaggerated bureaucracy where all the bad elements of being a person can come out. . . ."

The denizens of the Vatican are all too conscious of their foibles. They are all too aware of the dismay they cause outsiders. "If you don't like the heat," they are accustomed to say, with a wry smile, "then keep out of the kitchen." But it was precisely the combination of those shortcomings that proved as deadly for John Paul as if the gentlemen in the Vatican had collectively plotted to put digitalis in his coffee.

The conclave had chosen a pastoral pope, and they were delighted with their choice. As for his public reception, it was ecstatic. Father Farusi commented: "That Pope won enormous public affection from ordinary people. He was being thought of as even more popular than John XXIII; he was even holier, more humble, more modest, more simple. He was thought of as a holy pope, close to his people."

The corporate verdict in the Vatican, however, was a good deal less charitable. The new Pope was scorned for his waddling walk, his ungainly appearance, his askew zucchetto, his naive discourses—described by one cleric as *Reader's Digest* mentality." They mocked his attempts to speak to the masses, all those homespun homilies addressed to children. They wagged their heads and imitated his piping voice, saying, "There's more of Mama than of Papa in Almighty God." Members of the Curia disparaged his simple language, his habit of mentioning Pinocchio in the same breath as Augustine and Gregory the Great. He was referred to condescendingly with diminutives—"his little siesta"; he did not know the difference between true doctrine and "blasphemy." He was a pretend-Pope, like "Peter Sellers," a clown. There were endless stories of his gaucheries and faux pas, some of them apocryphal, like his popping out of the Sant'Anna Gate to look at the traffic, some of them true, like the dropping of the documents from the roof garden.

The conclave, the Church, had chosen a pastoral pope, a man of prayer, but the Vatican had refused to accommodate itself to the challenge or the opportunity. "They would have liked to change him," said Don Diego Lorenzi. They regarded him with condescension and Villot callously piled on the mountain of paperwork.

Then they began to be affronted, even scandalized; sharp tongues wagged when he pointed to himself and said: "Pity this poor Christ!" Before he died he confided in Sister Vincenza the chilling admonition: "You see that the crowd cries out 'Hosanna' at the beginning, and before long they are calling, 'Crucify him!' Only trust in God and put your faith in *Him*." As if to extend the simile to embrace the number of years in Christ's life, on the thirty-third day of his Pontificate he died.

He died alone at the very heart of the largest Christian community. He died without the last rites. He died of neglect and a lack of love.

Afterward, Don Diego said, "We did not deserve him."

The verdict of one Vatican official commenting on his death is typical of many that I heard: "The Holy Spirit did a good job: relieving us of him before he did too much damage." There were to be many other verdicts; theories were to proliferate both upstairs and below stairs in the palaces and offices.

Perhaps we shall never know the source of the theory that Archbishop Marcinkus and Cardinal Villot murdered the Pope with poison. A case has been made by the conspiracy theorists that Benelli got it going with innuendos and hints. This may be so. If it is true that Benelli had been cheated of the Secretariat of State by the death of John Paul I, he certainly had a powerful motive to wreak revenge on his old enemies. The conspiracy theorists have their uses in this strange hall of mirrors. But motive alone, as we have seen, is an insecure path to the truth.

New theories and innuendos continue to this day. Even as I prepared to leave Rome I was approached by a journalist who claimed that John Paul I was murdered by the CIA because he had been tipped off about the assassins of Aldo Moro. This same unattributable source then claimed that no less a person than Archbishop Marcinkus is a member of the CIA.

Within the space of one week: I read in a British paper an assertion that John Paul I was an active sodomite; I received an anonymous letter sent to the Secretariat of State claiming that one of its former personnel, a Father Kreishi, had been executed in Beirut in May 1988 for his knowledge of John Paul's assassins; and in the south of France a Luciani cousin was said to have announced to Agence France Presse that the family now believed that John Paul had indeed been murdered.

The whisperings, the rumors, the theories—farfetched, sensational, fantastic—all serve a purpose: they deflect attention from the most obvious and shameful fact of all: that John Paul I died scorned and neglected by the institution that existed to sustain him.

EPILOGUE

If we see only the negative aspects of secu-
larism . . . then we are going to keep our
religion out of politics and out of our economics and our law and everything else of
that kind. In fact we are going to let the world
get even more secular in a negative sense.

—EDMUND HILL, *Being Human*

And what of Marcinkus? I had found no evidence against
him in connection with the death of John Paul I, and
in this sense I believe he had been the victim of widespread
slander. But as my investigation drew to a conclusion I continued
to consider his role as a banker, and the enigma of his success and
survival in the Vatican.

Marcinkus seemed to me so much at odds with the ecclesiastical
milieu that his presence and style appeared surrealistic in the setting
of the Vatican. But by what combination of circumstances, or quirk
of fate, had he risen and remained at the top despite the scandals
that swirled about him? Had his strong, worldly character imposed
itself on an acquiescent institution? Or had he flourished in an ideal
element? The more I considered these questions the more I was
convinced that the answers lay in the dramatic upheavals that had
riven the Roman Catholic Church in the previous two decades.

The Second Vatican Council was intended to bring an era of

sublime papal isolation to an end. The new buzzwords were—
collegiality, consultation, outreach. Without a budget, or a thought
for the fiscal consequences, the Holy See had spawned new commissions, congregations and tribunals, and had come to resemble
a cross between a research foundation and an international government agency. To increase its financial woes, the Vatican began to
suffer the impact of massive wage-cost inflation in the early seventies. Its employees were now seeking annual pay reviews, clamoring for the same benefits accorded their colleagues in the secular
world: health plans, pensions, severance terms.

It was against this background that Marcinkus rose to prominence.
The brash, worldly priest from Chicago, protégé of powerful American cardinals, had made his mark as organizer of papal trips. He
was, by all accounts, the only cleric keenly aware of the physical
dangers that lay in store for a mobile pope abroad. The appointment
to the Vatican Bank clearly had much to do with the exercise of
patronage in an absolute monarchy: Paul VI was rewarding this
streetwise, physically powerful man who had saved his life on at
least two occasions. But, more importantly, during a period when
the world seemed to be encroaching on the Vatican sanctuary,
Marcinkus was seen as a priest who would deal confidently with
the secular domain, on its own terms. He belonged to that breed
of American prelates who could rub shoulders with businessmen,
talk the language of commerce with no sense of clerical coyness.

But what was his attitude toward business ethics? When I asked
him why he continued to do business with Calvi despite the Italian
banker's jail sentence for currency fraud, he said: "When Calvi was
in jail I *asked* somebody, 'Hey! What's going on?' And the fellow
says, 'Nah, if you're not caught, you're not worth anything.' " Taken
in isolation, his reply might be a fair reflection on some aspects of
Italian business mores, but in answer to my question I found it
deeply disturbing.

I had been in danger of misjudging Marcinkus. I had found his
apparent frankness and lack of ceremony appealing. Nor could I
feel censorious about his love for Havana cigars, good whisky and
the golf links. After all, was he not a priest who had managed to
reconcile the problem of "living in the world, with the world and
despite the world"? But his remark about Calvi signaled to me

paradoxically that his attitude toward commerce was as unenlightened as it was reprehensible.

It did not encourage me to give him the benefit of the doubt about his own business standards. The central issue remained the Vatican's part in the collapse of the Banco Ambrosiano. The letters of comfort, indicating the Vatican's control of the debtor Panamanian companies, were intended to buy time for Calvi so that he could put his house in order and decrease indebtedness. These letters were apparently supposed to inspire confidence by demonstrating a Vatican connection. Yet, as Marcinkus insists, there was no legally binding obligation for the Vatican bank to honor the companies' debts, proof of which existed in a letter from Calvi to the Vatican Bank absolving the Vatican of all responsibility. The letters of comfort were therefore, by his own express acknowledgment, a hollow, confidence-boosting exercise, with no consideration for the actual rights of the creditors.

The Vatican's involvement in the Ambrosiano affair illustrates the unacceptable face of traditionalist Roman Catholic morality: a disparaging view of the standards of the "secular" estate, coupled with a casuistic, as opposed to a consequential, appreciation of morality.

I have no evidence that Marcinkus was ever motivated by personal financial gain. He was no doubt anxious to help Calvi redeem Ambrosiano's fortunes, because the Vatican Bank stood to lose by a debacle as much as any creditor. One assumes, by the same token, that the Vatican also stood to gain by Calvi's success. Marcinkus's fatal flaw, it seemed to me, was his decision to adapt to the standards of Italian business practice to the detriment of the high moral claims of the institution he represents. The Vatican Bank, after all, is not just any bank; it is inextricably bound up with the moral stature of its auspices.

Marcinkus has had several years to contemplate the damage done to confidence both inside and outside the Church. His failure to resign, and the failure of the Pope to remove him, looks like an arrogant refusal to be accountable. Marcinkus admitted to me that his resignation had been anticipated by certain people inside the Vatican when the compensation payment fell due. He told me: "Then that killed them when they found out that I didn't have to go *anywhere* to get it." He added ruefully, "It didn't kind of clear us out completely; we had to kind of lower our capital level. But it kills me, because of the problems of tomorrow. I'm not thinking of the covering up of the deficit: that's secondary. It's tomorrow, your pensions and stuff. And once you're trying to run everything out of *ordinary* administration, that's when you get killed. If your company had used over the years the money for the pension fund, then they'd go broke. You've got to have the pension fund set aside."

It was an extraordinary statement. Did this mean that Marcinkus had saved the day and, incidentally, his job, but that the Vatican pension fund was now in jeopardy?

The stern lessons of the Ambrosiano fiasco are going to be felt for some years to come. As the Vatican pleads for financial assistance, the rumors of scandal and inefficiency have deterred Catholics the world over from digging deep into their pockets. The persistent secrecy, the apparent lack of candor when the Vatican does speak, hardly encourages the faithful to believe that there has been any salutary heart-searching.

Not the least of the consequences was the opportunity to speculate about a motive for the possible assassination of John Paul I. When the rumor that John Paul had been assassinated was first mooted, it remained a farfetched fantasy of Lefebvre's traditionalist faction. The Ambrosiano connection provided a context and receptivity for a plausible murder plot in the minds of non-Catholics and Catholics alike. In this sense Marcinkus was himself, ironically, the unintentional architect of the more recent conspiracy theories of John Paul's death.

But the most permanent and widespread consequence of the financial scandal is likely to have been its effect on the Church's moral authority. When John Paul II published his encyclical *Solicitudo Rei Socialis* in December 1987, he proclaimed that the Church takes a lead in giving to the poor "out of its necessity as well as its abundance." Turning to the question of Church treasures and the poor, he writes: "Faced by cases of need, one cannot ignore them in favor of superfluous church ornaments and costly furnishings for divine worship; on the contrary, it would be obligatory to sell these goods in order to provide for food, drink, clothing and shelter for those who seek these things." In the light of the Ambrosiano connection and the perception of Vatican wealth, these words were greeted with hollow laughter throughout the world, not least by Catholic journalists.

I finished my research in Rome on April 13, 1988, the Feast of Saint Martin, Pope and Martyr, the Supreme Pontiff from A.D. 649–655. Pope Martin was taken prisoner by the Emperor Constans and died of harsh treatment in exile. But far more agonizing than the emperor's brutality, as Martin made clear in his letters, was the Roman bishops' failure to alleviate his plight. His death, brought about with the acquiescence of his brother priests, was later deemed a martyrdom.

Browsing through the Office of Readings for that day in the library of the English College, I found a passage from one of Pope Martin's letters to his colleagues in Rome: "Christians have taken on pagan ways, showing none of that charity which human beings, even barbarians, regularly display in numerous compassionate deeds . . . But why am I anxious? The Lord is near. My hope is in his compassion that he will not delay long in putting an end to this course which he has assigned to me."

It was not difficult to find echoes here in the life and death of John Paul I. And yet, by the same token, I felt in the impression of déjà vu a sense of Rome's "still, sad music of humanity." Living and working in Rome for any length of time, that historic perspective steals upon one daily, harping on the persistence of human weakness, wickedness and folly, against the background of the spiritual longings of the Eternal City.

That evening I went down to attend the Mass of Saint Martin in the church of the English College, a little saddened that my quest was finally over. As on my first day in Rome I found the church in a blaze of light and flowers. The Mass celebrant, dressed in bright scarlet in commemoration of the martyred pope, was Monsignor Jim, with the snowy white beard. It was his eighty-fifth birthday.

His homily reflected on a long life in the Roman Catholic priesthood, on the ecclesiastical institutions that had flourished and declined in his own lifetime. "We all have to learn," he said, "the lesson of depending on nothing except God's mercy. . . . And yet, even at my age, after struggling to accept this truth throughout sixty years of my priesthood, I have to confess that I still move only at a snail's pace towards real assent to that ideal."

Dimly aware of the magnificence of the city in the gathering dusk outside—the hundreds of churches, the palaces and monuments, the countless works of Christian and pagan art—I sensed in his words a poignant expression of the intransigent tension between supernatural yearnings and temporal vanities, the sacred and the profane, so much a vital spring of Roman Catholic religious experience.

My investigation had precisely pointed up the consequences of a separation between religion and the world. At one point in my interviews, Marcinkus described his bank as being in a "hidden" place, and I took this, as I think he intended it, to mean a religious enclave separated from the secular estate. As I walked through the piazzas, the cortiles and the corridors of the Vatican, I sometimes felt as if I were indeed on board a floating palace, adrift from the mainland of life. The sense of otherworldliness was further reinforced by the apparent preoccupation with rituals and religious externals, casuistic legalism, the wearing of robes and the use of outmoded titles—Excellency, Eminence, Grace, Lord—tokens of a mental split between a sacralized institution and the "outside world."

This alienation within the Vatican has much to do, it seems to me, with a continuous attempt, despite the spirit of the Second Vatican Council, to patch up the old defenses against the perceived profanations of the world: a hankering after a fortress mentality, a retreat into a realm of private reference, a "pietistic" preoccupation with sacral trivialities. It is difficult in such an unaccountable institution to see that the emperor has no clothes. In such a "hidden" state of mind, it is easy to fool oneself into believing one is holy, to disguise evil for good. In these claustrophobic confines there is little room for a free, generous and spontaneous outflowing of love and compassion.

Paul in his letter to the Ephesians talks of Christ as one who has "broken down the middle wall of partition between us," eradicating the ancient divide between the sacred and the profane, the holy and secular. The New Testament was intended to mark the demolition of the divide between the clean and the unclean, to flout the pharisaic nit-picking and law keeping, to reject the belief that religion and God have nothing to do with secular life in the here and now.

My quest convinced me that the Vatican itself has not come to terms with the Christian challenge of bringing down the wall of hostility between God and secular society. My principal characters seemed to demonstrate two differing aspects of the same ghetto mentality. Despite his swashbuckling worldly veneer, Marcinkus proved to be as prejudiced against the prospects of carrying Christianity into the business world as any reclusive anchorite. And the men who surrounded John Paul I appeared to attach more importance to the externals of papal protocol than to genuine compassion and concern for his sufferings and inadequacies.

As for the "smiling Pope" himself, he will undoubtedly be remembered as a holy and humble pastor, but it is clear that his meekness, his diffidence, his preoccupation with purely pastoral and pietistic concerns did not bode well for a Church facing the "worldly" challenges of the eighties and nineties; even on the last day of his life he spoke of the dangers of stressing a "social" message at the expense of Christian evangelization, as if there were some contradiction between the two.

The *Osservatore Romano*, overcome by the suddenness of his passing and the brevity of his reign, described the event as an expression of "Divine Mystery"—a suitable euphemism for the real circumstances of his death. My inquiry has convinced me that the Vatican ignored, and continues to ignore, the dimension of human responsibility in the death of John Paul I—not only in the actions and omissions of those who surrounded him, but in his own acquiescence in the face of a death that might have been avoided.

APPENDICES

CERTIFICATO DI MORTE

Certifico che Sua Santità GIOVANNI PAOLO I, ALBINO LUCIANI,
nato in Forno di Canale (Belluno) il 17 ottobre 1912,
è deceduto nel Palazzo Apostolico Vaticano il 28 settembre 1978
alle ore 23 per " morte improvvisa - da infarto miocardico acuto ".
'Il decesso è stato constatato alle ore 6.00 del giorno 29 settembre 1978.

Città del Vaticano , 29 settembre 1978.

(Dott. Renato Buzzonetti)

Visto il Direttore dei Servizi Sanitari
    (Prof. Mario Fontana)

Vatican Memorandum Supplied to Episcopal Conference, June 1984

The death of Pope John Paul I

While the death of Pope John Paul I came as a great surprise only a month after his election to the papacy, the cardinals who gathered in daily meetings in preparation for the conclave saw no reason to question the report of Dr. Renato Buzzonetti, director of Vatican Health Services, that the death of Pope John Paul I was attributable to natural causes.

In addition, there was the fact that the Pope's health had been rather frail. Some time previously, he had complained of swollen ankles. His close relatives not only did not have any doubts regarding the naturalness of his death, but cited no less than three cases of similar deaths among relatives.

Pope John Paul I did not have it in mind to make revolutionary changes in the Vatican hierarchy, as can be seen from the following facts:

1. On August 27, he named Cardinal Villot secretary of state.

2. On August 28, he confirmed in their offices all the cardinal heads of departments and secretaries of the Curia "for the five-year term now running." This formula makes it clear that the Pontiff did not intend to make replacements then, but would at least wait for the scheduled expiration of each respective term of office in the event that any change would be made.

3. Following this general provision, which was published in the regular way in *L'Osservatore Romano*, the formal letter of confirmation in office was sent to each cardinal head of department, and to the superior prelates of the Roman Curia.

4. The intention of sudden sweeping change attributed to Pope John Paul I was, in reality, starkly opposed to his nature (i.e., out of character). As he had shown in his previous dioceses of Vittorio Veneto and Venice, as his biographer, Msgr. Giulio Nicolini, has noted, one of his outstanding pastoral gifts was prudence. Before taking decisions, he reflected, meditated, pondered for a long time. Then, when his thinking had matured, he acted decisively. Firmness was another of his gifts, but always with the most absolute respect for persons, according to Msgr. Nicolini.

5. It is not true that Pope John Paul I wished to send Cardinal Baggio to Venice as his successor. He had just confirmed the cardinal's appointment in the Congregation for Bishops, and in the presidency of the Latin American

episcopate scheduled for Puebla [Mexico]. Cardinal Baggio has himself directly denied the theory, saying, "Not only did he not ask me, but if he had asked me, I would have gone there—flying."

"The pages" and the Imitation of Christ

The pages found in the hands of Pope John Paul I after his death could not, therefore, have been lists of the prelates to be transferred.

Msgr. John Magee, the Pope's personal secretary, has indicated that it was the Pope's custom to review points of sermons and meditations for Wednesday audience discourses and Angelus talks on Sundays.

The theory that the Pope held in his hand the *Imitation of Christ* did not originate from any official Vatican source. No official document ever mentioned it. A report which circulated among journalists, with no ill-will intended, was picked up even by Vatican Radio (which does not have an official character) and was soon afterwards corrected, when the real facts were verified.

The sister or the private secretary?

While it makes no real difference whether the Pope was found dead by a sister, or, as the Vatican communiqué said, by the private secretary of the Pontiff, in fact, the secretary instantly ran to the bedside of Pope John Paul I when he was summoned by the sister who suspected that something might be wrong. The secretary touched the Pope to awaken him and discovered that he was dead. The secretary then called Cardinal Villot.

The Case of the *Wall Street Journal* against Marcinkus

"Vatican Bank Played a Central Role in Fall of Banco Ambrosiano," by Laura Colby, staff reporter of the *Wall Street Journal*, April 27, 1987

Rome—New information shows that the Vatican bank played a central role in the billion-dollar collapse of Italy's Banco Ambrosiano in 1982.

Since the scandal broke, the Vatican bank has sought to portray its involvement as innocent and at most peripheral. But for five years investigators have been sifting through thousands of pages of documents scattered from Luxembourg, Switzerland and Italy to Central and South America, and the documents tell a different story.

From them has emerged evidence that, for more than a decade, Vatican bank officials played a more prominent role than was previously believed in the tangled, fraudulent schemes of Roberto Calvi, the Banco Ambrosiano chairman who was found hanged under Blackfriars Bridge in London in 1982. In February, investigating magistrates in Milan, Banco Ambrosiano's headquarters, issued warrants for the arrest of three senior officials of the Istituto per le Opere di Religione, or IOR, commonly known as the Vatican bank.

The investigators' Banco Ambrosiano file contains thousands of pages, dating back to the early 1970s. Some of them, such as the now-famous letters of patronage issued by the Vatican bank, are widely known. But investigators say the file also documents dozens of transactions not previously known to the general public. The additional evidence was essential to the prosecutors' decision to bring indictments against the three Vatican-bank officials.

Confidential liquidators' reports and bank records made available to this newspaper show for the first time just how involved in Mr. Calvi's affairs the Vatican bank was. They describe in detail a series of financial transactions that took place over several years leading up to the Banco Ambrosiano collapse. These transactions, investigators assert, not only demonstrate the close relations between Mr. Calvi and the Vatican bank; they also show how Banco Ambrosiano's funds were used in ways not in its own best interests.

In one of the transactions, the documents show, the Vatican bank on Oct. 16, 1979, received two time deposits, one for $65 million and the other for 101 million Swiss francs ($69.2 million at present exchange rates), from the Lima, Peru unit of the Banco Ambrosiano. The Vatican bank turned around and lent identical amounts, with identical maturities, to a Panamanian company, United Trading. It appeared to be a routine banking intermediation operation, for which the Vatican bank received an interest-rate spread of one-sixteenth of a percentage point.

When the deposits matured in 1982 and the Banco Ambrosiano unit asked for its money, the Vatican bank declined, saying that it was United Trading that actually owed the Lima unit the money. But as it turns out, the Vatican bank controlled the entire share capital of United Trading and had for years. In essence, the Vatican bank had borrowed money from the Banco Ambrosiano unit and lent it to itself.

United Trading was involved in buying shares of Banco Ambrosiano and in other activities that haven't been fully explained, but it isn't clear what it used the money from the Lima bank for. In any case that bank wasn't repaid. Thus disappeared more than $100 million of the $1.3 billion initially lost in Italy's biggest bank failure, a failure that sent shock waves through the international financial community. Though creditors have since recovered some 70% of their losses, most shareholders of the Italian bank lost their investments.

Many questions about what happened and why remain unanswered. But investigators have assembled evidence strong enough to charge the three Vatican bank officials—Archbishop Paul Marcinkus, the bank's chairman; Luigi Mennini, its managing director; and Pelligrino De Stroebel, its chief accountant—with being accessories to fraudulent bankruptcy.

Such a charge implies that those accused either knew of the fraud or suspected it and went on with their business dealings anyway. "Without the complicity of the Vatican bank," says one Italian investigator, "Calvi would not have been able to do what he did."

There doesn't appear to be any evidence that the accused officials profited personally, and it remains to be seen whether the charges will lead to convictions.

Still, the warrants have put the church in the position of harboring fugitives from Italian justice.

The three officials, who maintain their innocence, have avoided arrest by remaining secluded within the walls of the Vatican, a sovereign state, requiring Italian authorities to request extradition through diplomatic channels. Italy and the Vatican don't have an extradition treaty. The Holy See hasn't indicated its response, but high-level Vatican sources say they expect it to fight the extradition requests. It has been fighting the arrest warrants.

In his first comment on the matter, Pope John Paul II last month defended Archbishop Marcinkus. "We are convinced that you cannot attack a person in such an exclusive and brutal manner," he said, "but we are taking the case with all seriousness, and we will have it studied by competent authorities."

Secular authorities have long asserted that what they call the fraudulent bankruptcy resulted from Banco Ambrosiano's lending huge sums of money through its overseas affiliates and the Vatican bank to a group of shell companies that had few, if any, ascertainable assets. The shell companies bought shares in Banco Ambrosiano, made an often dizzying series of loans to one another, and funneled funds to Calvi associates.

The Vatican has always insisted that it didn't own shell companies, but new evidence indicates that it did own at least some of them. The Vatican has also denied that it had any knowledge of their operations. Indeed, sources in the Holy See say the Vatican bank didn't even know of the existence of many of the companies until mid-1981. But investigators now dispute this.

One aim of all the shell-company transactions apparently was to ensure the independence of Banco Ambrosiano; the secretive Mr. Calvi feared a takeover. Counting the stake in the bank's shares amassed by the shell companies, the Vatican bank held 10%, giving it effective control at the time of the bank's collapse. Another goal may have been to support friendly politicians; Mr. Calvi also feared a Communist takeover of the Italian government.

Vatican sources say that it was Mr. Calvi who managed the shell companies and that the Vatican bank, therefore, wasn't responsible for them. Italian officials don't dispute that Mr. Calvi was the mastermind, but they say the Vatican bank shares the blame. They assert that it was aware of at least some of these companies' questionable activities and that its unique status as "an offshore bank in the center of Rome" enabled Mr. Calvi to operate under a veil of secrecy and escape supervision by the Italian authorities.

How did the Holy See get mixed up in all of this? Vatican sources say officials trusted Mr. Calvi because of Banco Ambrosiano's prestige as Italy's largest private bank and its unique role as a Roman Catholic bank; until a few years ago, one had to produce a baptismal certificate to buy its shares. And Vatican bank officials may have had their own political interest in maintaining the bank's independence. The profitable, discreet institution, with important holdings in publishing, regional banking and insurance, wielded much power in Italy.

The relationship was certainly profitable for the Vatican bank. During the eleven-year partnership, it acted as the intermediary for Mr. Calvi in countless operations like the loans to United Trading. It earned fees, commissions and interest, although just how much isn't known. As Archbishop Marcinkus, the Vatican bank's chairman, told the Italian press shortly before Banco Ambrosiano's collapse, the Vatican bank puts its money "where it does best."

By the late 1970s, according to evidence compiled by investigators and liquidators, the Vatican bank owned a number of Calvi-related shell companies. The bank itself acknowledged in the well-known letters of patronage, issued Sept. 1, that we directly or indirectly control "a series of Luxembourg and Panamanian companies and that it was "aware of their indebtedness." The letters—to the Lima, Managua, Nicaragua units of Banco Ambrosiano—were signed by Messrs. Mennini and De Stroebel.

Investigators in Milan see the letters as proof of a high-level agreement between Mr. Calvi and the Vatican bank. "There was an understanding that went far beyond ordinary banking intermediation," one Italian official says.

But Vatican sources have always said that the letters were issued at Mr. Calvi's request as he sought to shore up his collapsing empire, and that the Holy See didn't actually own the Luxembourg and Panamanian companies, and issued the letters to try to keep them from piling up further debts, the sources have said.

"Even in the period after the letters were issued," Archbishop Marcinkus wrote in a 1983 report detailing the Vatican's side of the story, "there was no type of intervention by the IOR—either direct or indirect—in the management of the controlled companies, even under the form of [giving] clearance or authorization for the execution of operations to interested persons or third parties."

Yet the archbishop's report appears to be contradicted by an Oct. 16, 1981 letter signed by Messrs. Mennini and De Stroebel. The letter, turned up by investigators in Luxembourg, gives clearance for Mr. Calvi to give orders on the Vatican bank's behalf, naming his "attorney in fact" for the companies mentioned in the letters of patronage. The letter raises two unanswered questions: If the Vatican bank really wanted to stop Mr. Calvi from borrowing more, why did it give him such power over the companies? And if it didn't really own the companies, how could it give the orders as to who was to manage them?

A little-known provision of a 1984 Geneva agreement with Banco Ambrosiano's Luxembourg unit supports the belief that the Vatican bank did actually own the shell companies. Under the agreement, the Vatican bank agreed to pay $250 million to the creditors in recognition of a "moral responsibility in the affair."

It also agreed to turn over to the creditors an assortment of "bearer shares" in its possession. These included 500 shares of United Trading, "forming the entire share capital"; 5,499 of the 5.5 million shares of a Luxembourg company called Zitropo Holding S.A.; and 44,944 shares of the 50,000 shares of a company called Manic S.A. Most of the shell companies were units of these three. In addition, the Vatican bank agreed to hand over to the same creditors 53,300 shares, or 23% of those outstanding, of Banco Ambrosiano S.A., the Luxembourg affiliate of the Milan bank. In return, the creditors agreed to drop any civil suits against the Vatican bank to recover their money.

Even Vatican sources say that the Vatican bank knew almost 10 years ago of the existence of United Trading, the Panama shell company that later ended up with the loans from Banco Ambrosiano's Lima unit. Vatican sources say that Mr. Calvi asked the Vatican bank to register United Trading's shares in the bank's name in late 1977 and that this was done in early 1978.

United Trading, investigators say, was also the recipient of further loans for which the Vatican bank was intermediary. The money was lent by the Bahamas unit of the Banco Ambrosiano to the Vatican bank and then passed on to United Trading. In these cases, too, the Vatican bank said that United Trading, not itself, was responsible for repaying the loans. Vatican sources say the bank had received written instructions from Mr. Calvi, as chairman of the Bahamas unit, empowering it to carry out the loan-intermediation operation. It was paid a commission.

Yet Pierre Siegenthaler, the president of the Bahamas unit, didn't know anything about such a letter, he told an investigating panel appointed jointly by the Italian government and the Holy See. According to the panel's report, he said the Bahamas bank's auditors "only accepted such a high exposure because IOR was the state bank of the Vatican. The auditors certainly would not have accepted such a huge indebtedness towards an unknown client company."

Thus, by using the Vatican as intermediary, Mr. Calvi apparently succeeded in tricking officials of his own bank into making shaky loans. At the time of Banco Ambrosiano's crash, United Trading's debts to units of the Milan bank totalled more than $200 million.

Another big debtor, the Luxembourg-based Manic, "was evidently incorporated by Calvi with the agreement of the IOR," according to a confidential 1985 report by liquidators of Banco Ambrosiano Holdings, the Luxembourg unit that grouped all of the Milan bank's overseas interests.

Manic was established in Luxembourg in 1973, say the liquidators, quoting from the company's charter, "to deal in shares, form and hold subsidiaries in Luxembourg and abroad, and to make and take loans with and without guarantees." Its initial capital was $50,000. Later that year, it increased its capital to $5 million, apparently through the sale of shares to the Bahamas affiliate of Banco Ambrosiano.

One month after Manic's establishment, says the liquidators' report, Roberto Calvi, as chairman of Banco Ambrosiano Overseas, signed an accord under which the Vatican bank subscribed to a $40 million bond issue by Manic and lent Manic $5 million against its entire share capital, taking possession of the shares and thus effectively gaining control of the company. Mr. Calvi, the report goes on, agreed to pay 10% interest on the total of $45 million with the understanding that once the loan was repaid, the shares would be returned to a holding vehicle of his choice.

This was not to be the case. When the $45 million was repaid to the Vatican bank in April 1979 via a transfer through Manufacturers Hanover Trust Co., the shares remained in the Vatican bank's possession, according to the 1983 report by Archbishop Marcinkus.

The Archbishop's report says this was because "the counterparty" never came to claim the shares. It isn't clear whether by "counterparty," he meant Mr. Calvi or, rather, the repaying entity. But according to the liquidators, the repaying entity was a company called Nordeurop, a unit of none other than United Trading, the company controlled by the Vatican bank. So the Vatican bank, indirectly at least, still controlled Manic. It is uncertain where the $45 million came from, but in September 1981, Nordeurop owed nearly $400 million to Banco Ambrosiano's Lima unit.

In the meantime, Manic had embarked on a course of action that was to prove disastrous for Banco Ambrosiano: It began buying, through nominee companies, shares of the Milan bank, and the purchases, according to the liquidators' report, were financed largely by loans—many of which were never repaid—from Banco Ambrosiano and its units. By the time Ambrosiano collapsed in 1982, says one published account, Manic directly or indirectly owned 3.7 million of the bank's shares, or 7.5% of those outstanding.

"The main purpose of Manic's transactions in Banco Ambrosiano S.p.A. appears to have been maintaining control of a significant block," the liquidators write. "The reason for Manic holding the shares in the names of various nominee companies was presumably to conceal the true ownership of the shares." For Banco Ambrosiano itself to have made such purchases, which exceeded the limits agreed to by its shareholders, would have been against the law, Italian legal experts say.

A Milan investigator is more blunt. "This was the secret strategy," he says. "Together they [Mr. Calvi and the Vatican bank] succeeded in controlling Banco Ambrosiano."

The Vatican bank maintains that it never administered Manic and had nothing to do with its operations. It also says that it never knew of the existence of Manic's Panamanian units until mid-1981, when it wrote the letters of patronage.

Yet there is evidence, in the form of letters addressed to the IOR's Mr. Mennini, that the Vatican bank did receive some information about Manic on at least three occasions. The letters, dated in 1975, 1976 and 1977, gave information on a capital increase and invited Mr. Mennini to attend the company's shareholders' meetings.

And investigators suggest that the Vatican bank could have learned about the activities of Manic's many subsidiaries through Archbishop Marcinkus, who since August 1971 had been one of the three directors of Banco Ambrosiano's Bahamas unit. One typewritten letter to the Bahamas unit, dated March 5, 1980, and signed simply "Manic S.A.," underscores the Bahamas unit's involvement in Manic's affairs:

"In connection with our various Panamanian subsidiaries which you are managing in our behalf, whose regular office is located in your premises, and for which you provide officers and directors, we hereby confirm that all corporate documents and files related to these companies are to be considered their exclusive property and are not to be made available to any third parties whatsoever, including your independent auditors."

How much of such information was available to the archbishop in his role as a director of the Bahamas bank is one of the many questions that remain unanswered. Vatican sources say the administered companies were never mentioned at the Bahamas unit's board meetings. They assert that the minutes of these meetings show that the archbishop repeatedly questioned proposals put forward by Mr. Calvi, who was the unit's chairman, to increase the tiny bank's line of credit.

But there were other warning signals about Banco Ambrosiano that the Vatican apparently failed to heed. In early 1982, for example, Carlo De Benedetti, currently the chairman of Olivetti and briefly deputy chairman of Banco Ambrosiano, met with a high Vatican official and expressed his concern at what was going on at Banco Ambrosiano. Mr. De Benedetti confirms the meeting.

Now, it is only a matter of time before the full details of the bank's long collaboration with Mr. Calvi are aired publicly. Magistrates in Milan say that if their extradition request is refused, they will try the three Vatican officials in absentia.

Meanwhile, Archbishop Marcinkus and Messrs. Mennini and De Stroebel remain behind the ninth-century walls of the Vatican, where they continue to run the affairs of the Vatican bank.

Marcinkus Replies to the *Wall Street Journal*

Memo prepared by IOR's lawyers re Laura Colby's article

1. The I.O.R. did not own and did not control UTC. The Vatican bank held *in fiduciary capacity* (a normal procedure in banking relationships) the share certificate of UTC *on behalf and upon written request of Banco Ambrosiano*. Said certificate was deposited with Banco del Gottardo, which also managed the company. The management contract stated that Banco del Gottardo would not make any transaction without written instructions from the I.O.R. The documents and the investigation carried out by the joint Commission (Italo-Vatican) have proved that the I.O.R. never gave any instruction whatsoever and that Banco del Gottardo managed UTC according to instructions received from Banco Ambrosiano and in particular from Mr. Calvi.

The I.O.R. would have had no need to borrow money from other banks to finance its own companies since it is a commercial bank (meaning its preoccupation is how to place money, not how to find it). UTC was financed with money coming from the Ambrosiano Group because it belonged to the Group and was directly managed by the Group in its own sole interest.

2. The accusation of the investigators is based only on conjectures and hypotheses that are not supported by any evidence.

In fact in their lengthy report they have not been able to indicate one specific fact that might prove that the I.O.R. executives were directly involved in the management of Calvi's companies, or that the I.O.R. was aware of the existence and unethical nature of Calvi's schemes. Since the I.O.R. was never involved in, and knew nothing of, the companies' operation, it is impossible to talk of complicity of the I.O.R. in helping Calvi pursue his fraudulent plans.

3. The Ambrosiano Group granted such large loans to the shell companies only because they belonged to the Group and were managed in the Ambrosiano's interest. In fact only the owner can finance his own companies at will, without the guarantees that are required for a loan to a third party. The I.O.R. *never did finance* the Ambrosiano's offshore companies; it merely acted as banking intermediary in some of the operations through which the Ambrosiano group was financing its own companies.

4. To this date, no "new evidence" has been produced by the judges. The documents that allowed first the joint Commission, then the Italian judges, to carry out their investigation were obtained only thanks to the I.O.R., who requested the banks and other financial institutions involved to hand over to the Commission copies of all the documents in their possession, *none excluded*, concerning the activity of the offshore companies and their relationship with the I.O.R. And, of course, the I.O.R. handed over all its own records. On the other hand, the liquidators of Banco Ambrosiano have been unable to supply the Commission with any document of some relevance.

5. It is an ascertained fact that the shell companies held over 10% of Banco Ambrosiano capital and therefore had de facto control of the bank. But the shell companies were never owned by the I.O.R. They belonged to the Ambrosiano Group, whose management had thus secured control of the bank. If the I.O.R. had been the controlling shareholder its behaviour would have been quite different. It would have placed on the Board its own people, first of all, since there was no obstacle—juridical or de facto—to the I.O.R. securing direct open control of a bank that, on top of everything else, had a strong Catholic tradition.

6. The criminal involvement of any subject can only be announced on the basis of specific facts and evidence, not of a judge's unsubstantiated hypothesis. Even the investigators concede that there is no document which proves that the I.O.R. was involved in, or aware of, Calvi's illicit transactions. To this date no witness has ever come forth to claim direct knowledge or evidence of any involvement of the I.O.R.

No other element or objective evidence has been brought forth to support the opinions and rumours, more or less extravagant, about a supposed direct involvement of the I.O.R. in the Banco Ambrosiano affair.

7. The commissions that I.O.R. received for its intermediation in some financing transactions are well known (0.0625%) and have been carefully ascertained by the joint Commission. No other payment or compensation of any kind was received by the I.O.R. for the above intermediation. The total amount of commissions paid to the I.O.R. is so modest that it could not possibly justify a complicity of the I.O.R. in Calvi's dealings in order to make an illicit profit.

8. In 1981 the I.O.R., having learned of the de facto connections that, through MANIC and UTC, linked it to a series of completely unknown companies, requested Calvi to sever immediately these connections. To help him in this, Calvi asked the I.O.R. to give him the letters of patronage dated September 1st "for use within the Ambrosiano Group only." The I.O.R. granted his request because (a) the de facto connections had indeed been created, though unbeknownst to the I.O.R., and did exist and (b) the financial statements of the offshore companies supplied by the Ambrosiano to the I.O.R. showed their assets would approximately cover their debts towards the various Ambrosiano Group banks.

It must be remembered that, in accordance with the commitment made by Calvi, the letters of patronage never circulated outside the group and had the effect of preventing further indebtedness of the offshore companies, which from that moment on did not raise further loans.

9. The authorization given Calvi to act as *attorney in fact* for the offshore companies was a direct consequence of the granting of the letters of patronage dated September 1st. It was given, on Calvi's express request, to formally empower him to manage the companies which the I.O.R. de facto controlled, though unwittingly so. The letter naming Calvi attorney in fact for the companies served only to confirm the situation previously "in esse," since the said companies had always been managed by Calvi without any instructions from the I.O.R. and unbeknownst to it. When the I.O.R. became aware of the situation its first step was to obtain Calvi's commitment that the companies' indebtedness would under no circumstance be increased. This in fact happened as there were no new transactions after September 1981.

Since the I.O.R. was not the real owner of, and had never managed, the companies it could not get involved in their management at that stage. On the other hand the I.O.R. did appear to be the holder of the companies' capital. Hence the need for the I.O.R. to formally entrust the management of the companies to their real owner.

10. The Geneva agreement of 1984, having taken note of the fact that the I.O.R. appeared to be the formal owner of the companies, and of the I.O.R.'s firm intention—stated from the beginning—to sever all ties with the companies of

which it was not the real owner, foresees the return to the Ambrosiano Group of the share certificates that had remained directly or indirectly in the I.O.R.'s name but of which the Ambrosiano was the real owner. It is not correct to say that the agreement indicates that the I.O.R. was the real owner of the shell companies. In fact the opposite is true because the agreement, accepting what the I.O.R. had stated and requested from the beginning, eliminated all formal ties between the I.O.R. and the offshore companies, which were turned over to their real owner—the Ambrosiano Group.

11. When the MANIC loan was repaid, the I.O.R. did not and could not know that the money was coming from Nordeurop, a company with which the I.O.R. has never had any relationship.

Equally, the I.O.R. did not and could not know that Nordeurop was a UTC subsidiary for the simple reason that UTC, according to the management contract with Banco del Gottardo, was not supposed to make any transaction without written instructions from the I.O.R., and no instructions had ever been given by the I.O.R. to Banco del Gottardo.

The repayment of the loan with money coming from another company anyway cannot imply that the latter controls MANIC.

12. It is quite true that the transactions carried out by MANIC (under Ambrosiano management) had the purpose of securing Calvi the control of Banco Ambrosiano. But it is not true that the I.O.R. was party to this plan and the facts prove it. In fact the I.O.R., as stated above, has never directly managed Ambrosiano by placing men it could trust on the Ambrosiano board, which would have been an absolutely normal thing for the owner to do. And there would have been no obstacles, juridical or de facto, to the I.O.R. securing direct, open control of a Catholic bank. On the other hand it would be against all common sense for the owner to let others manage, worse mismanage, an enormous fortune taking absolutely no interest in his investment.

13. The I.O.R. as creditor of MANIC—whose shares it held as collateral—received only on three occasions (1975, 1976 and 1977) the balance sheets of the company submitted for approval at the annual meetings. The I.O.R. never attended the meetings, nor did it ever give any instructions for the management of the company that was run by the Ambrosiano. It is symptomatic that the balance sheets sent to the I.O.R. did not indicate, among the participants, any of the subsidiaries involved in the Ambrosiano crack.

After 1977 and until 1981 no other information was ever sent to the I.O.R.

14. There were seven Directors on the board of Banco Ambrosiano Overseas Limited.

The bank was run by the General Manager (Pierre Siegenthaler) and the Chairman (Calvi), who had been given ample powers. Msgr. Marcinkus, as all the other directors, was only acquainted with the matters discussed at Board Meetings.

The minutes of the Meetings show that the activity of the Panamanian subsidiaries was never on the Agenda and was never discussed by the Directors. The MANIC letter to BAOL of March 6th, 1980 is an official letter confirming, with reference to the contracts of fiduciary management and domiciliation of the Panamanian subsidiaries, that all corporate files of the said companies were held by BAOL in a fiduciary capacity and should not be made available to third parties. This type of letter is absolutely normal in all fiduciary contracts with banks for the management and domiciliation of companies.

Transcript of a Letter of Comfort dated September 1, 1981

BANCO AMBROSIANO ANDINO S.A.

                                               LIMA—PERU
Gentlemen:

This is to confirm that we directly or indirectly control the following entries:
—Manic S.A. Luxembourg
—Astolfine S.A., Panama
—Nordeurop Establishment, Liechtenstein
—U.T.C. United Trading Corporation, Panama
—Erin S.A. Panama
—Bellatrix S.A., Panama
—Belrosa S.A., Panama
—Starfield S.A., Panama
—We also confirm our awareness of their indebtedness towards yourselves as of June 10, 1981 as per attached statement of accounts.

                    Yours faithfully.

              [signatures illegible]

                        ISTITUTO PER LE OPERE DI RELIGIONE

INDEX

Touche Ross, London, 121, 123, 127
Trafalgar Square, 30
tranquilizers, 311
Trocchi, Vittorio, 295, 296–97
Tully, Shawn, 123
Turkey, 65

ufficiale, 58
ufficioso, 58
Uganda, 65
Ulysses (Joyce), 110
United Nations, 84
United Trading (UTC), 128
Urban VII, Pope, 48

Vatican, 13
  Americans in, 66, 140–41
  employment in, 52
  financial worth of, 124, 338
  as foreign country, 276, 295, 342–43
  in John Paul I's death, 332, 343
  as obstacle, 301
  politics and gossip in, 91, 142–43,
    332–34
  security of, 30, 95
  women in, 157–58, 173–74, 187,
    205, 215, 303, 333–34
Vatican Bank, 17, 20, 43–44
  Banco Ambrosiano and, 57, 91, 121–
    128, 130–37, 339–40
  Calvi and, 125–28, 130–37
  investments of, 134–36, 254
  in John Paul I's death, 19
  Marcinkus in, 57, 65–66, 121–28,
    130–37, 170, 338
  moral stature of, 339
  physical appearance of, 71–72
Vatican City, 29, 312
Vatican Connection, The (Hammer), 123
Vatican Council II, 14, 16, 18, 113,
  337–38, 342
Vatican Gardens, 235, 282
Vatican Papers, The (Lo Bello), 47–48
Vatican Radio, 18, 30, 92, 196, 198–
  201, 205, 230, 250, 263, 295
Vatican Radiogiornale, 200, 203, 230, 263
Vatican Rumors, 185
Venerabile Collegio Inglese (English Col-
  lege), 36, 39, 41–46, 56, 119, 341
  ghosts in, 52–53

Venice, patriarch of, 243, 327
  Luciani as, 100, 138, 205, 207–8,
    254, 327
Via della Conciliazione, Rome, 29, 59,
  153, 199, 201
Via di Monserrato, Rome, 33, 41, 162,
  306
Villa Stritch, Rome, 22, 65, 73, 139,
  185, 256–57
Villot, Cardinal Jean, 17, 86–87, 144,
  310
  Banco Ambrosiano and, 86–87
  as camerlengo, 248
  death of, 96, 267, 325
  Humanae Vitae and, 21, 87, 209
  John Paul I and, 108, 109, 111, 112,
    211–12, 221, 235, 239, 241–43,
    259–61, 319–20, 329
  in John Paul I's death, 19, 20, 21,
    22–23, 86–87, 248, 259–61, 303,
    323, 325, 335
Vincenza, Sister, 111, 113, 334
  health of, 102, 216, 302, 329
  on John Paul I, 148–51
  in John Paul I's death, 18, 53, 86,
    102–3, 104, 181, 185–87, 214–16,
    241, 244, 247, 289, 290–92, 301,
    302–3, 319, 320–21, 323
Vraie Mort de Jean Paul Ier, La (Thierry),
  19

Wall Street Journal, 123, 128, 348–54
Warfarin, 307, 316–17
Warsaw, Poland, 190
Watergate Complex, Washington, D.C.,
  134–35
Weeke, Marjorie, 38–39, 53–56, 118,
  120, 153–54, 204, 210, 255, 262
Wilkins, John, 39–40
Willan, Philip, 182, 184, 257–59, 297
  interview with, 291
will to live, sudden death and, 330–31
Withers, Kay, 190–91, 296
Wojtyla, Karol, *see* John Paul II, Pope

Yallop, David, 20, 21, 22, 156, 256–57,
  290–93, 294, 297, 324
  interview with, 181–88, 216
Yankee Stadium, N.Y., 84

Zurich, Switzerland, 66, 132, 256

PHOTO CREDITS